Peace Talks®

Basic Family Mediation Course

Training Manual

Diana Mercer, Attorney-Mediator

Basic Family Mediation Course: Training Manual
Diana Mercer, Esq.

ISBN: 978-0-981093-0-2

Peace Talks® Mediation Services, Inc. 8055 W. Manchester Ave. # 201 Playa del Rey, CA 90293 phone (310) 301-2100 fax (310) 301-2102

www.peace-talks.com

Diana Mercer, Esq. is an Attorney-Mediator and the founder of Peace Talks® Mediation Services in Los Angeles, California (www.peace-talks.com). A veteran litigator, she now devotes her practice solely to mediation. Outgoing and down-to-earth, she makes clients and attorneys feel at ease in solving litigation disputes in civil cases, from divorces to employment law and real estate. She is the co-author of *Your Divorce Advisor: A Lawyer and a Psychologist Guide You Through the Legal and Emotional Landscape of Divorce* (Fireside 2001). She's an Advanced Practitioner Member of the Association for Conflict Resolution (ACR) and is admitted to practice law in California, New York, Connecticut, Pennsylvania and before the United States Supreme Court.

Interested to learn more? Visit Diana Mercer's Peace Talks® Mediation Services, Inc. web site, www.peace-talks.com or the Peace Talks® Mediation Services Blog, www.peace-talks.com/divorcemediation/index.php. Diana Mercer is the founder of Peace Talks® Mediation Services in Los Angeles (www.peace-talks.com) and the co-author of *Your Divorce Advisor: A Lawyer and a Psychologist Guide You Through the Legal and Emotional Landscape of Divorce*, (Fireside, 2001) www.yourdivorceadvisor.com. For free resources and planning tools for divorce and custody, visit our resource center at www.peace-talks.com/prepare.php

Table of Contents

DISPUTE RESOLUTION PROCESSES

AVOIDANCE	NEGOTIATION	ISSUE REVIEW BOARD*	MEDIATION	ARBITRATION	LITIGATION	SELF-HELP
VOLUNTARY	VOLUNTARY	VOLUNTARY	VOLUNTARY/ INVOLUNTARY	VOLUNTARY	INVOLUNTARY	VOLUNTARY/ INVOLUNTARY
NON – BINDING	AGREEMENT ENFORCEABLE VIA OTHER PROCESSES	AGREEMENT ENFORCEABLE VIA OTHER PROCESSES	AGREEMENT ENFORCEABLE VIA ARBITRATION OR LITIGATION	BINDING/ ENFORCEABLE BY JUDGEMENT	BINDING SUBJECT TO APPEAL	NON – BINDING
NO THIRD PARTY	NO THIRD PARTY	THREE-MEMBER PANEL WITH EXPERTISE RECOMMEND SOLUTIONS	THIRD PARTY NEUTRAL FACILITATOR	THIRD PARTY NEUTRAL DECISION MAKER WITH SUBSTANTIAL KNOWLEDGE IN THE DISPUTED MATTER	IMPOSED THIRD PARTY NEUTRAL/JURY WITH NO PARTICULAR EXPERTISE IN DISPUTED SUBJECT	NO THIRD PARTY
INFORMAL	INFORMAL	INFORMAL	INFORMAL	SOMEWHAT FORMAL	FORMAL	INFORMAL
NO EVIDENCE NEEDED	NO EVIDENCE RESTRICTIONS	NO EVIDENCE RESTRICTIONS	NO EVIDENCE RESTRICTIONS	NO EVIDENCE RESTRICTIONS	EVIDENCE RESTRICTIONS	NO EVIDENCE NEEDED
NO ADVOCATES	PARTIES CAN REPRESENT THEMSELVES OR CAN HAVE ADVOCATES	PARTIES CAN REPRESENT THEMSELVES OR CAN HAVE ADVOCATES	PARTIES CAN REPRESENT THEMSELVES OR CAN HAVE ADVOCATES	PARTIES CAN REPRESENT THEMSELVES OR CAN HAVE ADVOCATES	PARTIES USE ATTORNEYS	NO ADVOCATES
PRIVATE	PRIVATE	PRIVATE	PRIVATE	PRIVATE	PUBLIC	PUBLIC
NO OUTCOME	MUTUAL OUTCOME	MUTUAL OUTCOME	MUTUAL OUTCOME	OUTCOME BY OTHER	OUTCOME BY OTHER	OUTCOME BY OTHER
VERY EASY	EASY	EASY	NOT DIFFICULT	NOT DIFFICULT	DIFFICULT	VERY EASY

ADR - FOCUS IS ON THE PARTIES INTERESTS

COURT- FOCUS IS ON THE PROTECTION OF THE PARTIES RIGHTS AND HOW THE DECISION WILL AFFECT THE PUBLIC'S INTERESTS

Attorneys often forget the format of the proceeding and may need to be reminded of the focus of arbitration and mediation. The posture of win or lose is ingrained in the legal process and is difficult for most attorneys to modify their approach to settlement. A friendly reminder of the focus is often received in a positive light.

INTRODUCTION

Mediation is a by-product of failure or the inability of disputants to work out their own differences. Each party comes to the table locked into a position that the other party will not accept. The parties distrust each other and may be angry, frustrated, discouraged, and/or hurt. Their inability to reach a settlement may be due as much to the emotions of the case as the facts.

Mediation is negotiation carried out with the assistance of a third party neutral. The involvement of the mediator alters the dynamics of the resolution process. Depending on what seems to be impeding the agreement the mediator may attempt to:

1) Develop a process format that instills trust of the mediator. If the parties are willing to convene or meet for purposes of resolution, the 'mediation' or discussion process will provide them with a 'safe environment' and instill 'hope' of conclusion to their dispute.

2) Shift the focus from the past to the future. The past is history and cannot be modified. The future is theirs to determine and it can include closure.

3) Learn about those interests the parties are reluctant to disclose to each other. Be inventive on how to deal with these interests by developing possible solutions that meet the fundamental interests of both parties.

4) Help the parties understand each other's views. The mediator can have substantial knowledge in the particular subject at the heart of the dispute, if the parties so choose, or just be a great facilitator of communication.

Even though mediation is a dispute resolution process which can be practiced by any trained individual, it is not unusual that parties will select an individual who focuses on resolving conflicts in specific fields in which he/she has substantial knowledge. Having knowledge of the subject matter of the dispute enables the mediator to evaluate the input from both parties and assist them in judging their positions. Thus, the mediator has an opportunity to suggest solutions that might be perceived as more practical and applicable.

Although the goal of the mediator is to help the parties resolve their conflict, the ultimate goal must be to help them find an informed solution that is fair, reasonable, concluding, and most important, enduring. The mediator typically accomplishes these goals by following a proven road map to resolution.

1) CONVENE - Get the parties to the table.

2) OPEN - Get the parties to start the process feeling secure that it will be a fair process.

3) COMMUNICATE -Get their stories and by-pass the rhetoric.

4) NEGOTIATE - Help the resolution by encouraging flexibility and innovation.

5) CLOSE - Bring closure to the conflict by assisting the parties to make informed decisions.

MEDIATOR ROLE

A mediator's role varies from passive/indirect to active/direct. The various roles include:

- Convener
- Reality Tester
- Alternative Generator
- Gainer of Closure
- Educator
- Communication Facilitator
- Broker of Ideas
- Creator of Options
- Devil's Advocate
- Process Provider
- Referee
- Trust Builder

MEDIATOR STRATEGIES

- Control the process
- Record the history of the negotiations
- Make certain the participants are authorized to negotiate and settle
- Help determine the reasonable settlement range
- Review the advantages of settlement
    - Certainty
    - Immediacy
    - Economy
    - Privacy
    - Control
- Control tactics
- Stress the importance of cooperation throughout the process.

- Communication based tactics
    - Direct communication
    - Mediator as conduit
    - Reshaping
    - Clarification
- Procedural based mediation tactics
    - Caucus
    - Recess
    - Keeping the feet to the fire
    - Changing location if necessary
    - Using deadlines
    - Strategic suggestions
- Substantive based mediation tactics
    - Activation of commitments
    - Cost assessment
    - Deflating extreme positions
    - Mediator opinion in joint session
    - Clarification

MEDIATION STYLES

Facilitative - Focuses more on process than on content. Primary criterion is how well the options mutually satisfy the parties' interests. Strategies used:

- Joint sessions
- Controlled flow of process
- Build trust between the parties
- Listening
- Relating the learned facts to the other party
- Developing options that meet both parties' interests
- Dwell on the future without conflict
- Dwell on preserving relationships

Evaluative - Focus is on the substance of the case, the parties' rights, and the likely outcome. The mediator facilitates negotiations by being an agent of reality, and providing an opinion on which the negotiation is based. Strategies used:

- Active questioning
- Active listening
- Providing opinions
- Providing evaluations
- Using Caucuses
- Follow evaluation presentations with facilitative strategies
- Conclusion of the dispute
- Focus on the future without conflict and all the negative distractions that is inherent with conflict

Transformative - Focus on the parties' ability to make personal changes that will strengthen their empowerment and recognition. The mediator facilitates direct communication between the parties encouraging them to settle their differences by agreeing to make personal changes. Strategies used:

- Allow the parties to own both the process and the content
- Allow venting
- Discourage the use of caucuses
- Encourage personal commitments
- Encourage forgiveness

Shakedown (NOT ENCOURAGED) - Focus on the quantum portion of the case, since the parties have pre-concluded the complaining party is entitled to compensation. The mediator facilitates negotiations by being an agent of comparison of what may happen in the litigation arena. Strategies used:

- Providing opinions
- Analyze ability to pay
- Review insurance coverage
- Using Caucuses
- Focus on closure
- Demonstrate the possible economic impacts if settlement is not reached
- Encourage discussions of the settlement agreement

ORANGE PEEL

A story of the limitations of litigation and arbitration

Two sisters came home after school and simultaneously grabbed for the only orange in the fruit bowl. A fight broke out; each sister claiming they desperately needed and wanted the orange.

The mother arrived home just in time to break up the fight. The mother resolved the dispute by cutting the orange in half and giving each sister their proportionate share.

The mother controlled the process and did not take time to understand the 'underlying reasons for the claims'.

The one sister was baking a cake for school ad needed the orange peel for the frosting. The other sister was hungry and wanted the fruit.

By cutting the orange in half, the resolution was only partially satisfactory.

SPLIT THE CAMELS

A story of an early mediation

Anthropologist William Ury likes to tell the apocryphal tale of an old gentleman who, anticipating the day of his death, announced that his estate would be divided among his three sons as follows: one-half to the oldest, one-third to the middle son, and one-ninth to the youngest. The old gentleman eventually died, and his estate consisted of seventeen camels. The three sons attempted to divide up the estate according to their father's wishes but quickly found that they couldn't - at least not without doing violence to the camels. They argued and argued, to no avail.

Around this time, a village elder rode up on her own dusty camel, dismounted, and asked what the problem seemed to be. After listening to the three brothers, she offered to make her own camel available if that might help. And it did. With the addition of an eighteenth camel, the problem suddenly seemed soluble. The oldest son took his nine camels (one-half of eighteen), the middle son pried loose six more (one-third of eighteen), and the youngest son extracted two camels (one-ninth of eighteen). Nine plus six plus two equals seventeen. Almost before the three brothers what had happened, the old wise woman climbed on her own camel and rode off into the setting sun.

THE 6 STEPS TO CONVENING MEDIATIONS

First: Understand that convening is your #1 priority. Without mediation participants, our programs and practices are going nowhere.

Second: Have a clear vision of what you do. You can't encourage people to participate in mediation if you can't explain what it is. Develop your Elevator Speech: a one or two sentence explanation of what you do. Examples:

- Peace Talks® helps people get divorced without losing their shirt or their sanity; or
- We help busy lawyers like you settle cases.

How can you describe your practice in just a sentence or two?

Third: Understand what you're about and your practice's mission. Expand your elevator speech, draft a Mission Statement, and think about your Brand. You may never be Coca-Cola, but your practice and services need an identity.

For example, the Peace Talks® mission statement is: Our Mission: Peace Talks® Mediation Services is dedicated to providing a constructive, forward-thinking and peaceful ending to relationships. Marriages may end, but families endure forever. We provide a confidential, efficient and impartial atmosphere to help people resolve conflict and to create solutions with integrity and dignity for everyone concerned.

You may or may not share your mission statement with clients, but you need it in order to have a direction in your practice. You wouldn't leave on a trip without a map, and you shouldn't have a practice without a map, either.

Your brand is what you stand for, the kind of services that you provide, and your signature style. The Peace Talks® Brand includes:

- Honesty
- Trustworthiness
- Commitment to client education
- Down-to-earth service
- Going the extra mile
- Commitment to client service
- Commitment to the profession of mediation
- Really, the brand is about your values in your practice.

Fourth: Be prepared to discuss your mission, brand, and elevator speech in terms of value, benefits and results for clients. That's all clients care about: value, benefits, results. The good news is that mediation is full of value, benefits and results for clients. Brainstorm a list of what you perceive these to be. You'll use this list when you talk to clients about mediation.

90% of your discussion with prospective clients should be centered around value, benefits and results. Only 10% of the discussion will be about you and your qualifications. The same 90/10 rule holds true of all of your marketing materials, your web site, brochure, and any other descriptions of your practice or program.

When prospective clients call your office, they already believe you're qualified. They already think you're an expert. As a result, they don't really care about you and your qualifications. If they're calling you, you can rest easy: they're already sold on the fact that you're qualified.

Laypeople and many attorneys [generally] perceive all mediators to be equal. They assume mediators are all qualified. The way mediators can differentiate themselves is by describing their services in terms of value, benefits and results. Say it again: value, benefits, results. Value, Benefits, Results.

Price is not as important as you'd think. In Western culture, people believe that they get what they pay for. If it's free or inexpensive, it has no value. Prospective clients who are 100% price sensitive are always going to be a problem. You're never going to build a practice on price competition.

Fifth: Specialize. It's easier to market that way. You can accept any kinds of mediations that come into your office, but you're only going to market one or two specialties. You're also going to pick your geographical area. Marketing every service to every geographic area and to every individual is too difficult and expensive. The more you narrow it down, the easier it is to market.

It's counter-intuitive, but as we've narrowed the services that Peace Talks® offers, we've increased our income. In 2005 our gross income is 30% ahead from 2004 year to date, and we've cut back on the services that we offer and insisted on co-mediation in every case. The less we do, the more we make. It makes sense when you think about it, because the less you do the easier it is to describe what you do, including the value, benefits and results, and the easier it is for clients to conclude, "yes, this mediator can help me."

Sixth: Now it's time to think about what you're going to do when the telephone actually rings.

CONVENING MEDIATIONS: TURNING CALLS INTO CLIENTS

The key step in building a mediation practice is bringing in clients. This article is geared toward private mediation firms, but the same convening techniques and goals hold true for non-profits, HR and government agencies. Whether clients are paying you for your services or not, the key to keeping your mediation program alive is generating clients and demand for mediation. So when I reference "generating business" I mean paid or unpaid business.

When we think of generating business our minds naturally turn toward external marketing: speaking engagements, writing articles, networking, playing golf. We sometimes forget that our most valuable marketing contact-the client who actually telephones our office-is our most viable marketing prospect.

Consider how much time, effort, and money that it took to have that person actually contact your office. Every speaking engagement, networking luncheon, paid advertisement, volunteer mediation and Yellow Pages ad is designed to make the telephone ring. Yet when it does, few of us are as prepared as we need to be to turn that interested caller into a paying client. To ruin that golden opportunity by stammering on the phone, unprepared to discuss the concept of mediation and your particular type of practice, means that the rest of your marketing efforts are nearly wasted. So let's focus on what you do when the telephone rings.

That ringing telephone signals the beginning of a process called convening, or getting both sides to the table. Do you know what your call-to-client ratio is, i.e, how many times does it take the telephone to ring until a call turns into a paying client? Knowing your call-to-client ratio from each of your sources of referrals, as well as your overall ratio, is important in order to know which of your marketing plans is working, which is cost-effective, and where you should focus your most valuable asset: your time.

Telephone Calls

Who will take your telephone calls? Is it a receptionist, unskilled at mediation and unable to answer even the most basic questions about your services? Is it a Dispute Resolution Associate, trained in mediation and in convening? Will you take the calls yourself? A general receptionist is fine if you're taking the calls yourself to do the intake, but you may want to rethink the strategy of having your first line marketing person be someone who knows little or nothing about you or the mediation process. A Dispute Resolution Associate is a helpful addition to your staff (the general receptionist, with a 40-hour mediation training course, also enhances your ability to convene cases)

because he or she can answer many of the client's questions, assist with or independently handle the intake, and send out marketing materials. For beginning mediators and new practitioners, finances may dictate that you're doing your own intakes, but plenty of seasoned professionals choose to do so as well, because they feel they do their best selling themselves.

After you've decided who is doing the intake, what model will you use? Will you spend a few minutes taking down basic information, off the clock, and then send out your brochure, marketing materials, or a follow-up letter? Will you then schedule an orientation session? Or will you combine the orientation session with the intake session, with the telephone call lasting 15 minutes or half an hour with each party? Many lawyer-mediators prefer the short intake, coupled with an orientation session (either free, or for a modest charge), and many therapist-mediators prefer the long intake. Both work, and both have pros and cons. Have a plan for your intake so you handle it consistently, and you know what works for you.

You'll want to have an intake form handy for each call. You can combine prompts for yourself, such as concise ways to describe your background and services, as well as mediation in general, with blanks for basic information such as name and address of the parties. A critical part of the intake form is where the client heard about your services. You'll use this information to track the efficacy of your marketing efforts.

The next piece of information you need from the caller is whether or not the other party is aware of the first party's desire to mediate. Is the other party even aware that the call is being placed? How you handle the call from there will be based on whether or not the other party has already agreed to mediate.

For cases in which the parties have already agreed to mediate, your intake is then geared toward selling the potential client on your services. What do you offer that other mediators do not? Why should the client choose your services above someone else's? You may wish to write a short script or series of sentences, which you keep by the telephone in case you get tongue-tied on the phone.

Mediation Orientation Sessions

We offer a free orientation session in order to supplement the intake. Free orientations take place during regular business hours only.

It allows the parties to meet us together, at the same time, and to see how all of you interact. At some mediators' offices, these orientation sessions are conducted by Dispute Resolution Associates, trained mediators who convene cases for other mediators. Depending on the mediators' availability, it may be a mediator or DRS who is doing the orientation. The orientation session is free of cost as long as the focus is on the mediation process, and how mediation works, and not an actual mediation of the client's case. A distinct advantage of this model is that the clients may ask as many questions as they want, choose their mediator and pay the mediation fees without fear of biasing the mediator. The mediator meets the client for the first time at the first mediation session, eliminating any "conspiracy theories" about mediator favoritism of the party who called first, or who paid the bill.

At Peace Talks®, the Dispute Resolution Associate handles all telephone calls, sending out mediation information packages, and appointment scheduling, but the actual mediation orientation is conducted by one or both mediators who would serve as the mediators in the client's case. We practice this way because by meeting with the actual mediator, the mediator can use that time to build trust with the parties, let them know about common obstacles to reaching an agreement and to gather information for later planning prior to the session. The parties can decide if the mediator is a good fit for their case as well.

Once the orientation is complete, a mediation session is typically scheduled for another day. Although you could schedule the mediation to begin directly after the orientation session, if the clients have decided not to use your services, you then have several hours of empty time in your calendar. If you go directly into a mediation session from the orientation, it can put people under pressure to stay when they hadn't planned to do so. We typically only schedule things this way when someone is driving in from a long distance and they're almost 100% sure they want to mediate with our office.

Approaching the Opposition

If the other party has not agreed to mediation, or is unaware that the telephoning party is interested in mediation, you will handle the intake process differently. The first hurdle is how to contact the other party. Ask the calling party how best to approach the other party: Is it best if the telephoning party does it? Or should the initial call come from our office? Will you place the call yourself, or have someone else on the staff make the contact? Is it advisable to do it by telephone at all, or would a letter be more appropriate? These are issues which you can discuss with the caller to determine the most appropriate way to proceed. If the parties are represented by attorneys, you can contact the attorney who represents the other party easily enough, but make sure that your caller understands what you'll be doing, and agrees with your approach.

Information Packages

Once a call has come into our offices, an information package is sent to the caller, and the other side as well, provided the other side is aware of the mediation request. If the other side is unaware, discuss with the caller whether to send him or her 2 information packages, so that one might be shared with the other side via the caller, or whether it would be appropriate to send a package to the other side directly from your office, either before or after the desire to mediate has been communicated. Our policy is to never send an unsolicited package of information, which may give an unsuspecting adverse party an unnecessary shock.

Our information packages are made up of pre-printed brochures for our different services, articles and other information which feel is pertinent to the particular type of case involved. For example, you may wish to include your business card, copies of articles you've written, your firm newsletter, articles on mediation, your mission statement, your fee agreement, Association for Conflict Resolution brochures, copies of the Professional Standards for mediators, a short biography of yourself and your experience, pointers on how clients can prepare for their mediation session, and anything else which will differentiate your services in the marketplace as well as help gain the clients' confidence that you can help them settle their dispute. The advantage of using a simple pocket folder is that you can mix and match your materials for different types of cases. It's hard to cover all the bases in just one brochure, and even if you do, will the client have confidence that you have enough experience in his or her area of dispute to be of assistance?

We're convinced that only a small percentage of our prospective clients actually read the material we've sent, but that clients appreciate the fact that we're organized and we have materials to send out. We believe that it gives them a sense of confidence that we know what we're doing and that we're committed to client service.

Conclusion

Thoughtful convening is the bridge between marketing and building a practice. By determining in advance the procedures you'll use, what you'll say to clients, and how you'll cultivate those calls into paying clients is the key to developing a profitable practice.

Based on Concepts from Forrest S. Mosten

PRACTICE HINTS: THE INITIAL CONTACT

Few parties will know to ask directly about mediation or even know the term. Many will only generally understand that they can settle their dispute in a different way than usual. Mediation will typically be confused with arbitration, counseling or even meditation. You will need to sufficiently explain mediation over the phone so that the party understands enough that they are willing to find out more in the initial consultation session.

SPECIFIC POINTERS:

- Send material and brochures to both parties.
- Be willing to talk to the other party on the phone as you have done with the person who has originally phoned.
- Make sure to inform the parties that there is no way for either of them to compromise or lose any legal right they may have in coming to mediation.
- Do not become over involved in the discussion of substantive issues on the phone; the parties only need to decide how they want to do things (two attorneys or mediation), not what to decide about the issues.
- Explain that they are coming to the consultation session only for two purposes:
- to decide if mediation makes sense;
- to determine if they are comfortable with the mediator.
- Stress that in the consultation session you will not let them decide "on the spot" to mediate-attendance carries no obligation to mediation or to even proceed with a divorce.
- Suggest how to discuss mediation with a spouse, if necessary.
- Make sure to mention the consultation session fee.

The materials that follow in this section are available for your use, unless specifically noted otherwise. The brochures can be purchased in bulk from the Academy of Family Mediators and the Association of Family and Conciliation Courts.

What is divorce mediation? What is custody mediation?

Divorce Mediation and Custody Mediation are ways to resolve your divorce or custody dispute which lets you keep full control of the outcome. The only people making decisions are those involved in the dispute, unlike arbitration or litigation where a judge or an arbitrator makes the final decision.

Divorce Mediation and custody mediation typically consist of several joint meetings between spouses (or parents, if you are not married) which last 3-4 hours each. During those meetings, you and your spouse discuss the issues which need to be resolved in your case. The mediator is there to facilitate the discussion, assist with communication, provide information and suggestions, and use specialized training to assist the two of you to resolve your differences and write up an agreement which is fair to both of you, and, if you have children, in their best interests as well.

What happens at the first mediation meeting?

Many mediators offer a free mediation orientation so that you can meet the mediator(s) and decide if you'd like to try using mediation to settle your divorce or Family Law matter. Usually, the orientation lasts just 20-40 minutes. The mediator will explain the process, and you can ask any questions that you wish. The mediation orientation is about the mediation process, and not the details of your particular case. Ask if the mediator you're considering offers an orientation because getting divorced and choosing a mediator are very personal, very important decisions. Make sure you choose the right professional mediator and mediation office for your needs.

The actual Mediation process involves sitting down at a table in a neutral location where both parties will have the opportunity to present their stories in a balanced and non-confrontational way. Each person gets a chance to tell their side, and you'll decide in the session how the session will unfold, like who goes first and how long they speak, whether you'll stay in joint session or speak separately with the mediator, and whether you'll have your individual attorney present at the session.

Generally, mediation sessions are structured with a short intake, setting an agenda (a list of the issues) and then the decision of which issue to discuss first. Generally, you'll start with the smaller issues and work your way up to the tougher issues so that you can build some momentum. You'll work through each issue until there are no more issues left.

Ask if your mediator will write a summary letter about your session, including the agenda, tentative agreements, things to think about, and to do list for the next session. These letters are a lot of work for the mediator (ours are billed at 1 hour but usually take 2 or 3 hours to prepare) but they're very valuable. With a summary letter, everyone starts with the same "memory" of what happened in the session, and if you need to see an attorney, accountant, or therapist in between sessions, you can share your summary letter with him or her so that they know what you're working on.

Sometimes, people find they need more information before they can make an agreement or before the session can continue. When that happens, you can either go on to another issue, or stop the session and make another appointment, so that you'll have time to gather the information you need, or speak to your accountant, lawyer, or other advisor(s). Mediation works best when people don't feel rushed to make an agreement and when they have all of the information they need to make a good agreement.

Why mediation?

Mediation is the most practical and healthy choice for a person to make when facing a divorce. It helps you avoid the stress of litigation, saves you money, and helps you put the unpleasantness of divorce behind you as quickly and peacefully as possible. Generally, the agreements reached are more thoughtful and tailored to your individual circumstances, and your family's circumstances, than the typical court judgment. As a result, the adherence rate to mediated agreements is much higher than that of adherence to court orders.

Why is mediation cheaper?

Mediation is cheaper because it's faster and more direct. Most people come to mediation willing to work on the issues and to learn how to communicate better. That willingness translates into a less expensive divorce because resolving a case is almost always cheaper than taking it to trial. Rather than speaking through lawyers, you speak with each other (with the mediator's help, of course) about your goals and issues.

Even if lawyers are involved with your mediation, they aren't spending hours and hours in court waiting for the judge to be free to hear your trial or billing for endless back-andforth phone calls about the smallest details of your case. When you're using your lawyer, they're actually working on your case and helping to settle. Consequently, their fees are typically much lower than in a case which is brought to court to litigate.

Many mediators' fees are lower than local divorce lawyers. On average, clients resolve their cases with a mediator's help in 4 to 10 hours.

Why is mediation more effective?

Mediation is more effective because:

- you get a chance to fully discuss an issue before you agree on it
- you can try out agreements before the judge makes the divorce final
- you learn to communicate better which makes new and old issues less likely to turn into arguments, or worse still, days in court
- you can take time in between each appointment to think about whether or not a proposed solution makes sense
- if you need to change a solution before finalizing your divorce in court you can do it quickly and easily

What if we can't even talk? How can we mediate?

If you are willing to try to learn to talk to each other, then it's worthwhile to try mediation. Mediators are professionally trained to help people to build agreements and to learn to communicate with each other. If you're willing to try, a skilled mediator can get you talking.

As mediators, we've found that everyone who wants to reach an agreement and who is ready to reach an agreement will reach an agreement in mediation. If you don't want to reach an agreement or you're not ready to agree, there's not much a mediator can help you with. On the other hand, if you're in a lot of conflict, not speaking, and ready to go to court yet you're ready to and want to reach an agreement, a mediator can help.

If being in the room together is too difficult, ask to schedule separate sessions either at different times or at the same time, but in separate rooms (called a caucus). This can let you take advantage of the benefits of mediation without the stress of being together in the same room.

What happens if we don't agree in mediation?

Even if you cannot agree on everything, you will probably be able to agree on some things. Each issue that you resolve in mediation translates into less time in court, less legal fees and less aggravation for you. And, for those issues you could not agree upon, at least you understand what those issues are, and where you stand. At the very least, you will feel like you tried your best to reach an agreement before resorting to court intervention.

Sometimes new information, proposed solutions, or the passage of time makes it possible to resolve a previous disagreement, so even if you don't resolve your issue immediately, you may be able to resolve it a week or a month later, without having to go to court. Because mediation is flexible, you're free to schedule an additional appointment at any time. You're also free to stop the mediation at any time if you don't feel you're making progress toward resolution.

WHAT DOES IT COST TO GET DIVORCED?

As a divorce professional, I hear a lot about how easy it is to get divorced. I'm assuming that the people who say this have never been divorced, because after 19 years in this field, 12 as a divorce litigation attorney with the nickname "Jaws", I don't think there's anything easy about divorce at all.

Emotional toll and costs aside—and we all know people who have paid too dearly with these non-monetary factors-divorce can get expensive fast. Lots of clients ask how much their case will cost. It's hard to estimate a total for legal fees before a case begins because it's hard to know how long it will take. There are some predictors, however: acrimony and agreement-readiness.

The single best predictor of the cost of a divorce is acrimony. The more unresolved emotional business, the more expensive the process gets. Ironically, it's rare that the reason people end up in court is because they have a legal question which needs the helping hand of a judge. People end up in court because they've stopped talking, there are too many hurt feelings, or because they don't know of any other way to end their relationship.

When both spouses are ready to get divorced and want to reach an agreement, fees generally stay low. Even if you have complicated finances or a complicated parenting plan, solving a divorce case is mostly about willingness to try to agree.

Lots of people pin the high costs of divorce on the lawyers themselves. I suppose sometimes that's true, www.owingsmillsmediation.com/openletter.htm, Frank letter from divorce lawyer about why folks practice like they do but if you're using an ethical lawyer, generally the costs become high when clients ask the lawyer to help in ways that the lawyer isn't trained to help. Bills get high when clients call every time a question pops into their minds, rather than saving questions on a notepad by the phone to ask all at once. Or, clients will ask the lawyer to file papers requesting a court hearing when really a settlement conference would make more sense. Again, it probably all comes down to whether you're ready to reach an agreement and whether you're emotionally prepared to reach an agreement.

Nowadays there are a variety of ways to resolve the dissolution of a relationship: Alternative Dispute Resolution models including self-help, paralegals, mediation, Association for Conflict Resolution, www.acrnet.org, and Collaborative Divorce, www.lacfla.com, have all entered the modern day lexicon in addition to the traditional divorce litigation model.

These estimates are based on my 12 years of experience as a divorce litigator followed by 7 years in a mediation-only law practice. They're Los Angeles numbers, so if you live in a more rural area you can reduce these estimates by 30% to 50%. The contrast is still the same, though: you can save a great deal of money and time, as well as stress, by using mediation before choosing litigation. Here's the chart that lays it all out: www.peace-talks.com/compare.php

Mediation	Litigation*	Life Beyond Divorce	Savings by Using Mediation Instead of Litigation	Time Value of Money (Savings) Over 20 Years**	Total Savings By Using Mediation
3 sessions at 3 hours each, $625 per hour * plus preparation of paperwork and consultation with independent attorneys to review settlement options: $8500**	Low conflict divorce, with some negotiation but uncontested final judgment. Both spouses have attorneys who charge $375 per hour: $40,000	Trip to Hawaii for two, two weeks, all-inclusive package including room with a view: $10,000	$31,500	$71,811	$71,811: Enough for over 7 trips to Hawaii
3 sessions, paperwork, consultation attorneys to options: $12,500	Limited contested divorce case, no children, trial on common financial issues: $70,000	1976 Rolls Royce Silver Shadow classic automobile, fully refurbished: $15,000	$58,000	$91,682	$91,682: Enough for 6 classic Rolls Royce cars
5 sessions, preparation of paperwork and consultation with attorneys to review settlement options: $18,000	Contested divorce case with custody issues which settles right before trial date: $125,000	Undergraduate education, 4 years in-state tuition, Indiana University (Bloomington): $29,000	$107,000	$234,450	$234,450: Enough to send 8 children to CSU for an undergrad college education
6 sessions, paperwork, consultation with attorneys to review options: $21,000	Fully contested custody case which proceeds to trial: $275,000	Law School education, 3 years' tuition, Southwestern Law School , Los Angeles , California: $105,000	$254,000	$556,545>	$556,545: Enough to send 5 people to law school ***and*** buy a classic Rolls Royce
8 sessions, paperwork, consultation with attorneys to review options: $25,000	Fully contested custody and financial issues case involving child custody evaluators and forensic valuation experts for business, pensions, etc.: $350,000	4 bedroom, 2 bath home with water view, Ft. Lauderdale, Florida: $425,000	$325,000	$712,115	$712,115: Enough for a house in Ft. Lauderdale with enough left over to send a child to college *and* law school, and $ 75,000 to spare.

* Think I've exaggerated the costs of litigation? Consider this quote from the presiding judge of the Los Angeles County Superior Court at the Beverly Hills Bar Association meeting in September 2002: "By the time we see [divorce] cases in court, most people have spent all of their community assets on the divorce itself. By that time, we're just dividing debts and allocating attorney's fees."

** For this calculation, I've used a 4% simple interest rate and subtracted the cost of mediation from the cost of litigation. This figure represents the amount of money you'd save by mediating your divorce instead of litigating, and how much that savings would be worth if you invested it at 4% interest for 20 years.

SAMPLE MEDIATION AGREEMENT LETTER

November 7, 2003

Ms. Nancy Lott
5540 Garth Avenue
Los Angeles, CA 90056

RE: Mediation

Dear Nancy:
Thank you for your call this afternoon about mediation. Mediation is a very good process for completing a divorce with less cost, time, and overall stress than traditional litigation. It also gives you the opportunity to develop a settlement that is tailored to your family, and that makes sense for everyone. I've enclosed some information about mediation, and about our firm. You may also want to take a look at our web site, http://www.peacetalks.com.

Because mediation is a new concept for many people, we offer a free mediation orientation for people who are considering using our services. The orientation typically takes about 30 minutes, and it gives you a chance to meet us and to ask any questions you have about the process. If you need our assistance in deciding how to approach your husband about this, please let us know. I've enclosed an extra brochure which you can pass along to him if you wish.

Please let us know if you'd like to schedule an orientation, a mediation session, or both. Although it's not required, many people going through mediation either have attorneys, or consult with attorneys, before signing a mediated agreement. If you need a referral to an attorney who can represent you individually but who believes in the mediation process, please let us know. If you've already hired an attorney, you may wish to share this letter and discuss of the benefits of mediation with him or her.
Take care, and I wish you all the best.

Very truly yours,

Diana Mercer,
Attorney-Mediator

Peace Talks Mediation Services, Inc.

8055 W. Manchester Ave., Suite 201
Playa del Rey, CA 90293
Telephone (310) 301-2100
Fax (310) 301-2102
e-mail: mediator@peace-talks.com
www.peace-talks.com

AGREEMENT TO MEDIATE

I have read the attached Mediation Agreement completely and understand its contents. I have initialed each page to indicate my understanding and agreement of the terms.

This is an agreement between **Peace Talks Mediation Services, Inc.**, **and **hereinafter "parties," and Tara Fass, LMFT, and Michelle Kazadi, Esq., hereinafter "mediator," to enter into mediation with the intent of resolving issues related to the dissolution of our marriage.

Dated	MEDIATOR, Tara Fass, LMFT
Dated	MEDIATOR, Victoria Simon, Ph. D., LMFT
Dated	MEDIATOR, Michelle Kazadi, Esq.
Dated	MEDIATOR, Grace K. Lee, Esq.
Dated	MEDIATOR, Stephanie Maloney, CDFA
Dated	MEDIATOR, Diana L. Mercer President, Peace Talks Mediation Services, Inc.
Dated	, Client
Dated	, Client

Party #1 ______
Party #2 ______

MEDIATION AGREEMENT

Peace Talks Mediation Services, Inc., the parties and the mediator understand and agree as follows:

1. ESTABLISHMENT OF MEDIATION RELATIONSHIP

The undersigned wish to retain the services of Peace Talks Mediation Services, Inc., and Michelle Kazadi, Esq., Grace K. Lee, Esq., Diana L. Mercer, Esq., Tara Fass, LMFT, Stephanie Maloney, CDFA, Peter W. Ballas, MBA, and/or Victoria Simon, Ph.D., LMFT, to mediate disputed issues with regard to the dissolution of our marriage.

All references to "mediator" apply to any person designated by the mediator to assist in the mediation process.

2. NATURE OF MEDIATION

The parties understand that mediation is an agreement-reaching process in which the mediator assists parties to reach agreement in a collaborative, consensual and informed manner. It is understood that the mediator has no power to decide disputed issues for the parties. The parties understand that the mediator's objective is to facilitate the parties themselves reaching their most constructive and fairest agreement.

3. RIGHT OF CONSULTATION WITH LAWYER AND OTHER TRUSTED ADVISORS

We suggest that you don't go through this process alone. Reach out to people and professionals you trust. Consider consulting with a lawyer, accountant, financial planner, therapist, friend, family member or other trusted advisor at any time during the mediation process, and especially before signing the final settlement agreement. We recommend that you consult with these advisors early in the process to establish a relationship with counsel you trust so that when you review the agreement, you will be reviewing it with a professional who has familiarity with your circumstances. Many attorneys, accountants and other Trusted Advisors will work on an hourly basis (no retainer, no minimum fee). Please let us know if you would like a referral. If you'd like for us to share any information with them directly, we can give you a release for all mediation participants to sign.

4. MEDIATOR REPRESENTS NEITHER PARTY

The parties acknowledge that the mediator does not represent the interests of either party and is not acting as an attorney or the parties' personal therapist. The parties acknowledge that the purpose of mediation is to facilitate the ultimate resolution and agreement between the parties regarding the issues, problems, and disputes presented in

Party #1 _______
Party #2 _______

mediation and that the mediator does not act as an advocate, representative, fiduciary, lawyer, or therapist for either party. The basic legal information which we provide is no substitute for individualized legal counsel.

The staff at Peace Talks is committed to sharing legal information with clients, and helping clients to make informed decisions, but we cannot give you individualized legal advice. While mediation may encompass more than the usual legal remedies, we believe that family mediations also operate within the framework of the legal system. At Peace Talks you may choose to make a creative or unconventional decision, but you will not make an uninformed decision. Because there is no mediator certification or licensing in California, there is no standardization of mediation practice from firm to firm beyond the basic mediators' ethical rules. If you have any questions about how our practice may differ from others, please let us know.

We often talk about taxes and tax ramifications during our mediation sessions. Please understand that, in compliance with regulations issued by the Internal Revenue Services, any federal tax advice contained in any communications with or from this office are not intended to be used and may not be used by any person to avoid any penalties under the Internal Revenue Code. (IRS Circular 230). That said, we do our best to be helpful, but you want to be sure to speak with your accountant or tax professional with regard to all of your tax issues.

5. IMPARTIALITY OF MEDIATOR

The parties acknowledge that although the mediator will be impartial and that the mediator does not favor either party, there may be issues in which one party may be reasonable and the other may not be reasonable. A common criticism of mediation is that mediators skip the difficult discussions in favor of reaching a quick agreement. That will not happen at Peace Talks. The mediator has a duty to assure a balanced dialogue and to diffuse any manipulative or intimidating tactics.

6. CONFIDENTIALITY

Mediation Sessions and Work Product: It is understood between the parties and the mediator that the mediation will be strictly confidential. Mediation discussions, written and oral communications, any draft resolutions, and any unsigned mediated agreements shall not be admissible in any court proceedings. Only a mediated agreement signed by the parties is admissible in court. Most people agree that they will share the summary letters and draft agreements with their attorneys, accountants, or other advisors, and to this extent they would not be confidential, although they would not be admissible in court as evidence.

Between Session Telephone Calls and Letters: Unless otherwise agreed, the content of between session telephone calls and letters *is not* confidential. For example, if we receive an e-mail from one party, the other party will receive a copy of that e-mail along with the response.

Caucuses in Mediation Sessions: Unless otherwise agreed, the individual sessions (caucuses) held during a mediation session at the office are completely

confidential, and the discussions held with one party *will not* be revealed to the other party without the first party's specific agreement.

Party #1 ______
Party #2 ______

Court Testimony: The parties further agree to not call the mediator to testify concerning the mediation or to provide any materials from the mediation in any court proceeding between the parties. The mediation is considered by the parties and the mediator as settlement negotiations. The parties understand the mediator has an ethical responsibility to break confidentiality if s/he suspects another person may be in danger of harm. The only other exceptions to this confidentiality of the mediation are with regard to the mediator's duty to report reasonable suspicion of child abuse; the mediator's ability to defend himself/herself in any legal action; in the event of a joint written waiver of confidentiality by the parties; use and admission into evidence of this Agreement to Mediate to establish the confidentiality of the mediation process, or otherwise as may be required by law.

Financial Disclosures: This confidentiality does not extend to the parties' mutual financial disclosure requirements, which are required by law.

Security System: As part of our security system, cameras in our office record video (but not audio) 24/7. These recordings are systematically deleted every 30 days, and are used only in the event of a security problem in our office.

E-Mail: We often use e-mail to correspond with clients because it is fast and convenient for many people. Our e-mail is not specially encrypted for security, and passes over the internet like any other e-mail. If you do not wish for us to send you e-mail, please let us know. We send all important letters, court papers, and agreement copies by U.S. Mail in addition to e-mail.

7. RIGHT OF MEDIATOR TO WITHDRAW

The mediator will attempt to resolve any outstanding disputes among the parties as long as both parties make a good faith effort to reach an agreement based on fairness to both parties. Parties must be willing and able to participate in the process in order for it to work. Mediated agreements require compromise, and parties agree to attempt to be flexible and open to new possibilities for a resolution of the dispute. If the mediator, in his or her professional judgment, concludes that agreement is not possible or that continuation of the mediation process would harm or prejudice one or all of the participants, the mediator shall withdraw and the mediation conclude.

8. TERMINATION OF MEDIATION WITHOUT CAUSE

The mediation may be terminated without cause by any party at any time. No reason must be given, either to the other parties or to the mediator.

Upon termination of mediation, the mediator will not counsel either party or represent any party against any other party, in any court proceeding, adversary negotiation, or for any other reason involving a dispute between the parties except the mediator or Dispute Resolution Associate may discuss with either party individually how to recommence the mediation process.

9. VOLUNTARY DISCLOSURE OF POSSIBLE PREJUDICIAL INFORMATION

Party #1 ______
Party #2 ______

The parties agree that, while mediation is in progress, full disclosure of all information is essential to a successful resolution of the issues. Since the court process may not be used to compel information during the mediation process, any agreement made through mediation may be rescinded in whole or in part if one party fails to disclose relevant information. Since the voluntary disclosure of this information may give one party an advantage that may not have been obtained through the traditional adversarial process, the parties agree to release and hold harmless the mediator from any liability or damages caused by voluntary disclosure of prejudicial information in the mediation process that may be used in subsequent negotiations or court proceedings. The mediator has no power to bind third parties not to disclose information furnished during mediation.

10. THE MEDIATOR DOES NOT PROMISE RESULTS

Each party acknowledges that, since mediation is a process of compromise, it is possible that any party might agree to settle on terms that might be considered to be less favorable in comparison to what they party might have received from a Judge after a contested court hearing, or through negotiation in which one or all of the parties have retained legal counsel. The mediator makes no representations that the ultimate result would be the same in kind or degree as might be concluded through negotiation or a contested trial on one or all of the issues. Any questions concerning fairness should be addressed to the mediator as they occur. In addition, parties should consult with independent legal counsel to review compromises made during the course of mediation, and all provisions of a final agreement prior to executing any court documents.

11. FILING OF COURT DOCUMENTS

Once an agreement is reached, in whole or in part, or at any time the parties desire to file any court documents to confirm the agreement and to obtain court order or judgment based thereon, the parties understand that the mediator may not represent either party in a court of law. However, if parties agree to act as their own attorney(s) *In Pro Per*, the parties may authorize the mediator and Peace Talks staff to prepare court papers and to monitor all paperwork through the court system. In performing such work, Peace Talks' attorney-mediators are performing their neutral mediator functions and will take no action without the mutual agreement and authorization of all parties.

12. MEDIATION FEES

Our list of fees and services is attached to this agreement (pages 9 & 10).

General terms: Fees for the mediator(s) are billed on an hourly basis for time spent with the parties in mediation as well as for time outside of the mediation sessions to study documents, research issues, prepare correspondence, respond to and initiate telephone calls, prepare draft and final agreements not covered by a flat fee arrangements, and do such other things as may be reasonably necessary to facilitate the parties' reaching full agreement.

Time involving two or more mediators is billed at a rate of $625 per hour, and time involving one mediator is billed at a rate of $575.00 per hour. Our office works on a

Party #1 ______
Party #2 ______

co-mediation model, so time in mediation sessions is billed at $625 per hour unless otherwise specified. The $575 billing rate will be used for single-mediator tasks such as between-session telephone calls and letters, and between-session drafting and research. Mediation Summary letters and drafting time is billed at $625 per hour. If we spend time working on your file, we bill for that time; for example, we bill for telephone calls and e-mail, with the minimum time increment billed being .2 hours (two tenths of an hour).

Fees for the Dispute Resolution Associate are also billed on an hourly basis with the minimum time increment billed being .2 hours. The Dispute Resolution Associate is a paralegal and paralegal tasks are charged at a rate of $225 per hour. Such billable tasks include, but are not limited to, discussions about your case or case status other than scheduling appointments, assistance with completing financial disclosures, and requests for additional copies of any portion of your file. There is no charge for purely administrative tasks handled by the Dispute Resolution Associate, *e.g.*, making and confirming appointments, monthly status letters, and directions to our office; however, sending duplicate copies of letters or documents which have previously been sent to you will be billed at $225 per hour with a minimum fee of $50 per request.

Payment in full for the first mediation session plus all requested follow up work, such as mediation summary letters, the administrative fee, as well as any flat-fee paperwork, is due upon signing of this agreement. We do not ordinarily require a retainer, and for appointments during regular business hours you simply pay for the time and services that you use when you use them.

Non-Refundable Appointment Deposit: To schedule each mediation appointment a non-refundable $200 deposit must be paid in advance and is **forfeited** if you cancel or reschedule your mediation session less than 72 business hours of the scheduled time. This deposit will be credited to your final mediation appointment bill. Cancellation and rescheduling: Saturday, Sunday or Monday appointments must be canceled or rescheduled no later than 11:00 am on Wednesday. Tuesday appointments must be canceled or rescheduled no later than 11:00 am on the preceding Thursday. Credits and Refunds of Deposit: If your appointment is canceled or rescheduled *more* than 72 business hours in advance of the appointment time, your $200 deposit will be credited to your next mediation session provided your next session is held within 6 months of your originally scheduled mediation appointment. After 6 months, your $200 deposit is forfeited. Your deposit is non-refundable. If you prefer to pay for mediation time in advance as a flat fee package, we have some options in addition to our usual "*a la carte*" billing, so let us know if you're interested.

The parties shall be jointly and severally liable for the mediator's fees and expenses.

From time to time, Peace Talks pays referring attorneys a referral fee. Fee sharing (*e.g.*, this referral fee) is permitted by the ethical rules for attorneys in the State of California provided that it does not increase the amount you pay us for our services, that you're aware that a referral fee may be paid in your case, and that the referring attorney is not involved in your case (*i.e.*, there no conflict of interest). If you would like to know if Peace Talks is paying a referral fee in your case, please just let us know.

As a token of our appreciation to you, when you refer friends or relatives who become clients of Peace Talks, we will send you a small gift, *e.g.*, a gift certificate. This is not a referral fee and should not be interpreted as a request to solicit business.

Party #1 ______
Party #2 ______

Should payment not be timely made, Peace Talks may stop all work on behalf of the parties, including the drafting and/or distribution of the parties' agreement, and withdraw from the mediation. If collection or court action is taken by the mediator to collect fees and/or expenses under this agreement, the prevailing party in any such action and upon any appeal therefrom shall be entitled to attorney fees and costs therein incurred.

Late Arrivals: Our billable time begins at time that your session is scheduled to begin. We dedicate uninterrupted time for your appointment and are ready to begin at the scheduled time, and you will be charged accordingly. We appreciate a telephone call if you will be late, but you will be charged beginning with the time the appointment was originally scheduled.

Early Arrivals: We encourage you to arrive early and spend some time in our client library. There are a number of books and materials available for you to use, and several good videos. If you are already involved in mediation and have hired our office to do your paperwork, arriving early will give you a chance to finalize your paperwork with our legal assistant.

The mediators will not speak with either party (other than to offer beverages, start a video, etc.) prior to the arrival of the second party unless we have both parties' permission to do so.

Cancellations and Rescheduling: You are welcome to cancel or reschedule an appointment with 72 business hours advance notice to our office. With less than 72 business hours' notice, you will be charged a flat fee of $200 for cancellation or rescheduling. If you cancel or reschedule an early, late, weekend or [previously] rescheduled appointment less than 72 business hours before your scheduled session, you forfeit your $200 deposit. For early, late, weekend and rescheduled appointments which are canceled or rescheduled more than 72 business hours in advance, the $200 deposit will be credited toward the next mediation session within 6 months. Remembering your scheduled mediation date and time is your sole responsibility, and we generally will not call or e-mail to confirm appointments.

13. CO-MEDIATION

We feel that a therapist and a lawyer or financial professional working together provide the fullest view possible of the divorce process. Divorce isn't just a legal process; it's an emotional process as well. Using both types of professionals, we can help you navigate both sides of the issues. Even with the slightly higher fees, many clients find that they resolve their cases faster and more thoroughly than if just or a lawyer or just a therapist mediated with them alone. Please let us know if you'd like to discuss the benefits of co-mediation further.

14. MEDIATION AND BINDING ARBITRATION

All disputes between Peace Talks, the parties and the mediator regarding any aspect of our professional relationship will be resolved by mediation, and if not resolved, to be followed by binding arbitration administered through the County Bar Association

Party #1 ______
Party #2 ______

Should payment not be timely made, Peace Talks may stop all work on behalf of the parties, including the drafting and/or distribution of the parties' agreement, and withdraw from the mediation. If collection or court action is taken by the mediator to collect fees and/or expenses under this agreement, the prevailing party in any such action and upon any appeal therefrom shall be entitled to attorney fees and costs therein incurred.

Late Arrivals: Our billable time begins at time that your session is scheduled to begin. We dedicate uninterrupted time for your appointment and are ready to begin at the scheduled time, and you will be charged accordingly. We appreciate a telephone call if you will be late, but you will be charged beginning with the time the appointment was originally scheduled.

Early Arrivals: We encourage you to arrive early and spend some time in our client library. There are a number of books and materials available for you to use, and several good videos. If you are already involved in mediation and have hired our office to do your paperwork, arriving early will give you a chance to finalize your paperwork with our legal assistant.

The mediators will not speak with either party (other than to offer beverages, start a video, etc.) prior to the arrival of the second party unless we have both parties' permission to do so.

Cancellations and Rescheduling: You are welcome to cancel or reschedule an appointment with 72 business hours advance notice to our office. With less than 72 business hours' notice, you will be charged a flat fee of $200 for cancellation or rescheduling. If you cancel or reschedule an early, late, weekend or [previously] rescheduled appointment less than 72 business hours before your scheduled session, you forfeit your $200 deposit. For early, late, weekend and rescheduled appointments which are canceled or rescheduled more than 72 business hours in advance, the $200 deposit will be credited toward the next mediation session within 6 months. Remembering your scheduled mediation date and time is your sole responsibility, and we generally will not call or e-mail to confirm appointments.

13. CO-MEDIATION

We feel that a therapist and a lawyer or financial professional working together provide the fullest view possible of the divorce process. Divorce isn't just a legal process; it's an emotional process as well. Using both types of professionals, we can help you navigate both sides of the issues. Even with the slightly higher fees, many clients find that they resolve their cases faster and more thoroughly than if just or a lawyer or just a therapist mediated with them alone. Please let us know if you'd like to discuss the benefits of co-mediation further.

14. MEDIATION AND BINDING ARBITRATION

All disputes between Peace Talks, the parties and the mediator regarding any aspect of our professional relationship will be resolved by mediation, and if not resolved, to be followed by binding arbitration administered through the County Bar Association

Party #1 ______
Party #2 ______

pursuant to the Code of Civil Procedure and not by litigation in court. By this provision, the parties and Peace Talks are both giving up the right to have any such dispute decided by a judge or a jury and we are each giving up the right of appeal.

The prevailing party in any arbitration between us will be entitled to reasonable attorney's fees and costs. Any litigation or arbitration between us will take place in Los Angeles County and California State law will apply.

It is important for you to know that under current California law a mediator has complete immunity from suits regarding negligence or malpractice or any other cause of action. This means that you cannot sue our mediators for any damage to you arising out of the mediation relationship.

Before signing this agreement, you have a right to consult your own attorney about the legal consequences to you of signing this agreement and specifically waiving the right to use the courts in any fee dispute and using arbitration instead.

15. FILE RETENTION AND DESTRUCTION

You will receive copies of every important document in your case as the case proceeds. Our office policy is to keep copies of your documents, not originals. Once your case is closed, we will retain your file for 5 years. If you would like your file returned to you after 5 years, please keep us informed of your current address so we can send it to you. If you do not request the return of your file we will destroy your file after 5 years. If you are filing court papers, the court [generally] keeps your court papers indefinitely. A copy, or certified copy, can be obtained by requesting it from the court. For Los Angeles County, you can request these copies online at www.lasuperiorcourt.org or at 111 N. Hill Street, Room 112, Los Angeles, CA 90012.

16. EXECUTION OF MEDIATION AGREEMENT

By signing this Mediation Agreement, each party agrees that he or she has carefully read and considered each and every provision of this Agreement and agrees to each provision of this agreement without reservation.

Mediation Fees:

Hourly fees:

Co-Mediation (2 mediators together)	$625.00
Summary Letter and drafting rate	$625.00
Single Mediator Rate	$575.00
Paralegal	$225.00
Parenting Plan Mediation *	$475.00
Post-Judgment Mediation Sessions **	$375.00

* Parenting Plan Mediation will be held with a therapist-mediator alone, at Peace Talks' option, with no attorney-mediator present, and will cover only parenting plan mediation issues, not child support or any financial issues.

**Post Judgment Mediation Sessions: This fee is a special rate for clients who completed their divorce mediation through Peace Talks and who are returning to discuss post-judgment matters, including but not limited to parenting plans, child support modifications, spousal support modifications, etc. Clients opting for this special post-judgment rate agree that Peace Talks may elect to provide one or two mediators, at their option, and that Peace Talks may choose which mediator(s) work with clients at this special rate.

Party #1 ______
Party #2 ______

Mediation Summary letters are prepared after each session and are billed at 2 to 4 hours of the regular single mediator hourly rate, depending upon the actual time to complete the letter given the mediation session's complexity and length. Your mediation summary letters provide a personalized road map of how you will get through this process with the maximum amount of efficiency and success. It provides a written record of the progress made in each session, memorializes the next steps to take, and summarizes the information and discussion to share with your trusted advisors.

Administrative Fee: A one-time, non-refundable administrative fee of $150 is due at the time you make your first mediation appointment. This fee covers the cost of convening your case and setting up your file with this office.

Paper Preparation (Flat Fees):

Petition and Response:

Petition and Response (no minor children)	$375.00
Petition and Response (with minor children)	$475.00

Petition/Response Papers include at no extra charge:
Case Cover Sheet
Summons
UCCJEA Statement
Notice and Acknowledgment of Receipt
Proof of Service
Actual mail service of papers and copies

Court Filing Fees: *Please make your checks payable to "Clerk of the Superior Court".*

Petition	$320.00
Response or Agreement (whichever is first)	$320.00

Judgment Package:

Judgments (no children):	$1995.00
Judgments with Parenting Plans:	$2295.00

All judgment packages include at no extra charge:
Typing and service of Income and Expense Declarations
Typing and service of Schedule of Assets and Debts
Declaration of Disclosure (one for each party)
Continued on next page:

Appearance, Stipulation and Waivers
Declaration Re: Default or Uncontested Divorce
Judgment
Notice of Entry of Judgment
Declaration Re: Service of Declaration of Disclosure
Mail service of papers and copies

Party #1 ______
Party #2 ______

Proof of Service
Child Support Case Registry Form
Wage Assignment (if requested)
Stipulation for Waiver of Final Declaration of Disclosure
10 minute signing appointment (for signing and notarizing papers only, no mediation time)
Filling in blanks on judgment (*e.g.*, account numbers) when e-mailed in advance of any appointment

Miscellaneous fees:

Early, Late and Weekend appointments: (Weekdays before 10:00 am and after 6:30 pm)	$200 non-refundable deposit plus an additional $50 per hour surcharge
Quitclaim deed or Inter-Spousal Transfer Deed (includes recording, recording fees, and copies)	$375.00
Preparation of Income and Expense Declarations and Schedule of Assets and Debts (financial disclosures)	billed at regularly hourly rate
Divorce paperwork only (no mediation time)	$300.00
Expedited papers fee (prepared and mailed within 7 days)	$150.00
Faxes (each)	$ 40.00
Federal Express letters and packages (Fed Ex bill plus)	$ 40.00
Courier deliveries surcharge (courier bill plus)	$ 40.00
Telephone calls (minimum charge)	.2 of mediator's hourly rate
Copies of complete file **	$200 + 25 cents per page
Duplicate copies of letters or documents previously sent to you **	$ 40.00 minimum but billed at regular hourly rate

** clients are given a copy of every document that crosses our desk, *e.g.*, mediation summaries, Petition, Response, Judicial Council forms, all court paperwork, bills and correspondence. The $200 charge + 25 cents per page charge is for making a duplicate copy of the documents you've already received.

Party #1 _______
Party #2 _______

Adapted from Forrest S. Mosten's *Agreement to Mediate (2000)*

Institute for Conflict Management, LLC
1541 Ocean Avenue, Suite 200
Santa Monica, California 90401
Tel: 310.319.0011
Fax: 310.319.1104
www.ICMadr.com

SAMPLE PRE-MEDIATION LETTER

CLIENT INFORMATION

Jared Knowels
ADF Business Systems
PO Box XX42
Los Angeles, CA 90049
T: 555-453-4409
F: 555-453-0866

This information is intended to assist you to maximize and economize your mediation experience. My goal is to assist you to most effectively, comfortably and confidently represent yourself in mediation. In mediation, you will be making all of the decisions. The mediator has no decision-making power. Thus, it is important for you to consider how you can best represent your interests in mediation, as well as the results that you would like to create in mediation.

How long will the mediation take and how much will it cost?
Unfortunately, it is hard to predict with precision how long a mediation will take or how much mediation will cost. These issues depend primarily on how agreeable the participants are. Generally, for divorce, business and organizational matters, we meet between two and six times for approximately two hours each meeting. The cost of a comprehensive mediated agreement generally ranges between $1,000 and $3,000. I will be as specific as possible in these regards once I have a better understanding of your situation.

What if we already agree on lots of issues?
Fantastic! The first thing that we want to do in mediation is to identify what you already agree on. We will use those points of agreement as a foundation for your overall Agreement. The standards that make sense to you on certain "easy" issues can often be applied to resolve other issues. We will want to be sure that your Agreement is well-informed and that you are aware of the many issues that you may want to consider. What is included in your Agreement is up to you. Our goal is to support your well-informed decision-making.

What are our chances for success?
Over the years, approximately 90% of mediating parties at The Mediation Center have reached comprehensive resolution. This high success rate is due to most participants being highly motivated to reach agreement.

Institute for Conflict Management, LLC
1541 Ocean Avenue, Suite 200
Santa Monica, California 90401
Tel: 310.319.0011
Fax: 310.319.1104
www.ICMadr.com

SAMPLE AGREEMENT TO MEDIATE

AGREEMENT TO MEDIATE

This is an Agreement between ____________________ and ________________ and, ______________________________ hereinafter "mediator," to enter into mediation with the intent of resolving the following issues: ______________________
____
____.

The parties and the mediator understand and agree as follows:

1. Nature of Mediation
The parties hereby appoint ______________, as mediator. The parties understand that mediation is an agreement-reaching process in which the mediator assists parties to reach agreement in a collaborative and informed manner. It is understood that the mediator has no power to decide issues for the parties. The parties understand that mediation is not a substitute for independent legal advice. The parties are encouraged to secure such advice throughout the mediation process and are advised to obtain independent legal review of any formal mediated agreement before signing that agreement. The parties understand that the mediator has an obligation to work on behalf of all parties and that the mediator cannot render individual legal advice to any party and will not render therapy nor arbitrate within the mediation.

2. Scope of Mediation
The parties understand that it is for the parties, with the mediator's concurrence, to determine the scope of the mediation and this will be accomplished early in the mediation process.

3. Mediation is Voluntary
All parties here state their good faith intention to complete their mediation by an Agreement. It is, however, understood that any party may withdraw from or suspend the mediation process at any time, for any reason.
The parties also understand that the mediator may suspend or terminate the mediation if he feels that the mediation will lead to an unjust or unreasonable result; if the mediator feels that an impasse has been reached; or if the mediator determines that he can no long effectively perform his facilitative role.

4. Confidentiality
It is understood between the parties and the mediator that the mediation will be strictly confidential. Mediation discussions, any draft resolutions and any unsigned mediated agreements shall not be admissible in any court or other contested proceeding. Only a mediated agreement signed by any parties will be so admissible. The only other exceptions to this confidentiality are if all parties waive confidentiality in writing or in an

Institute for Conflict Management, LLC
1541 Ocean Avenue, Suite 200
Santa Monica, California 90401
Tel: 310.319.0011
Fax: 310.319.1104
www.ICMadr.com

What if we don't reach agreement?
In mediation, all discussions and materials, with very few listed exceptions, are confidential. If no mediated Agreement is reached, evidence of the mediation discussions, mediation materials and any draft mediation resolution will not be admissible in court or any other adversarial proceeding.

Who pays for mediation?
Responsibility for mediation fees is an issue to be decided by mediation participants. Participants are encouraged to consider sharing fees to some extent so all will benefit from expeditious and economic resolution.

What about our own attorneys?
As a mediator and attorney myself, I am ethically bound to advise you to have any mediated Settlement Agreement reviewed by individual legal counsel prior to your signing that Agreement. In practice, I have found that it works best for mediating parties to obtain one to four hours of individual legal advice throughout the mediation process. This legal advice may be best obtained early in the mediation, by legal counsel's review of a near-final draft Agreement, and by counsel's review of the final Agreement. This level of consultation will dramatically elevate your comfort and confidence in the final agreement.

What about utilizing experts?
It may make sense, in a particular case, for mediation participants to retain mutually trusted experts. For example, participants may desire a trusted valuation of real property, personal property or a business. It is also not uncommon for mediating parties to choose to jointly consult with an accountant or tax expert. Mediation participants with parenting concerns may find it beneficial to obtain the thoughts and recommendations of a trusted child psychologist. Mediation participants may choose to jointly retain an impartial advisory attorney who, based upon an agreed-upon set of facts, may render an advisory non-binding opinion on how a court might resolve the identified issues.

What else can I do to prepare?
Perhaps the most important thing any mediating party can do to ensure a satisfying and successful mediation experience is to prepare for the mediation discussions by seeking clarity as to his or her desired outcomes and perceived standards of fairness. Stated otherwise, "What do you want?" and "How will you know that it is alright to agree?"

Thank you for your kind attention. I look forward to working with you.

Sincerely,

Institute for Conflict Management, LLC
1541 Ocean Avenue, Suite 200
Santa Monica, California 90401
Tel: 310.319.0011
Fax: 310.319.1104
www.ICMadr.com

action brought by any party against the mediator. The parties agree not to call the mediator to testify concerning the mediation or to provide any materials from the mediation in any court proceeding between the parties. The mediation is considered by the parties and the mediator as settlement negotiations. All parties also understand and agree that the mediator may have private caucus meetings and discussions with any individual party, in which case all such meetings and discussions shall be confidential between the mediator and the caucusing party.

5. Full Disclosure
Each party agrees to fully and honestly disclose all relevant information and writings as requested by the mediator and all information requested by any other party, if the mediator determines that the disclosure is relevant to the mediation discussions. In family mediation cases, each party agrees to fully and accurately disclose all income, assets and debts.

6. Mediator Impartiality
The parties understand that the mediator must remain impartial throughout and after the mediation process. Thus, the mediator shall not champion the interests of any party over another in the mediation nor in any court or other proceeding.

7. Coordination with Legal Counsel
The parties agree that the mediator may discuss the parties' mediation process with any attorney any party may retain as individual counsel. Such discussions will not include any negotiations unless the parties instruct the mediator that their attorney(s) have negotiating authority. The mediator will provide copies of correspondence, draft agreements and written documentation to independent legal counsel at a party's request.

8. Mediation Fees
The parties and the mediator agree that the fee for the mediator shall be $___ per hour for time spent with the parties and for time required to study documents, research issues, correspond, telephone call, prepare draft and final Agreements, and do such other things as may be reasonably necessary to facilitate the parties reaching full Agreement. The mediator shall also be reimbursed for all expenses incurred as a part of the mediation process.

A payment of $___ toward the mediator's fees and expenses shall be paid to the mediator along with the signing of this agreement. Any unearned amount of this retainer fee will be refunded to the parties. The parties shall be jointly and severally liable for the mediator's fees and expenses. As between the parties only, responsibility for mediation fees and expenses shall be: ____.

Institute for Conflict Management, LLC
1541 Ocean Avenue, Suite 200
Santa Monica, California 90401
Tel: 310.319.0011
Fax: 310.319.1104
www.ICMadr.com

The parties will be provided with a monthly accounting of fees and expenses by the mediator. Payment of such fees and expenses is due to the mediator no later than 15 days following the date of such billing, unless otherwise agreed in writing. There shall be a 1.0% monthly service charge on accounts not paid by the last day of the month.

Should payment not be timely made, the mediator may, in his sole discretion, stop all work on behalf of the parties, including the drafting and/or distribution of the parties' Agreement, and withdraw from the mediation. If collection or court action is taken by the mediator to collect fees and/or expenses under this Agreement, the prevailing party in any such action and upon any appeal there from shall be entitled to attorney fees and costs therein incurred.

DATED this ____ day of ________________________, 200_.

MEDIATION RULES AND PROCEDURES

1 Mediation Procedures Part of Parties' Agreement: When the parties, either by pre-existing contract or subsequent agreement, determine that a dispute that has arisen between them should be resolved through mediation under the authority of the Institute for Conflict Management, LLC (ICM) or under these Procedures, they shall have made these Procedures a part of their mediation agreement.

2 Party-Agreed Procedures: The parties may agree on any Procedures that are consistent with applicable law and the overall goal of resolving the dispute. The parties shall immediately notify ICM at the time of filing, in writing, of any party-agreed Procedures. The party-agreed Procedures shall be enforceable as though contained herein.

3 Amendment of Procedures: ICM reserves the right to amend these Procedures without notice. The Procedures in effect on the date of the commencement of the mediation shall apply, unless the parties have specifically agreed otherwise.

4 Conflict with Law: If any of these Procedures, or as modified by the parties, conflict with any mandatory provision of applicable law, the provision of law shall govern. No other Procedure shall be affected.

5 Commencement of Mediation: Mediation may be initiated either by:

5.1. filing with ICM a fully executed Submission to Mediation Agreement form along with the appropriate filing fees as shown in ICM's current Mediation Fee Schedule; or by,

5.2. any party to the dispute filing for mediation through ICM and requesting that ICM the other party to join in a Submission to Mediation on a form provided ICM. However, a party need only provide the names, addresses and telephone numbers of the parties to the dispute, a Request for Mediation by ICM and a brief description of the dispute and the remedy sought. Upon receipt of the Mediation Agreement form and the appropriate filing fee, ICM shall commence administration of the mediation; or by,

5.3. submission of a contractual provision between the parties requiring them to engage in mediation to resolve their dispute, along with written evidence of the intent of all parties to comply with the requirement and the appropriate filing fees.

6. Determination of Commencement

6.1. The mediation process is deemed commenced when ICM confirms in writing that the above requirements for initiation have been met. The date of commencement of the mediation is the date that ICM mails notification to the parties of the commencement of the proceedings.

6.2. If a party in interest fails or refuses to agree to participate in the mediation process per the parties' contractual agreement (or Submission to Mediation Agreement), ICM shall confirm in writing the failure or refusal of the party to participate. If a party contests the enforceability of a mediation agreement executed as a condition of the parties' initial contract, ICM shall suspend administration of the Procedures, or other related steps, in order to allow the party contesting the enforceability of the contractual mediation clause to seek judicial determination of its enforceability. ICM shall comply with such judicial determination.

7. Notices: The parties agree that all notices necessary for the commencement or continuation of these proceedings may be served by Certified Mail, facsimile transmission or telephone notification with written confirmation via First Class Mail. The date of service of the notice shall be the date the item is post-marked or transmitted by facsimile, whichever is earlier.

8. Parties may be Represented: Any party may be represented in the mediation by anyone of their choosing. Such representative may be an attorney or non-attorney advocate. The names, addresses and telephone numbers of such persons shall be communicated in writing to Institute for Conflict Management. The parties shall ensure that their representatives are fully prepared for all scheduled mediation sessions and that the representative has complete settlement authority at all sessions. Failure to do so may result in the imposition of sanctions as provided herein.

9. Selection of the Mediator: Upon commencement of the mediation, ICM shall appoint a qualified Mediator to serve the parties in resolving their dispute. If the parties have otherwise agreed on a specific ICM Mediator, that Mediator shall be appointed subject to availability. A single Mediator shall be appointed unless the parties request or agree to co-mediation. If the parties have an agreement or contract provision specifying the method of appointing a Mediator, that designation or method shall be followed.

10. Mediator Qualifications: No person with a financial or personal interest in the outcome of the mediation shall serve as Mediator. Prior to accepting an appointment, the prospective Mediator shall disclose any possible conflict of interest, bias or information likely to create a presumption of bias or any potential scheduling conflict that would prevent a prompt meeting with the parties and finalization of the matter. Upon receipt of such information, ICM shall either replace the Mediator or immediately communicate the information to the parties to secure a written waiver.

11. Challenging the Selection of the Mediator: If any party knows or believes that there is some reason why the appointed or designated Mediator should not serve in that capacity, that party shall immediately notify Institute for Conflict Management. A party's failure to so notify ICM shall be deemed a waiver of the party's objection to the Mediator in these proceedings and may not later constitute grounds to nullify the settlement agreement. If

ICM determines that the appointed Mediator should be disqualified, ICM shall immediately appoint a substitute Mediator from its panel.

12. Mediator Vacancy: If the appointed or designated Mediator is disqualified, or becomes unwilling or unable to serve, ICM shall immediately appoint a substitute Mediator from its panel.

13. Good Faith Effort: By agreeing to mediate under these Procedures, the parties undertake to participate in the mediation, to negotiate, and to make good faith efforts to settle the dispute. Parties who mediate their dispute under these Procedures agree to carry out any settlement agreement without delay.

14. Authority of the Mediator: The Mediator is not empowered to impose a settlement on the parties. Rather the Mediator's authority extends only to those processes that the Mediator determines may best facilitate an agreeable resolution of their dispute.

> 14.1. Sanctions: In certain circumstances, where a party has failed or refused to mediate in good faith, or is egregiously dilatory in preparing to participate in the mediation, the Mediator may impose monetary sanctions which must be paid prior to proceeding with the Mediation. Such behavior may include, but is not limited to, actions causing delay, failure to disclose information known to be relevant, failure to make a good faith effort to prepare for a pre-mediation conference or mediation session, failure to abide by a Case Management Order, or failure to designate and provide a representative vested with adequate authority to settle the entire amount of the claim.

15. Disclosure of Confidential Information: The Mediator is authorized to conduct joint and separate meetings with the parties and to make oral and written recommendations for settlement. Any separate meetings shall be confidential. If the Mediator is advised that information conveyed during such meeting is confidential, the Mediator shall not disclose that information to the other party.

16. Pre-Mediation Conferences: In some cases the parties or the Mediator may deem a pre-mediation meeting between the Mediator and the parties essential to the expeditious mediation of the claim. Any party, or the Mediator may notify the parties and schedule such a conference before a mediation session is scheduled.

> 16.1 Procedural Matters Only: The sole purpose of the conference shall be for the discussion of procedural matters. The merits of the respective parties' cases shall not be discussed with the Mediator, nor shall any testimony or evidence of any kind be submitted at that time.
>
> 16.2 Discovery Procedures: The Mediator shall set discovery Procedures and an evidence exchange schedule with submission deadlines to assist in defining the issues, and the nature and extent of the claims. The Mediator may include this, and

other procedural issues discussed in these Procedures, in a written Case Management Order to ensure that all parties to the dispute fully understand their rights and responsibilities.

16.3 Additional Pre-Mediation Conferences: Additional meetings may be ordered by the Mediator prior to commencement of the Mediation to ensure compliance among the parties, to further define issues, and to release nonessential parties whose lack of responsibility for any portion of the damages alleged in the claim may be early determined.

17. Neutral Experts: The Mediator may obtain neutral expert advice concerning technical aspects of the matter. The parties shall equally divide the costs of such expert(s). Neutral Experts may include those knowledgeable of engineering, design or construction matters, or they may be neutral attorneys whose legal expertise is needed on matters of discovery, construction defect, delay claims or damages, or other construction contract issues. The latter, for example, might be brought into the pre-mediation conference to serve as a discovery referee.

18. Memorandum of Issues: At least ten (10) days prior to the first scheduled mediation session, each party shall provide the Mediator with a brief Memorandum of Issues setting forth its position with regard to the matters that need to be resolved. At the discretion of the Mediator, the parties may mutually exchange such memoranda.

18.1. At the first session, the parties shall produce all information reasonably required for the Mediator to understand the issues presented.

18.2. The Mediator may require any party to supplement such information.

19. Suspension of Civil Claims: If a matter has been submitted for mediation after civil litigation has been commenced in court over the same claim or dispute, or if a matter has been submitted prior to or in lieu of filing the case in court, the parties must stipulate in writing that any civil action is being held in abeyance pending the outcome of the mediation process. A party may be required to provide the Mediator with proof that a pending civil action is no longer calendared on the court docket. In the absence of such stipulation and/or appropriate proof, ICM shall suspend the mediation process until such stipulation or proof has been supplied.

20. Setting Mediation Sessions: ICM shall set the date, time and place of each mediation session, taking into account scheduling information provided by the Mediator and the parties. The mediation shall be held at any convenient location agreeable to the Mediator and the parties, as determined by ICM.

21. Privacy of the Mediation Process

21.1. Attendance of Non-participants at Hearings: Mediation is a private and confidential proceeding. Only those having a direct interest in the mediation shall be entitled to attend the conferences and sessions, provided, however, that ICM personnel or panel members may observe for quality assurance purposes.

21.2. Such observers shall be bound by the same confidentiality requirements set forth in these Procedures as the Mediator and ICM. Any record or report created by the observer shall be the sole property of ICM, and no party shall be allowed a copy thereof, or to compel production and/or inspection for any reason.

22. Confidentiality of the Mediation Process: Neither the parties, the participants, nor the Mediator shall disclose any confidential information obtained in the course of the mediation. Under California law, all records, reports or other documents received or made by the Mediator while serving in that capacity shall be private and confidential.

22.1. The parties agree that no effort shall be made to compel the Mediator to divulge such records or to testify in regard to the mediation in any adversarial proceeding or judicial forum. The parties shall maintain the confidentiality of the mediation proceedings at all times.

22.2 Generally, California law deems any of the following information inadmissible as evidence in any subsequent arbitration or judicial proceeding:

22.2.1. the views expressed or suggestions made by another party with respect to possible settlement

22.2.2. any admissions made by a party during the mediation sessions;

22.2.3. any documents, notes, or other information prepared for, obtained during, or created at the mediation sessions;

22.2.4. any proposals made, or personal views expressed, by the Mediator;

22.2.5. whether or not a party had expressed a willingness to enter into negotiations or accept a settlement offer, proposal or agreement.

23. No Record of Proceedings: Mediation is not a proceeding of record. No party or participant shall make a video, audio or stenographic record of the mediation proceedings.

24. Closure of Mediation: The mediation shall be terminated when:

24.1. the parties have executed a written settlement agreement;

24.2. the Mediator in his/her discretion declares, in writing, that further efforts at mediation are not likely to produce a settlement agreement; or,

24.3 when a party or the parties declare in writing that further mediation sessions are not likely to produce an agreeable settlement and therefore request termination of the mediation.

25. Commencing Arbitration: If the parties fail to reach a mutually satisfactory settlement through mediation and the mediation process has been terminated, a party or the parties may request that ICM initiate arbitration proceedings under either a pre-existing contract or by subsequent agreement of the parties. Upon execution of a written agreement to arbitrate the dispute, the ICM Arbitration Procedures and Procedures shall govern the dispute.

26. Immunity of Mediator and Institute for Conflict Management:

26.1. Neither ICM, its employees or associates, nor any Mediator shall be subject to subsequent judicial proceedings relating to the mediation, nor shall they be liable to any party for any act or omission in connection with the mediation conducted under these Procedures.

26.2. The parties expressly agree that these Procedures govern and waive any rights to name the Mediator(s), ICM, its employees or associates for any reason in subsequent litigation.

26.3 The Mediator(s), ICM, its employees and associates invoke all state statutes and other laws conferring immunity upon them individually and/or in their official capacities with regard to the mediation. ICM and its panel further invoke all laws limiting disclosure of these confidential and private proceedings.

27. Interpretation of These Procedures: The Mediator shall interpret and apply these Procedures insofar as they relate to the Mediator's authority to facilitate a settlement between the parties. ICM retains the sole and exclusive right to determine any procedural question that arises under these Procedures.

28. Mediation Fees and Expenses

28.1. The fees for mediation services under these Procedures shall be those listed in ICM's schedule of fees in effect at the time the mediation is commenced as provided herein. Fees for mediation services governed by any other set of Procedures may differ from those of ICM, and will be set on a case-bycase basis.

28.2. Any expenses, incurred by the Mediator, ICM's representatives, or Neutral Experts requested by the Mediator, that are reasonably related to the mediation, shall be borne equally by both parties, unless they agree otherwise.

29. Parties to Bear Their Own Expense: The expenses incurred by a party to participate in mediation including, but not limited to, travel, lodging, meals, witness fees, duplication costs, etc., shall be solely borne by the respective party.

GLOSSARY

Advocate: An attorney or non-attorney agent who represents a party involved in mediation, arbitration or other form of alternative dispute resolution process.

Alternative Dispute Resolution, or "ADR": Any method used to resolve a dispute short of civil litigation. Such methods include negotiation, facilitation, conciliation, Issue Review Board™ mediation and arbitration.

Arbitration: A process in which two or more persons voluntarily agree to let an Arbitrator, or panel of Arbitrators, decide their dispute. This decision may be legally binding on the parties. An Arbitrator is a neutral selected to conduct an arbitration hearing and render a decision in a dispute.

Binding Arbitration: Arbitration of a dispute where the Decision of the Arbitrator is final and legally binding on all parties to the arbitration. State or Federal law may provide a limited right of review. The prevailing party may compel compliance with the decision under applicable State or Federal law. Non-Binding Arbitration is the same in every aspect as binding arbitration, except that the Decision of the Arbitrator is advisory only. This method allows any party to immediately commence litigation in a court of law as though the arbitration never occurred.

Business Days: Monday through Friday, except recognized state and federal holidays.

Case Manager: An associate of ICM responsible for the management and administration of disputes submitted to ICM for resolution.

Claimant: The party initiating mediation or arbitration by submitting the appropriate filings with ICM.

Conciliation: A process whereby a neutral from ICM's panel is selected by the parties to review issues arising during the course of construction and to make a non-binding Recommendation for immediate resolution.

Days: Calendar days, including Saturdays, Sundays, excluding state and federal holidays.

Decision: The written award signed and dated by the Arbitrator(s).

Demand For Arbitration: The form used to initiate arbitration proceedings when a contractual obligation to resolve a dispute through arbitration exists. The form sets forth the complaint and relief requested or remedy sought.

Discovery: The process of obtaining evidence and documents from an opposing party.

Issue Review Board(r) (IRB(r)): Referred to by some as a Dispute Review Board. An IRB(r) is a panel of neutrals established prior to commencement of construction to maintain familiarity with a project throughout construction. The IRB(r) meets regularly, and as requested by the parties, to review issues and make non-binding Recommendations for their resolution. The owner and contractor each select a neutral from ICM's panel. The two neutrals then select a third who becomes the Lead Member of the IRB(r). All of the neutrals must be approved by both the owner and the contractor.

Litigation: A lawsuit filed in court to enforce a right or obtain a remedy.

Mediation: The process by which a neutral third party assists the parties to a dispute in reaching a mutually acceptable settlement. The Mediator serves as the neutral third party who is chosen by the parties.

Miscalculation of Figures: A mathematical error in an arbitrator's Decision.

Mistake of Fact: A true error in an Arbitrator's Decision including such things as dates, times, places or names, but not a conclusion of the Arbitrator with which the party disagrees.

Negotiation: The process of submission and consideration of offers and counter-offers until an acceptable offer is made and accepted.

Panel of Arbitrators: Usually three to five Arbitrators, at least one of which is neutral to the parties, empowered to determine the outcome of a controversy.

Parties: Includes any and all persons or legal entities (companies, corporations, etc.) that have an agreement which includes a mediation and/or arbitration provision, or who have signed appropriate forms or agreements under ICM's Rules and Procedures, and who have a recognizable interest in the outcome of the dispute.

Party Arbitrator: Any person appointed by a party to be their selected Arbitrator in a panel of Arbitrators.

Request for Clarification: A form used to ask the Arbitrator to clarify a Decision that is ambiguous or uncertain as to what action is required of a party.

Request for Correction: A form used to ask the Arbitrator to correct a Mistake of Fact or Miscalculation of Figures that appears on the face of the Decision.

Respondent: The party against whom the Claimant has filed for mediation or arbitration.

Response to Demand for Arbitration: The form used by the Respondent to answer the Demand for Arbitration of the Claimant. The form may set forth a general denial or denial of specific issues of the Claimant's Demand. The form may also set forth a counterclaim and relief sought by the Respondent.

Sanction: A fine or penalty, which may be imposed by a Mediator or Arbitrator on a party for failure to comply with any of the Rules or Procedures, or to follow a directive of the Mediator or Arbitrator.

Submission to Arbitration: The form used by the parties to submit a dispute to arbitration where no prior contractual obligation exists. The form is the parties' agreement to arbitrate and confers authority on ICM to initiate the arbitration proceedings.

MEDIATION AND DOMESTIC VIOLENCE

What is "domestic violence" and where will you draw the line?

How will you know when you've got a domestic violence issue?

Screening Procedures

Ways to ask about domestic abuse:

- Tell me about your situation
- Do you feel you can tell the other party what you really want?
- Is there any reason why you and the other party should not sit down to try and work out [any issue]?
- Do you feel comfortable meeting with the other party to discuss these issues?
- Do you have concerns about sitting in the same room as the other party?
- Do you have concerns for your safety?
- Do you have any orders for protection in effect? Have you ever gotten an order of protection?
- Are you afraid of the other party?
- Has the other party ever threatened or hurt you?
- Have you been abused?

For more screening suggestions, there's a great article on mediate.com. Search "domestic violence" for their very thorough article on domestic violence screening. Excerpt attached; reprinted by permission.

"Red Flags" That Abuse has Occurred in a Relationship[1]

1. Observation of threatening, controlling, intimidating behavior toward one party to the mediation by the other;
2. The report or observation of obsessively jealous, possessive, suspicious or accusatory behavior toward one party to the mediation by the other;
3. Unusual timidity or fearfulness of a party in mediation. Efforts by a party in mediation to avoid any conflict with the other party, the potential abuser. The party may also dismiss what sounds to you as abusive behavior;

---

[1] Adapted from "Recognizing and Working with Domestic Abuse" by Denise Wilder, MSBA Family Law Forum, March 1996, Vol. 8, No. 1

4. References to the other party's "anger problem". A suspected victim says that the children don't like to visit the other party;
5. A party, the suspected victim, assumes responsibility for the other party's problems, behavior, etc.
6. Physical, social and/or financial isolation of one party by the other (e.g., limiting phone use, travel, contact with friends or family, or access to money);
7. Unusual history of injuries-frequency or severity. Often injuries are attributed to "accidents" or "clumsiness";
8. Unstable job history of a suspected victim-possibly due to injury or harassment at the workplace by the potential abuser;
9. The suspected victim moved out of the house in a hurry, is staying with a friend, has no personal belongings;
10. A party is very concerned about confidentiality;
11. A party seems anxious or in a hurry;
12. Alcohol or drug abuse, along with other red flags.

What are the risks in mediations where there has been domestic violence between the parties?

- For you
- For them
- For the process

Will you handle mediations in which there has been domestic violence? Will you have a choice?

Pros and cons What's in between?

- No-never appropriate
- Yes-if the abused party is clear about wanting to mediate
- Yes-if screening and you feel the abuse wasn't that severe
- Yes-always, with safeguards

What does saying "no" to handling those kinds of mediations may mean

For you and your practice

For the participants

If you decide to handle mediations in which there's been domestic violence between the parties, what are the issues?

Safety Planning

Before Mediation

- Use screening techniques
- Be prepared to make referrals if mediation isn't appropriate
- Make sure mediation session won't violate TRO or Domestic Abuse orders---if the parties still wish to mediate, enter into written agreement & file with court that mediation will not violate "no contact" orders. This agreement protects both sides.

During Mediation

- Only mediate if you're experienced, or better yet, co-mediate with an experienced mediator
- Use separate waiting areas and stagger arrival and departure times
- Use an escort or an advocate for the abused party to/from/during the mediation session
- Invite both parties' attorneys to attend the mediation
- Use caucuses-and perhaps use them exclusively, never meeting with the parties in the same room
- Use ground rules, and let the parties know you can terminate the mediation at any time at your discretion. Put this in your Mediation Agreement
- Be alert for signs of intimidation
- Plan the room set up and seating arrangement
- When you terminate the mediation, stagger departure times, let the abused person leave first, provide an escort
- Mediate when other people are around in the building
- Have an "emergency" plan in case abuse arises during the mediation or your physical safety is threatened

In the Agreement

- No provisions that require contact between the parties
- Consider using trial or temporary agreements to see if workable (e.g., supervised visitation with neutral 3rd party) with report back time frame to neutrals.

Adapted from Family Law Mediation Training (Summer 2001) Domestic Abuse Supplement

Some Domestic Violence Statistics[2]:

Type of Violence or Incident	Est. % of Total DV
Ongoing / episodic male battering	10-18%
Female initiated violence	13-15%
Male-controlling interactive violence	20%
Separation engendered & post-divorce trauma	17-25%
Psychotic and paranoid reactions	5%

[2] Adapted from Leslie Ellen Shear's Anatomy of a Parenting Plan presentation for the AFCC-California, February 20, 2004

ATTORNEY-MEDIATOR AREAS OF EXPERTISE

As an attorney mediator in a practice where most family law clients are not represented by counsel and who request a lot of information and guidance on the law, it's helpful to know something about the topics below. You're not acting as either party's attorney, of course, but in order to provide the kinds of information that clients request, it's helpful to be very knowledgeable about some things and conversant in others.

- Community property and debts, exceptions
- Separate property: reimbursements, Moore/Marsden, tracing, Epstein/Watts
- Taxes and divorce: spousal support deductibility, exemptions for children, head of household, mortgage deductions, reading tax returns
- Real estate and mortgages: types of mortgages, mortgage resources, calculating equity, closing costs, capital gains, buying a house, appraisals and comparative market analyses
- Retirement Plans: different kinds of retirement plans and methods for dividing them
- Self-employment issues and small business valuations
- Miscellaneous assets: royalties, residuals, stock options, ESOPs, deferred compensation, lawsuits
- Child support and child support add-ons
- Spousal support factors
- Move-aways (custody)
- Infant overnights
- Credit, credit reports
- Basic court procedure
- Basic financial planning

Sources to gain this knowledge[3]:

- *Los Angeles Times* Sunday Real Estate Section (read every week)
- *Los Angeles Times* Sunday Business Section. Read Kathy M. Kristof's and Liz Pulliam Weston's columns each week
- IRS Publications for divorced people
- David Bach (author of financial planning books)
- Pension Appraisers (www.pensionappraisers.com)

---

[3] From Jerry Cohen, CPA, CDFP

- Your Divorce Advisor
- CEB Family Law annual volume
- Rutter Group (more complete than CEB but harder to read)
- Certified Divorce Financial Planners

I have 2 suggestions:

1. the California CPA Education Foundation (www.educationfoundation.org) has a 2 day class (9/11 & 9/12) at Lax on Family Law Practice: How and Why;
2. The Institute for Divorce financial Analysts (www.institutedfa.com) offers courses and trainings.

MEDIATION ORIENTATION

- **Answer clients' questions first**
- Product vs. Process
- Legal information & education vs. legal advice
- Joint sessions vs. individual caucuses
- Balanced Discussion
- Time and cost*[4]
- Paperwork
- Attorneys' roles, mediation friendly attorneys
- Typical first session
- Mediation summary letters
- Win/win outcomes and how they work
- Why mediation works and litigation doesn't work
- Mediator Styles—Facilitative vs. Evaluative explanation since there's no licensing for mediators in California
- Featured twice in Consumer Reports[5]
- Offer more information
- What is the next step for us to serve you? Would you like for us to set up an appointment or would you like some time to think about it? $200 deposit to secure date/time

Mediation Planning

Mediation planning helps you become a strategic mediator. No longer just grateful that a client has come in the door, and no longer flying by the seat of your pants, you're thoughtfully planning out your office procedures, case management procedures, and your actual mediation sessions in a thoughtful and ever-expanding way.

We were introduced to the concept of the strategic mediator by Forrest Mosten at his May 2004 advanced family mediation training. Mosten is also quick to credit Christopher Moore's *The Mediation Process* (Wiley/Jossey Bass 2003) and Michael Lang and Allison

---

4 Cost: 85% of Peace Talks® clients complete the entire divorce (paperwork, court fees, mediation time, mediation summaries) for $8500 or less and 60% complete the entire divorce for $6500 or less. Only 3% exceed $10,000. A typical LA attorney's retainer is $10,000, and you're just getting started. At Peace Talks®, you're done with money to spare. Family Law Presiding Judge Marjorie Steinberg told the LA Times Magazine May 4, 2008 that it's not unusual for a divorce to cost $100,000. Time: Most clients are done in 2-3 mediation sessions over 2-3 months.

5 February 2008 Consumer Reports & June 2006 Consumer Reports Money Adviser

Taylor's *The Making of a Mediator.* (Jossey Bass 2000) with these ideas and we've summarized them here before telling you what we're doing in our own practice.

A strategic mediator approaches each mediation as follows:

- Develop a theory
- Develop a goal for the case (in most cases, the goal is an agreement)
- Develop a strategy to get to the goal (you may do this individually for each issue)
- Develop an intervention based on the strategy
- Reflect on what went well and what the mediator could have done differently after the parties are gone.

Each strategy may have many possible interventions, but it's good to have a few thought out beforehand.

A strategic mediator is also thinking about:

- The next statement or action to create baby steps toward agreements;
- How to create awareness of the progress and underlying interests;
- How to motivate discussions;
- How to guide without directing;
- Giving the parties the best opportunity to agree.

The plan is to move along the continuum of mediator competence (adapted from The Making of a Mediator, Michael Lang and Allison Taylor, Jossey Bass 2000):

- **Apprentice:** unconscious incompetence
- **Novice:** conscious incompetence
- **Practitioner:** unconscious competence
- **Artist:** conscious competence

Preparing for a Session

At least 30 minutes before clients come in, we start by being debriefed by our Dispute Resolution Associate, Keisha Chandler, about her telephone experience in convening the case to date. How the clients have behaved on the telephone, what they've told her and how they've told it to her, and what they've failed to tell her can all provide clues as to what we might be facing in the mediation room.

Depending on the outcome of that discussion, we're not above sprinkling Holy Water or lighting white sage to clear the air. It may sound very "California", but every little bit helps. We even had our space feng shui'ed just in case it actually works. The idea is to have the space and physical environment set the tone for calm and peace.

Before the clients arrive, we get comfortable, adjust the room setup and make sure the water pitcher and snacks are ready. If it's a second or third appointment, we discuss the last session and develop a probable agenda. The mediators define their own agendas and consider likely impasses and agreements so that we're prepared for what may come up during the session. We distribute copies of previous mediation summary letters so clients can mark on them as we fine-tune previous tentative agreements.

When clients arrive, they're offered a seat in the client library or in a caucus room. Our Dispute Resolution Associate offers them coffee, tea, and sodas. We make a fresh pot of coffee if it's the afternoon. The client library is stocked with hard copies of our worksheets and forms, books on divorce, mediation, and parenting, and it also has videos like Children, the Experts of Divorce and it's Still Your Choice. There is a landline telephone clients can use as well as a table to write on. It's not uncommon for some participants to be chronically late (see the discussion on Ambivalence above!) so we make sure that clients have plenty to keep them occupied while they wait.

The mediators don't greet clients except to say "hello" until both parties have arrived. We want clients to be assured that we are neutral and that we don't use one person's early arrival as a conspiracy theory opportunity. It can be a little awkward ignoring someone sitting in the next room, but most clients appreciate our explanation. After all, if we hold good boundaries with them, we'll do the same when it's their spouse who arrives first next time.

This may all sound like a bit much, but one client described it as, "There was a feeling of abundance with all the snacks and drinks and extra telephones, and I felt like I didn't have to worry about my case because there would be enough to go around." Another client said, "You're lending me a book and giving me a folder of information, but when I hired my lawyer for three times as much money, all he gave me was a piece of paper saying he was my attorney." Having a client-centered office is an important part of success in the mediation room. The mediation environment should be part of the solution, not part of the problem.

Knowing Your Customer

We like to say that our clients are very nice people having the worst day of their lives. That said, Los Angeles presents us with a very diverse population. It helps to be prepared.

Anticipating racial, ethnic, socio-economic and cultural differences and related planning

Some categories of diversity come to mind easily, e.g., racial, ethnic, religious, gender and nationality issues. Others are not so quickly identified but can influence the climate in the mediation room as much or more than those which are more obvious:

- Cultures torn by war

- Traumatized cultures
- Persons with a traumatic personal history
- Geographic differences between regions of one country or state, e.g., New Yorker and Californian, Southerner and Northerner
- Degree of practice within a religion, or Atheism
- Political leanings, from Conservative to Liberal, but also lifestyle politics, like a vegan lifestyle
- Socio-economic class

This list is by no means exhaustive, but designed to help you think about the different issues that create diversity issues in the mediation room.

Within these diversity labels, other nuances exist which are influenced by all of the above, for example:

- Mores about openness to therapy and helping professions
- Trust in the government
- Trust in the court system, and justice system
- Willingness to communicate with persons inside and outside the family about personal problems or family secrets
- How trauma is handled
- Parenting styles, e.g., authoritarian, laissez-faire
- Acceptable gender roles
- Tolerance for conflict
- Negotiating styles

All of these things can influence what happens in the mediation room.

As a mediator planning for a mediation session, and using good case management, it helps to anticipate where some of the diversity issues may create conflict or impasses to settlement. To advance-plan a session with new parties based only on their anticipated ethnic or cultural backgrounds would likely do more harm than good, making it difficult to abandon pre-conceived notions about who the parties are likely to be as individuals once you've started to work with them. Yet, to completely ignore and fail to anticipate likely diversity issues would be equally as irresponsible.

If you find yourself working with particular groups of people often (whether it's Koreans, Jews or Southerners), it would be worthwhile to learn more about that group's culture and their norms and mores. It not only gives you insight into their culture, but also credibility in the mediation room when you can convey that you understand some of the clients' backgrounds.

This section is only a very brief introduction to a vast opportunity to explore diversity in mediation, but a fascinating line of inquiry and an opportunity to bring a higher level of artistry to your mediation practice.

PRACTICE HINTS: CONSULTATION SESSION

PURPOSE

The Consultation has two fundamental purposes:

- For the parties to determine if mediation makes sense for them; and
- To determine if they are comfortable with the mediator.

Reassure the parties that participating in the consultation session does not mean that one or both have decided to divorce or to mediate, only that they are willing to hear about the mediation process.

TASKS

There are four primary tasks in this initial meeting with the client:

- To give the parties sufficient information about the mediation process so that they can make an informed decision to mediate (e.g., rules of mediation, how mediation fits into the formal legal process and the role of attorneys, the estimated time and cost of mediation).
- To sufficiently engage the parties on a personal level in order to establish confidence in the mediator (and subsequently in the process).
- To begin obtaining the parties commitment to the mediation process.
- To obtain an initial assessment of the parties: e.g., the dynamics and timing of the decision to divorce (who is leaving whom, level of acceptance), parties' psychological states (self esteem, ability to negotiate), complexity of issues, stresses.

SPECIAL ISSUES

- Before you can begin the substance of the session, you may need to negotiate with one or both of the parties being present. Often, and especially in mandated mediation program, one or both of the parties feel forced into mediation. That sentiment must be addressed directly so that their participation, even in the consultation session, is shifted from feeling involuntary to voluntary.
- At the end of the session, if one person is anxious and the other is still considering whether to mediate, help the parties to negotiate a time frame within which to decide so a clear decision is made without either feeling pushed.

WRITTEN INFORMATION AND MATERIAL TO BE GIVEN TO CLIENTS (FORMS)

- Client reading list

- Legal process of divorce
- Rules of Mediation
- Agreement to mediate (given at consultation to be reviewed only - not signed)

GRAPHICS

The use of graphics is especially effective in the initial consultation session and throughout the mediation process:

- The parties identify with a picture of their family
- The flipchart focuses the parties' attention on the common issues.
- An agenda keeps the mediator organized and on track and gives the clients a sense of organization.
- Graphics allow for visual as well as audial information to be transmitted.
- There is too much information to take in by didactic modes of communication alone.
- Graphics allow "anchors" to be set.

Mediation Session Planning and De-Briefing

Therapist Mediator:________________________________

Attorney Mediator: ________________________________

Clients: ______________________________________

Session Date: ____________

Debriefing or Pre-Session Planning (circle one) Anticipated Agenda (for today's session or the next session):

Problems we encountered in the session:

Possible interventions next time:

Future issues to consider or anticipate:

Possible interventions:

MEDIATION CONFIDENTIALITY AGREEMENT

_______________________has been appointed by the Institute for Conflict Management to preside as the Mediator in the matter of _________________________________v _____________________________.

_______________________will assist the parties in seeking a settlement in the above entitled case. The undersigned parties acknowledge, understand and agree to the following:

1. Role of Mediator: The Mediator is an impartial, neutral intermediary, whose role is to assist the participants in reaching a settlement by negotiation. The Mediator cannot impose a settlement but will assist the participants towards achieving their own settlement. The Mediator does not act as an attorney or advocate for or give legal, tax or other professional advice to any participants. In this regard, no professional-client or fiduciary relationship is created between any participant and the Mediator.

2. Attorney Consultation: The participants acknowledge that they are free to consult an attorney at any time during the mediation process. In the event the dispute is settled, the participants may have the settlement agreement independently reviewed by their own counsel prior to signing it.

3. Applicable Statutes/Confidentiality: The mediation is conducted pursuant to______________ ________, and _______________________and other sections or successor sections of the ____________________ _______and any Federal law counterparts, if applicable, governing, among other things, the confidentiality of mediation proceedings. The Mediator may not testify in any proceedings pursuant to these statutes and the participants shall not seek to have the Mediator testify. Subject to certain limited exceptions set forth in the Evidence Code and case law, statements made during the mediation are confidential, are generally not subject to discovery outside the mediation process, and are not admissible in any subsequent proceeding. However, written or oral agreements reached by the parties in the course of the mediation may, under certain circumstances, be admissible in a subsequent proceeding. Post-mediation communications between the Mediator and any participant related to the mediation shall be confidential. The participants agree that the Mediator may consult with colleagues about this matter and may describe this matter to colleagues for educational purposes so long as the Mediator does not disclose the participants' names or any other information which would specifically identify the participants.

4. Limited Liability, Release and Indemnification: The participants hereby agree to release the Mediator from any and all claims arising out of their failure to reach agreement or their decision to enter into any agreement or any other aspect of the mediation process. Further, the Mediator makes no representation that the participants will reach an agreement on any of the issues, disputes or controversies discussed in the mediation. Any party who brings any claim, action or proceeding of any nature against the Mediator or who seeks to have the Mediator testify shall be responsible to indemnify the Mediator for any expenses, loss or damage incurred, including, without limitation, attorney's fees and expenses incurred in connection with such claim, action or proceeding brought by such participant.

5. Mediator Compensation: The parties have submitted a retainer fee to compensate the mediator for a specified period of time. If the participants are unable to resolve their controversy within this

retained time frame, but desire to continue the mediation and pay the Mediator's hourly fee of $____ _______, those participants expressly agree to do so within seven (7) days of today's date.

6. Potential Conflicts of Interest: The Mediator is unaware of any actual or potential conflicts of interest which would amount to grounds for disqualification in accordance with ________________ _______ (applicable to judges and by reference to mediators).

To the extent any actual or potential conflicts of interest exist, the mediator does not believe same will affect his/her capacity to be impartial. By signing this Agreement, the participants expressly waive the conflicts and potential conflicts disclosed, if any. If either participant believes that the Mediator is not impartial, said participant should immediately terminate the mediation at the signing of this agreement.

Dated ________, 20__

Witnessed:

Party A________________________________

Party B________________________________

Mediator ______________________________

Agenda

- Parenting Plan, Interim Parenting Plan
    - Decision Making
    - Day-to-Day Schedule
    - Vacations, Holidays and Travel
    - Other Parenting Issues
    - Interim Parenting Plan
    - Step Up Plans
    - Telling the Children
- Child Support
    - Monthly Amount
    - Add-on expenses, like work-related childcare, sports, lessons, camp, etc.
    - College and post-high school education (optional)
- Spousal support, spousal support buy-out
- Separation plans
- Boundary issues, communication, changing nature of the relationship
- Interim support & interim financial arrangements
- Move out expenses
- House, mortgages
- Apartment or rental home: occupancy of apartment, security deposit
- Other real estate: rental properties, apartment buildings
- Bank Accounts
- Retirement Assets, e.g., 401(k) plan, IRA, Pension, Profit Sharing plans
- Savings, investments, stocks, mutual funds (non-retirement)
- Cars, RV's, other vehicles
- Frequent flier miles
- Insurance: Health insurance, Car insurance, Life insurance
- Personal Property, Pets
- Debts, student loans, personal loans or loans from family
- Filing taxes for 2008, back taxes, tax loss carry forward
- Business(es)

- Separate property claims, reimbursement claims
- Intellectual property: patents, trademarks, copyrights, songs, books, scripts, works in progress
- Stock Options
- Privately held investments, limited partnerships
- Season tickets, football tickets, Lakers tickets
- Frozen embryos, eggs or sperm
- Injury settlements and lawsuits, workers compensation, car accidents
- Timeshare(s)
- Mediation Fees
- Paperwork, paperwork timing
- Date of Separation
- Legal separation or divorce choice
- Social Security Benefits (protected by federal law & only if married > 10 years)

Mediation Session Structure

Each session should follow this basic structure:

At every session: tell the clients the outline of what you're going to do in that session, and if there are particular goals (yours or theirs), articulate those goals.

What you'll tell clients you'll be doing:

- Review and sign fee agreement;
- 10 minute intake;
- Brainstorm agenda;
- Work from easiest agenda items to hardest agenda items;
- By the end of the first session we should have been able to outline all of the things we need to talk about, get tentative agreements on the easier things, and at least lay out many of the options and things to think about for the more difficult agenda items so that you can use the time in between sessions to think about what might work the best for you;

- Don't worry about taking copious notes because we will do a summary letter for you that will lay everything out, along with a "to do list" of things you'll want to do or think about before the next session.

For subsequent sessions, you might start by saying:

- Are there any updates or things you'd like to tell us about since the last session?
- We looked at your file and thought that this list might be the remaining agenda items-are there any things you'd like to add or delete?
- Are there any goals in particular you'd like to accomplish by the end of this session?
- Did you get a chance to ____________ ?

If this is the first session, summarize each paragraph of the fee agreement, ask clients if they have any questions, and have them sign the fee agreement and initial each page. This is done off the clock (no charge to clients, but mark it down on the timesheet as "orientation" time).

Why? Clients must agree to mediate, and to our office procedures, before a mediation starts. If they won't sign the fee agreement, they'll never reach an agreement in mediation, either. If you can't settle the small, easy stuff, the

challenging stuff will never fall into place. Also, by doing each session this way clients can never claim that they did not get a chance to read the fee agreement.

Intake: Do as much of an intake as you'd like, but try to keep it to 15 minutes or less unless the clients orally agree that they'd like to take more time doing the intake. Don't let the intake devolve into an excuse to avoid the tough mediation ahead. Tara Fass, LMFT likes to do a therapeutic intake, but only do an intake this way if you know how you'll be using that information. Diana Mercer, on her own, would not do much of an intake. It's up to you, but just be sure you know why you're doing the intake you're doing.

Agenda: The agenda is brainstormed. No one idea is more important than another irrespective of where it appears on the list. You'll include big issues as well as small issues, agreed-upon issues as well as controversial issues.

When someone throws out a new issue in the middle of the session, acknowledge it and write it on the agenda. You might not talk about it at the moment it's brought up, but you want the client to know you heard and that you'll talk about it eventually.

There are sample agendas and an article about agenda order in this handbook.

Paperwork: Divorce or legal separation paperwork might be an agenda item. If clients want to do the paperwork as part of the session, if you'll give the Dispute Resolution

Associate the information (for Petition and Response, for example) early in the session the clients can sign the papers before they leave.

That can put things a little out of order agenda-wise, so tread lightly. I'll often ask, "Did you know if you wanted to do the divorce paperwork as part of today's session? I realize that this is an odd time to ask, as we're just starting the session, but if you've already made up your mind I can get the DRS started on the paperwork while we're here in the session and then you can sign it before you leave. If you haven't decided yet, we can just make it an agenda item and not worry about doing everything today."

There are 2 emotional things you'll need to know for the divorce paperwork: who's the Petitioner, and does the wife want a maiden name or different name back. Legally, it doesn't matter who the Petitioner is, but since it's officially the person who's asking for the divorce, it often matters to people emotionally. As for the maiden name, it's totally the wife's decision. Husband cannot demand that she take her name back (although it's up for negotiation, of course).

Paperwork timing: We find that it's best to sign and file the papers at the first meeting. Because California has a 6 month waiting period, if you wait until the people have an agreement then they have to wait an additional 6 months before they're divorced. By getting the papers filed early, the 6 months start ticking ASAP. If they need longer than 6 months to finish their agreement, that's okay with the court. If they finish in shorter than 6 months, you can submit the agreement as soon as it's ready and the court will "pre-approve" the agreement.

No pushing, though. Sometimes people aren't ready to do the paperwork at the first session.

The parties don't need an agreement - or even an agreement that they can reach an agreement-to file the Divorce papers. The Petition and Response are really just their names, date of marriage, date of separation, children's names & dates of birth. The rest we fill in as "I want everything" on each person's paperwork so that if they end up having to go to litigation they won't have to amend the petition or response. If they have an agreement, the court never even looks at the requested relief. It's a little counter-intuitive, but it can save them money if things fall apart later on.

When we sign papers as part of the session, we have clients sign the Petition and Response at the same time. We also have the Respondent sign the (undated) Notice and Acknowledgement of Receipt. This is so we don't have to chase them down to sign the form once the papers are filed. We send the Petition to the court for filing and hold the other papers in the file until it's time to send them in. Once they've been filed with the court, we send the clients copies. Clients also take unfilled copies of all the papers they sign with them on the same day that they sign the papers. Put everything in a blue pocket folder or the client will lose it immediately.

Mediation Agenda Order

After much experimentation, we've found that starting with the easiest items and working up toward the more difficult agenda items works best. Tackling the easiest issues first lets mediation participants get used to the mediation process and gives them a chance to settle into the rhythm of the session. It also lets them see the progress they're making in mediation, and illustrates for them what we as mediators have come to know: most couples are closer to an agreement than they think.

By working up to the more difficult issues, we also get a chance to accumulate all of the facts so that we (the mediators) can begin to formulate hypothesis about where the difficult issues lie and where to anticipate impasses. In our more evaluative moments, we can start to formulate our own proposals and suggestions for settlement. In our more facilitative moments, we can start to see the ruptures and trouble points and begin to think of ways to help couples rebuilt the trust necessary to reach an agreement.

Typically, by the end of the first session we've handled or tabled the easiest issues and those will become the "tentative agreements" in our first summary letter. We've also outlined all of the more difficult issues, pinpointed the numbers on financial issues or identified the disagreements in the parenting issues, and we've discussed the elements of the issue with the clients and outlined possible settlement options for them to think about before the next session. These topics typically become a "to do list" in a mediation summary.

For example, if a family law mediation couple is not sure what to do with their home, we might start the discussion as follows:

- How much is the home worth?
- What do you owe?
- Did either of you contribute some pre-marital money or a gift from a parent that you're seeking to be reimbursed? If the other person doesn't agree, can you put together the paperwork showing the pre-marital or gift money?

If both parties would like to keep the home and buy out the other person's interest, the next line of discussion might be:

- Can either of you afford to own the home on your own? If you can afford it, is that the best way to spend your money? Will all the peanut butter and jelly sandwiches be worth it?
- If you can afford the home, can you handle all the maintenance by yourself? Is that how you'd like to spend your free time?
- What kind of a mortgage loan do you have? If it's a variable rate loan, can you handle an increase in payments?

- Would you be in a position to refinance and remove the other person's name from responsibility?
- Would you be in a position to refinance and borrow enough money to pay off the other person's interest? Or are there other assets which can be traded off against the equity in the home? And if so, is this the most desirable way to allocate your money?

By the time you've broken down the agenda into these bits and pieces, you've taken some of the emotionality out of the decision and turned it more into a data conflict (see Christopher Moore, *The Mediation Process*, pages 64-65, Wiley/Jossey-Bass 2003), which lets people take back some power in making their own decision. By investigating the facts behind the decision "I want to keep the house", asking people to speak with a financial planner about asset allocation and a mortgage broker about available financing options, they start to see the house in terms of "is this the best decision for me?" rather than a competition against their spouse.

Resistance to Agenda Order

Although trial and error has taught us that starting with the easiest issues and working up to the most difficult issues is the best formula for success in our practice, we often encounter resistance to this agenda order. Clients often want to start with the most difficult issue, wanting proof that mediation can really work.

The problem we've found with starting with the most contentious issue is that the discussion can quickly devolve into low road behavior without our having gotten to know the clients well enough to help them manage this behavior and overcome impasse. The clients don't know us well enough to trust that we really are impartial and that we have their best interests in mind. We make the hidden transparent by directly asking them to make the initial leap of faith into our agenda order and explaining why we think it helps them make the best progress.

Figure 2.1. Circle of Conflict: Causes and Interventions.

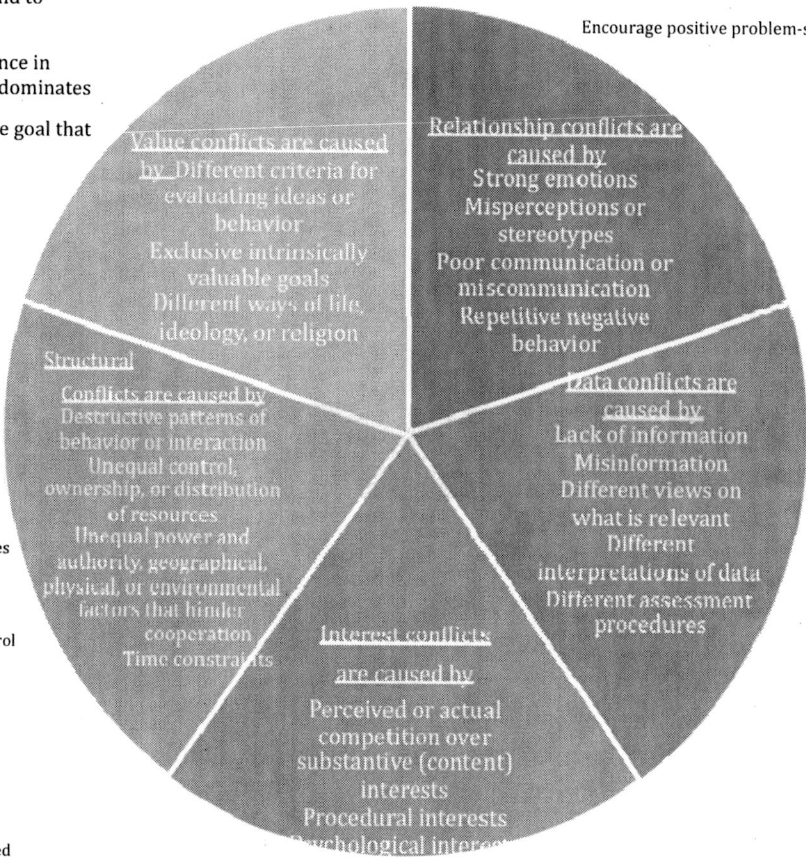

Possible Relationship Interventions

Control expression of emotions through procedure, ground rules, caucuses, and so forth

Promote expression of emotions by legitimizing feelings and providing a process

Clarify perceptions and build positive perceptions

Improve quality and quantity of communication

Block negative repetitive behavior by changing structure

Encourage positive problem-solving attitudes

Possible Value-Related Interventions

Avoid defining problem in terms of value

Allow parties to agree and to disagree

Create spheres of influence in which one set of values dominates

Search for superordinate goal that all parties share

Value conflicts are caused by Different criteria for evaluating ideas or behavior
Exclusive intrinsically valuable goals
Different ways of life, ideology, or religion

Relationship conflicts are caused by
Strong emotions
Misperceptions or stereotypes
Poor communication or miscommunication
Repetitive negative behavior

Structural Conflicts are caused by
Destructive patterns of behavior or interaction
Unequal control, ownership, or distribution of resources
Unequal power and authority, geographical, physical, or environmental factors that hinder cooperation
Time constraints

Data conflicts are caused by
Lack of information
Misinformation
Different views on what is relevant
Different interpretations of data
Different assessment procedures

Interest conflicts are caused by
Perceived or actual competition over substantive (content) interests
Procedural interests
Psychological interests

Possible Structural Interventions

Clearly define and change roles

Replace destructive behavior patterns

Reallocate ownership or control of resources

Establish a fair and mutually acceptable decision-making process

Change negotiation process from positional to interest-based bargaining

Modify means of influence used by parties (less coercion, more persuasion)

Change physical and environmental relationship of parties (closeness and distance)

Modify external pressures on parties

Change time constraints (more or less time)

Possible Data Interventions

Reach agreement on what data are important

Agree on process to collect data

Develop common criteria to assess data

Use third-party experts to gain outside opinion or break deadlocks

Possible Interest-Based Interventions

Focus on interests, not positions

Look for objective standards and criteria to guide solution development

Develop integrative solutions that address needs of all parties

Search for ways to expand options or resources

Develop trade-offs to satisfy interests of different strengths

From Christopher Moore's *The Mediation Process* (Wiley/Jossey Bass 2003)

Figure 2.2. Mediator Process of Building and Testing a Hypothesis

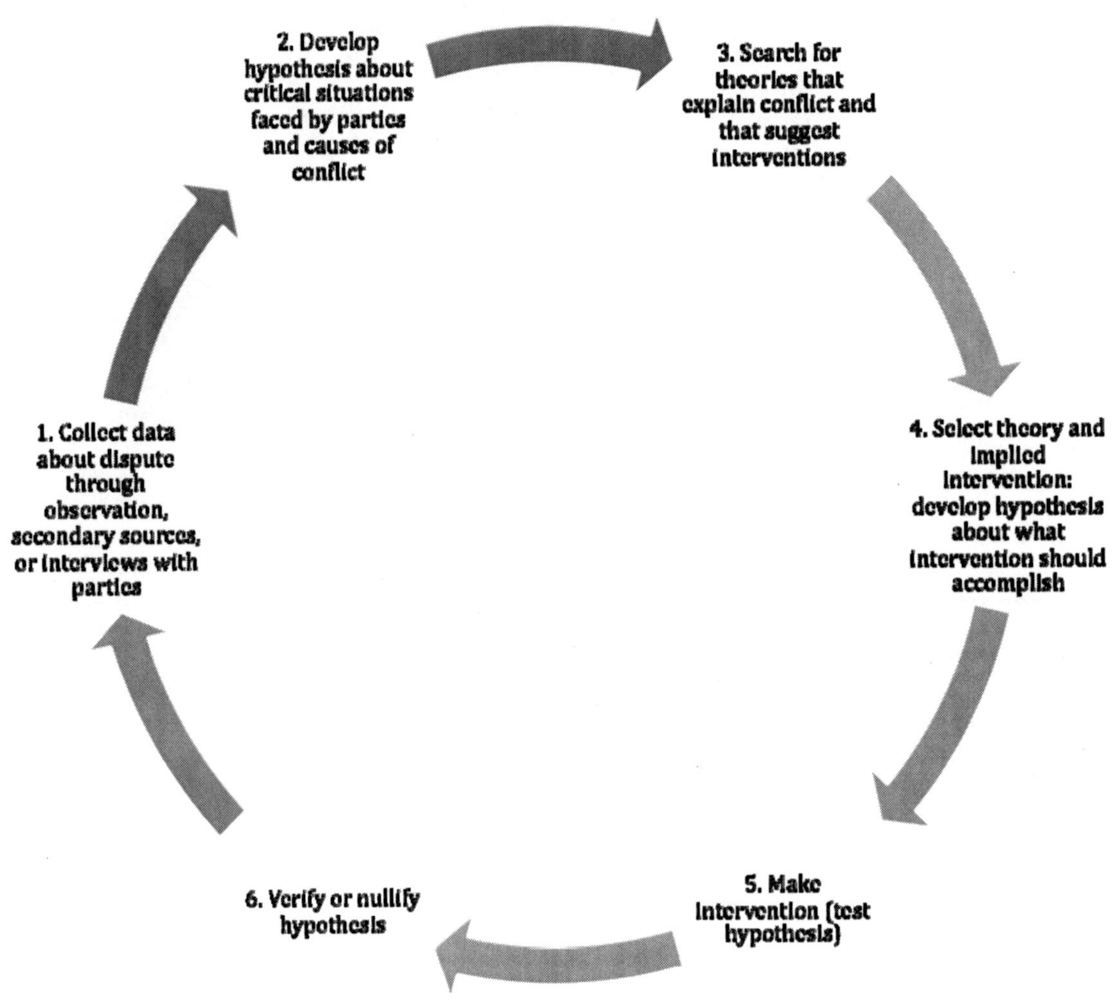

From Christopher Moore's *The Mediation Process* (Wiley/Jossey Bass 2003)

There are also a few shorthand words of persuasion we use as well:

- Gentle persuasion: If these other issues are truly simple, it will just take a few minutes to get them all down on paper, and then we can get to the issue which is really troubling you;
- Forcing the issue: Do you know how you're going to handle your 2005 taxes? Tell me about how you're going to do that (i.e., mediator forces the issue by picking what appears to be the easiest issue) and let's get it out of the way quickly;
- Reality testing: Is that really the easiest agenda item? Surely the car lease is an easier issue;

Even when there is a time constraint making a contentious issue a quasi-emergency, we'll start with something simple, or break the issue down into simpler issues so as not to jump right into the hardest discussion without a warm-up.

Summary Letters as Mediation Tools

We insist on doing summary letters. In our practice, it used to be optional, but in the name of saving a few dollars too many clients went without the summary letter and too many mediations fell apart between sessions because neither client had an accurate record of what went on during the session. Our case management compromise (so far) is that we bill for 1/2 an hour to a full hour for the summary letter, but in reality it takes us 2-3 hours to write. It's worth it to us not to have the mediations fall apart, and the clients see it as a manageable expense. We also don't give them the option of refusing a summary letter-it's just too valuable a tool both for the clients and the mediators.

What the mediation summary letter does: Without asking people to make a decision on the day of the mediation, the agreement about the issue is simply that they will investigate their options. The summary letter will outline the discussion, questions to ask their advisors, and the to-do list so that the clients don't have to take copious notes during the session.

The other advantage of the summary letter is that it gives both the clients and the mediator an "institutional memory" of what went on at the session. A good, detailed summary letter can eliminate much of the he said/she said. Even if the mediator makes a mistake in the summary, at least everyone is starting from the same place.

The summary letter can also flesh out discussions that didn't quite get finished, or which might be too technical to be of use during the session. A good example of this is the explanation of how Qualified Domestic Relations Orders work. "There's a special court order you can use to divide up a pension, so don't worry about how that will happen," might suffice for the mediation session itself, but ultimately the client will need more detail than that. The summary letter is a good place to make sure the clients get the information they need to make a good decision.

We also use the summary letters to ask the clients to expand their range of options between sessions. We'll ask them to think of different ways to resolve things, or whether they would consider a particular solution, even on a temporary basis. The summary letter is also an opportunity to acknowledge high points in the mediation, point out progress made, and gently encourage clients to keep thinking about certain issues.

Conclusion

It's the mediator's job to develop case management protocols which help mediation participants to succeed in reaching an agreement. Simple office procedures and thoughtful rules within your mediation structure, like how to set the agenda and tackle agenda issues, can go a long way toward providing structure for settlement discussions.

Figure 2.3. Twelve Stages of Mediator Moves.

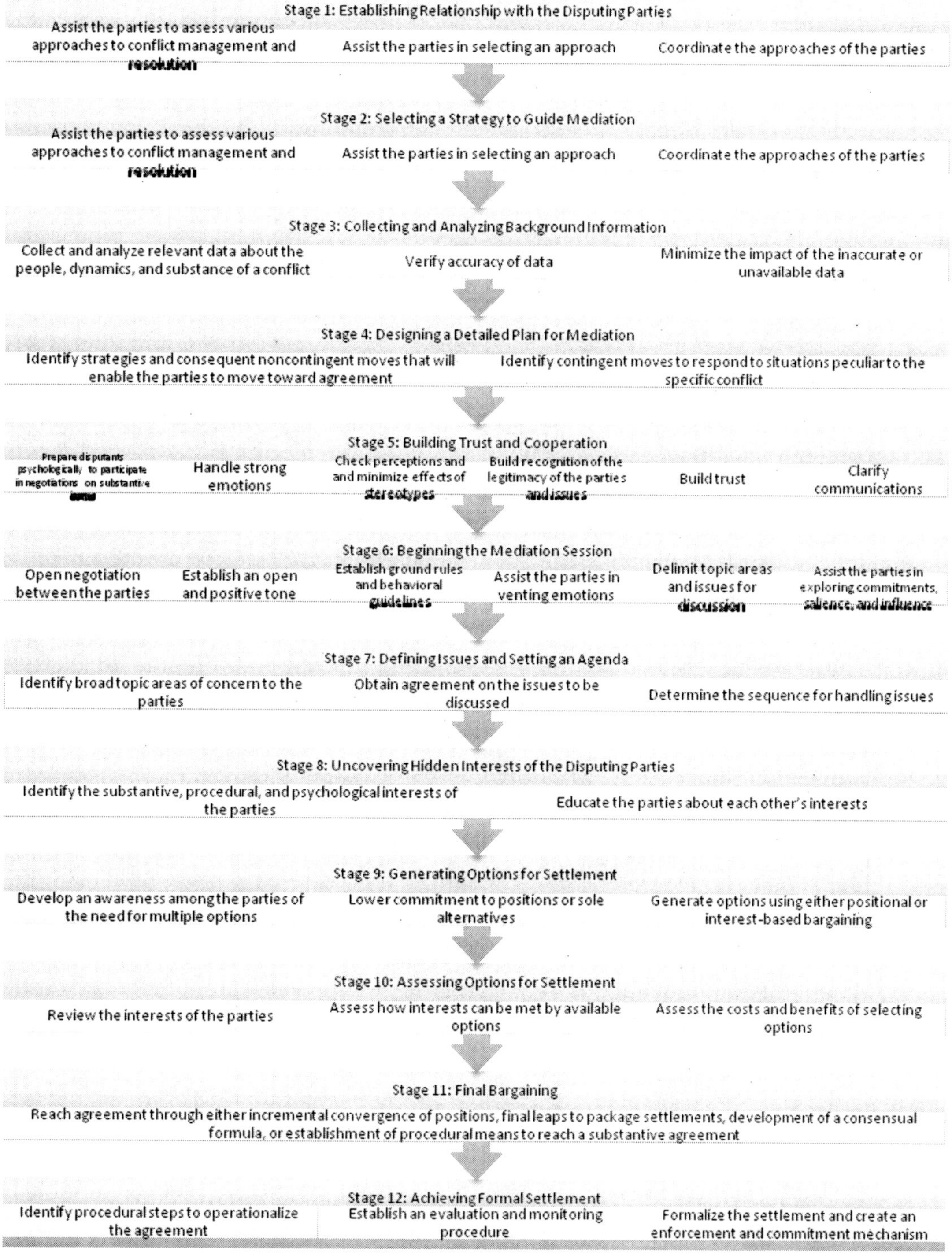

Stage 1: Establishing Relationship with the Disputing Parties

- Assist the parties to assess various approaches to conflict management and resolution
- Assist the parties in selecting an approach
- Coordinate the approaches of the parties

Stage 2: Selecting a Strategy to Guide Mediation

- Assist the parties to assess various approaches to conflict management and resolution
- Assist the parties in selecting an approach
- Coordinate the approaches of the parties

Stage 3: Collecting and Analyzing Background Information

- Collect and analyze relevant data about the people, dynamics, and substance of a conflict
- Verify accuracy of data
- Minimize the impact of the inaccurate or unavailable data

Stage 4: Designing a Detailed Plan for Mediation

- Identify strategies and consequent noncontingent moves that will enable the parties to move toward agreement
- Identify contingent moves to respond to situations peculiar to the specific conflict

Stage 5: Building Trust and Cooperation

- Prepare disputants psychologically to participate in negotiations on substantive issues
- Handle strong emotions
- Check perceptions and and minimize effects of stereotypes
- Build recognition of the legitimacy of the parties and issues
- Build trust
- Clarify communications

Stage 6: Beginning the Mediation Session

- Open negotiation between the parties
- Establish an open and positive tone
- Establish ground rules and behavioral guidelines
- Assist the parties in venting emotions
- Delimit topic areas and issues for discussion
- Assist the parties in exploring commitments, salience, and influence

Stage 7: Defining Issues and Setting an Agenda

- Identify broad topic areas of concern to the parties
- Obtain agreement on the issues to be discussed
- Determine the sequence for handling issues

Stage 8: Uncovering Hidden Interests of the Disputing Parties

- Identify the substantive, procedural, and psychological interests of the parties
- Educate the parties about each other's interests

Stage 9: Generating Options for Settlement

- Develop an awareness among the parties of the need for multiple options
- Lower commitment to positions or sole alternatives
- Generate options using either positional or interest-based bargaining

Stage 10: Assessing Options for Settlement

- Review the interests of the parties
- Assess how interests can be met by available options
- Assess the costs and benefits of selecting options

Stage 11: Final Bargaining

- Reach agreement through either incremental convergence of positions, final leaps to package settlements, development of a consensual formula, or establishment of procedural means to reach a substantive agreement

Stage 12: Achieving Formal Settlement

- Identify procedural steps to operationalize the agreement
- Establish an evaluation and monitoring procedure
- Formalize the settlement and create an enforcement and commitment mechanism

Adapted from Christopher Moore's *The Mediation Process* (Wiley/Jossey Bass 2003)

MEDIATION: STAGE I BEGINNING THE SESSION

Welcome the parties to the session and thank them for attending.

Introductions: ask if it is all right for everyone to be on a first-name basis.

Housekeeping:

- If you'd like to take a break, just ask
- Location of restrooms, drinks, access to telephones
- Anything else?

Explain the mediation process: in simple terms:

- Mediation is voluntary-for it to work, the participants have to want it to work
- Mediation is a way to reach an agreement or settlement without giving the decision-making power to someone else
- The goal is to assist you in developing a written agreement that everyone is comfortable with.
- What mediation is about-making an informed decision about how to resolve your issues based on your personal situation. It's not about sticking your head in the sand and ignoring the legal aspects of your situation, or about one party browbeating the other into an agreement. It's about working together to resolve the situation in a way that everyone is satisfied.
- Mediation has basic components: outlining the issues in dispute and setting an agenda, discussing each item in turn and the options for resolving each item, and reaching an agreement on that issue.
- Sounds simple, but in the middle, things can take some twists and turns and sometimes things aren't resolved right away, maybe you need to think about it some more or you need more information, and that's why we schedule mediation sessions for 3 hours at a time.
- Mediation is confidential, and mediator cannot be subpoenaed to testify [exceptions if you are a mandated reporter]
- What you do and what you don't do-will you answer legal questions? Calculate child support? Make outside referrals? Take them on as individual therapy clients?

Explain the role of the mediator(s):

- Neutral party to facilitate communication
- To assist the parties in reaching an agreement

- Not judges or jury, and won't decide who's right or wrong
- Ask if there are any questions about the process

Get an Agreement on the Ground Rules

This process establishes the mediator as in control of the session, and begins the agreement process.

- No interruptions. One person speaks at a time. Each person will be given a chance to speak, but the mediator decides who will speak and when. You each have a pad of paper and a pen, and you'll use that to write down each thing you'd like to discuss concerning what the other person has said. That way you won't forget the specific comments you'd like to address when it's your turn to speak, but you won't need to interrupt.
- Speak directly to the mediators unless you're asked to speak to each other
- No negative looks or gestures. Please follow the basic rules of politeness
- Be honest. This procedure is voluntary, and if you're not going to participate in good faith, it's not worthwhile to participate at all.
- Explain the caucus procedure: It may become necessary to meet individually with one or both parties. This is called a caucus. Anyone may request a caucus at any time. Everything in the caucus is confidential just as everything in the mediation is confidential, and what you say will not be revealed to the other person unless we get your specific permission to do so.
- The mediator(s) may take notes during the session, but those notes are confidential and they'll be destroyed when your case is concluded.
- Ask the parties if they have any additional ground rules to add
- Ask the parties if they're prepared to honor the ground rules that have been set.

Initial forms:

- Go over agreement to mediate, and have them sign if they have not already done so. Questions?
- Have all parties sign one copy and check for the signatures
- Collect all of the forms

What if I want a script?

I don't use a script, but some people do. Becoming a really good mediator is all about establishing your own personal signature-how you do what you do. Some people like scripts, especially just starting out, so here's one I've lifted from a well-known mediator[6]:

- Introduce yourself
- Be on a first-name basis
- Thank parties for agreeing to mediate: *I am very confident that we will reach ant agreement in this matter. The fact that you are here demonstrates to me, as I hope it demonstrates to each of you, your willingness to resolve the concerns that you have between each other. It is that willingness to work things out that will cause us to reach an agreement.*
- Housekeeping Time constraints (ask if there are any-court hearing scheduled? Pick up kids by 6?)
- Have you ever participated in a mediation before?

The Mediation Process

At this time I want to describe the actual mediation process to you. It is much like what we are doing now. We are going to sit across from each other and each of you will talk and tell your side of the story. You will have all the time you need to say what's on your mind, and you will also have time to respond to what each other says. During that time I will be listening to each of you and I'm going to ask that each of you listen to each other as well.

To be able to listen, there are 2 ground rules I want to establish at the outset of the mediation:

1. One person speaks at a time. I have been in your position before where someone that I am in dispute with is telling their side of the story and I wanted to respond to what they were saying as soon as they said it. I few did that here, I think you can see that our discussions could quickly become arguments. To satisfy your urge to respond, I have supplied you each with pens and paper. While one person is speaking, the other one should write down his or her responses to what is being said, without stopping listening, and I promise you that we will get to your responses.
2. No name-calling. Now, I'm not saying that either of you will resort to name calling. All I am saying is that I have heard it before. What happens is that name-calling can turn constructive dialogue into destructive dialogue. We're going to make progress here today, and name calling can hurt that progress.

---

[6] Reprinted from and based on a Mediation Script, Copyright John Biancardi, Copyright registration number TX4-294-558

Mediator's Role:

My role in this process is to:

Facilitate the process Regulate the activity during the meeting Listen, and I'll ask that each of you also listen Be neutral. I will not take sides or advocate for either of you. My job is to remain impartial. I will assist you in reaching a settlement, but I cannot decide it for you. I'm confident that you will reach an agreement.

Confidentiality:

What is said here in this room stays in this room. It makes having discussions easier, and it prevents gossip. I know that everyone has friends or relatives who will be very curious as to what was said and what happened during the mediation. My best advice is that you speak only in generalities. You can let them know that you said everything that you needed to say, that you reached an agreement, and that the dispute is now over.

A confidentiality agreement between the parties and the mediator is an absolute must. Mediation can only be effective if people willingly disclose information to reach settlement. Confidentiality agreements protect people from future litigation if mediation should fail. By signing an confidentiality agreement, you're agreeing to honor your commitment to the mediation process, and acknowledging the California State Legislature's commitment to mediation, outlined in California Evidence Code Section 1119. The agreement to mediate which you signed includes a confidentiality agreement.

Caucus

There may be a need for me to meet separately with each of you during the mediation. That private meeting is called a caucus. I can ask to meet privately with each of you, and you can also request to meet with me in private, at any ty, and everything said in the caucus is considered confidential, and will not be spoken about during the mediation unless you choose to bring it up.

Attorneys

Attorneys are allowed to be here in the mediation with you. However, all dialogue will be between the actual parties to the dispute. We can certainly make allowances for attorneys to speak during the mediation. But what I will ask is that if either of you want to speak to your attorney, or if the attorneys want to speak to their clients, please call for a break or caucus and confer with each other outside of the meeting. When you return to the meeting, I will ask that the parties communicate what they feel needs to be discussed.

Voluntary mediation:

Please recognize in each other that you are here as volunteers, as I mentioned earlier. That tells me, and I hope it tells you, that you are willing to resolve this matter. Your presence means that we have already made some progress toward a successful resolution of this dispute.

Involuntary mediation:

I know that you are here because you have been ordered to participate in a mediation try and work out your differences. The reason you have been ordered here by the (court/company) is because it has been its experience that your type of case lends itself to resolution through the mediation process. All I ask is that since you are here, let me and the process try to work for you. Remember, even though your participation here is mandatory, the agreement that I'm confident you will reach can only be entered into on a voluntary basis.

SAMPLE MEDIATION OPENING SCRIPT – LONG FORM

Good morning. My name is ________. I will be your mediator today. Let me tell you briefly what my qualifications are. I am a (*Lawyer, passed my first bar exam in 1982and have been in litigation practice since then. I am also a mediator certified by The Institute for Conflict Management, (ICM) and I have been participating in alternative dispute resolutions since about 1987.)*

You are to be commended for agreeing to participate in mediation, which is a proven, successful process. Since you are here by agreement I know that you are committed to making the process work for you and in attempting to reach the best resolution for your dispute.

At the outset I should clarify that I have no connection with this case and that I know what I know about this case from the confidential position statements and other materials you have sent me. My knowledge of the parties and their positions is limited to what you have presented me.

While this has allowed me some familiarity with your contentions, it is not enough for me to have formed an opinion or any preconceived ideas about the nature of your dispute or how it should be resolved.

Also, in case there is any question, I want to explain the mediation process. I am not a judge or a decision maker. My job is to facilitate communication and to help each of you think and communicate more clearly with the hopes that you will be able to reach a settlement.

My job is to probe and ask questions. My job is to help each of you explain your case to me in a manner that will help you reevaluate both your position and that will help you reevaluate the position of the other party with an eye towards reaching a resolution of this dispute.

By *(Texas state)* statute the mediation process is confidential. I will do everything in my power to assure that the process remains confidential. The pre-submission materials and any materials you give me here today are either returned to you or destroyed at the end of the mediation. My notes are destroyed at the end as well.

However, let me warn you that any information that can be independently discovered is not confidential as to the parties. Regardless of that, I as a mediator cannot be compelled to come into court and testify as to any part of the mediation except that the case did or did not settle. That the case did or did not settle is the only disclosure that I will make as to the case. The reasons, so-called "fault" and other matters are all the subject of absolute privilege as far as I am concerned.

STARTING THE MEDIATION

Prepare the group for mediation:

A) Introduce yourself. Make sure the parties have met each other and the people they have surrounded themselves with and have knowledge of the reason they are attending.

B) Define the necessity for and the use of confidentiality in the mediation process.

C) Define mediation and your role in the process.

D) Reinforce the impartiality of your position.

E) Describe the mediation procedures you will be using.

F) Explain unusual terms such as caucus and no lunch break.

G) Give logistics (bathrooms & rest areas).

H) Lay out the guidelines you expect them to follow (i.e. regarding good manners, etc.).

I) See if there are any questions in regards to your background or the process.

J) Discuss power and responsibilities of the parties in dispute.

K) Get busy. Remember that as you enter your caucuses there may be an attempt on the part of each party to get you on their side. This is a sand trap that you will have to watch for at all times. Remember, you are not the decision-maker, but you do have the responsibility of helping them work out a mutually acceptable agreement. Good luck!!!!

SAMPLE MEDIATION OPENING SCRIPT - SHORT FORM

In circumstances where parties are strongly committed to mediate and have a reasonable understanding of the process, a mediation may begin with a short "mediator's opening statement." This is typical in civil and commercial mediation where parties are represented by legal counsel, and in other situations where parties are relatively "sophisticated" and when the practicalities of the situation (e.g., multiple parties, parties from out of town, emergency) necessitate moving forward with negations.

Good morning. I am ______________, your mediator today, which means that I am here to help you and to aid your efforts to resolve your conflict. To help you, I will stress three things:

One, your voluntary participation. The mediation process exists for your benefit – which is why it can be voluntary. I will be helping you make your own choices in your own self interest by examining your essential needs and positions.

Two, I will emphasize symmetry or fairness. This means that I will treat every side equally and act only inside the limits you authorize.

Three, confidentiality. What we talk about in private remains private unless you say otherwise.

To start the process, I will ask each side to put their issues on the table and to tell us about their case. You can take the time you need, but most people take about five to ten minutes to describe things. When both sides have finished, we will then break into separate groups or caucuses and go from there, as the matter requires.

(Complaining Party), I would like you to start by sharing some information about your case. What would you like to tell us?

THE PSYCHO-LEGAL INTAKE IN MEDIATION

Mediators can benefit from borrowing and combining intake techniques used by therapists and lawyers. Therapists often do a psychologically based intake as part of their clinical practices. Most family lawyers do an intake geared which is financial-fact based. These two intake styles can be combined to create a valuable mediators' tool: the psycho-legal intake[7].

Benefits: The purpose of the psycho-legal intake is to learn a little more about the clients than a straight fact-based intake. This extra information will help you plan your mediation session, to anticipate where impasses may occur, and to help you deal with the parties' in a sensitive, client-focused way.

The psycho-legal intake has several benefits for the mediation process. In addition to the information gleaned during the intake, taking the time to do a psycho-legal intake helps the mediators build a relationship with the clients. It helps the mediators access and align with the clients and their dread that goes along with facing the task at hand. It helps mediators to work with them during what may be the worst moment of their lives (the first few minutes with the reality of the decision to divorce setting in) which ultimately helps clients commit to the buy-in to mediate and to stay with the mediation process when the going gets tough.

For clients, the intake begins to move them from reluctance to go into their history to feeling the release offered by articulating their issues and naming the relationship ruptures. This helps clients move toward the peace of mind that comes with both repair and agreement. The intake helps create the ambience for conflict resolution by creating an atmosphere of 'reverie'1 about the past that enhances emotional memory and taps into both the clients' grieving as well as their desire to heal. It is the mediators' job to start clients on this path.

How to being: A thorough, useful mediation intake combines a bit of both professions' standard intakes. The psycho-legal questions include a developmental history of the spousal relationship and parenting history, including new partnerships and how the children are responding to the divorce, along with some basic financial information. The challenge is to make the intake useful to mediators, who may or may not be therapists or attorneys, and short enough that mediation clients can tolerate what feels like small talk when they're hoping to get down to business.

The psycho-legal intake begins with what may sound like routine, nuts-and-bolts questions. What you're looking for as a mediator, however, goes beyond the words the parties use to answer. As long as this list of questions may seem, typically the intake only takes 10

[7] This concept is similar to psychoanalyst Elizabeth's Weiss, LCSW's idea of analyst's reverie.

minutes or so, though may take longer particularly if clients are interested in exploring this material together with you.

To being the psycho-legal intake:

Parties' Relationship

- Ask the clients' ages. Ask nicely.
- Ask them to turn back the hands of time to ask how their relationship started and when they met. Get as much detail as possible. These questions need a light touch. It's not about probing, but about asking:
    - When did the parties meet? How?
    - Did they befriend each other first, and if so, when did this move into a dating relationship? When did they get serious?
    - Realize that some people met as a result of an affair and this is particularly shameful if an affair is now part of the problem in the divorce.
    - When were they engaged? Did they live together before they were married?
    - Were their friends and/or family supportive of the decision to marry?
    - When did the relationship start to take a corner and there was a realization that something was not right?
    - What has been done about this? Therapy? Is this the first separation?

Children and Parenting

- Ask about the decision to have or not have children.
    - If there are no children, gently ask about how they arrived at that decision. You may hear about painful infertility treatments or a serious disconnect on this issue, which can foreshadow the impasses in the mediation session.
    - Ask if the children were planned pregnancies. How this is answered will give you a lot of information about how the parties came together and coexisted. Was there anything unusual or difficult about the pregnancies?
    - Ask about the division of labor with regards to child rearing. How did this arrangement come about? Was it discussed and agreed upon or not?
    - Has it been a satisfactory division of labor?
- How about the children? Ask to see their photographs. What feeling do you get when you look at them?
- What are the blended family issues, if any? Ask about any other step and/or half sibling custody and visitation arrangements in the household.
- Are the children on any regular medications and if so, for what?

- Do they have any chronic conditions? Any conditions they've been tested for? Any conditions they are watching over time to see how it develops?
  - There may also be a disconnect on this too, with one parent more concerned and the other more dismissive.
- Are the children currently in therapy or have they been in therapy and if so, what kind?

Post-Separation

- Ask what kind of parenting schedule they've been following post-separation, acknowledging that the mediation will explore this in depth when the parenting plan is addressed.

The Role of Anniversaries:

When constructing this timeline through sensitive history take of different types anniversaries including various milestones and ruptures in the individual lives of the parties, the life of the couple and the children's lives as well as how that all applies to the timing of appointments.

Anniversaries you're looking for:

- Traumas of all kinds;
- Dates clients got serious about the relationship, moved in together and got married;
- Wedding anniversaries;
- Children's birthdays;
- Anniversary of the death of a parent.

Purpose: When you're asking these seemingly innocuous questions, here's what you're looking for:

See if the words match the body language. If they don't, then sensitively talk about it. Does one party bristle at what the other says about something that sounds neutral to you?

Watch for people who gloss over difficult subject matter as well as for those who catastrophize. This will give you an idea of what to expect from them during the mediation session, and help you to develop interventions to assist them.

Understand that clients may find certain subject matter taboo and move away from such material. By finding a way to address it in the mediation session, you may be able to help avert impasse and to bring the parties to a new level of understanding and cooperation.

Many people react consciously or unconsciously to anniversaries. Be sensitive to the fact that clients may be extra emotional or appear to over-react to stressors near the anniversary of their physical separation, a parent's death, or other event.

Watch for parties who describe things differently. When discussing how they met, a topic which most people wouldn't find controversial, do the parties seem competitive or contemptuous? Or has one party completely forgotten the details? These observations will tell you a great deal about what kinds of difficulties to expect in negotiations.

Reading Between the Lines: How can you listen more closely for what people are indirectly telling you especially when clients telling you everything is simply "fine" or "awful"? What is really going on?

At the very least, prod for more details. For example, for the clients who say that their child is "fine", ask if the child has any health-related needs, is in therapy, takes any medication, does well in school, and is adjusted socially. If the child is truly "fine", these questions will just take a few seconds. If the answers to these questions take a long time, then you know that "fine" wasn't really the answer. The same goes for the basic questions about the relationship that you're asking as part of the psycho-legal intake, like "when did you meet? Were you friends first, or did you start dating right away?" You're looking for more than the factual answers.

Common Elements in Divorces: For the other questions, you're also looking for some common elements in many divorces. By finding out a little bit about the parties, you'll have a chance to develop some hypothesis about how to help them, when to expect to need to slow down, and what kind of negotiation styles to anticipate. All of the information in the psycho-legal intake will help you in your mediation planning.

You're looking for these types of threads in your intake:

- **Unplanned Pregnancy** - unplanned pregnancies may lead to a marriage in which one or both parties are not committed to the relationship, or a marriage in which the parties are emotionally immature and either or both never fully accepted taking on the role of parenting and forever resented the imposition and adaptation of lifestyle required by parenthood.
- **Affairs** - affairs create trauma in the breakdown of a marriage especially if one party was in denial and/or taken by surprise. Although the popular culture likes to label affairs as "the" reason a marriage broke down, as mediators affairs are a sign of a breakdown in a relationship that was already happening such that there was room for a third party to step in. The affair didn't start the breakdown of the marriage; the breakdown of the marriage permitted the affair. Affairs happen for a variety of reasons; for example, sometimes it's that one party felt invisible, hence the surprise, sometimes it was a way to feel alive again, and sometimes

the affair was a way to get the other party's attention or make it impossible to remain in the relationship.

- **Unilateral Decision to Divorce** - Usually one party initially broaches the subject of divorce. Statistically, the person who initiates the divorce has considered it for a year before bringing it up. Rarely are people on the same emotional timeline for divorce. So that one party doesn't feel completely responsible for 'ending' the marriage, you can reframe the separation as the marriage situation being such that it wasn't "leaving" per se, but that the situation was such that it was impossible to stay. Relationships are a two-way street and while there may be comparative negligence there is also contributory negligence perpetrated by both parties.
- **Birth of the First Child** - While the parents may be delighted to add a baby to their family, the move from a dyad to a triad is highly stressful even under the best of circumstances.
- **Launching of the Last Child** - When the children begin to leave for college or move out on their own, this can be a stressful time for parents who are redefining their roles in life. Chronologically, this timing often coincides with a mid-life crisis, the stressors related to caring for a couple's own elderly parents, or other mid-life passage issues.
- **Other Life Altering Events** - Even positive life events can be sources of stress with negative consequences to individuals and their partners in life. The obvious life-altering events are negative changes, e.g., the death, sickness or divorce of a child, close relative, mentor or friend, physical move of the household, loss of a job or promotion at work, but positive changes can also be stressors, e.g., achievement a milestone such as a the attainment of an educational degree, professional license, sale of a business, winning a prize or getting sober.

Although therapists are trained to use the psychological information in the psycho-legal intake in a more complex way than attorneys are trained, as an attorney this information is useful because even observing how a couple communicates the information they're telling you can be a valuable clue as to how they'll behave in the mediation session and where impasses might occur. By probing a little deeper into the intake information, even if it's only 10 minutes' worth of information, you'll have a better idea of what to expect in the mediation session. Couples with lots of trauma points or with major disagreements about basic, non-controversial facts like when they met will present a different challenge than couple who agree on the basic intake information and who demonstrate a high degree of cooperation in the intake. Knowing this in advance helps you strategize and develop hypothesis about the mediation session (as well as future sessions) and to anticipate where impasse may arise as well as how to deal with it.

PRACTICE HINTS

This is the first meeting with clients after the consultation session and after they have decided to mediate; it is the second actual meeting.

PURPOSE AND TASK

To structure the process; the underlying assumption is that clients adopt a crisis mentality because they have no information, or are confused by misinformation and overwhelmed. The mediator needs to organize information and issues to diffuse the crisis. Setting an agenda for the whole process and each individual session can be critical for the parties to see what they have accomplished and what yet needs to be done-much like a "Trip-tik" from the Auto Club laying out your route from New York to San Francisco (use that metaphor with clients).

WRITTEN MATERIALS TO BE GIVEN TO CLIENTS

- Agreement to Mediate (should have been received by clients before session either by mail or given in consultation session)
- Financial Profile
- Client History

DESIGN OF THE SESSION

The session begins with exercises calculated to allow for general assessment and to understanding how the parties conceptualize their future relationship after the divorce and their notions of fairness, and then to move directly to the specific tasks such as setting the agenda, addressing immediate issues and homework assignments (information gathering).

The specific exercises are:

1. **Relationship Expectations:** This is not therapy. The mediator is simply trying to establish where the relationship is now and where they hope it might be in the future. The purpose is to pierce the myth of finality that when they go to court and have a final agreement their relationship is over.
2. **Goals/Interests:** Fairness It is important to establish common ground. Don't let parties discuss specific plans; it is too early in the process and they don't have enough information or awareness of options. Focus on "protection of the children", "financial responsibility and security for each" and the "equitable distribution" of property. Identify the standard of fairness they choose to use-their personal standard rather than a legal standard (what court would do) or a mathematical standard (50/50=fair) early in the process before discussion of specific difficult topics takes place in later sessions.

3. **Agenda Setting**: Give the parties the issues that need to be addressed; they do not typically know or are not able to distinguish them on their own. Financial responsibility issues will be lumped together with property division issues, or if left to develop an agenda ad hoc, they'll list specifics "my coins", "the kids' college education", etc. Direct the parties' participation in thinking about which will be the easier or harder issues. Protect both parties from feeling that the discussion and tentative resolution of an issue early on will be "set in stone"-all issues are always open for review. Remember that parties will often confuse themselves viewing all issues as inextricably connected with every other issue-the agenda is merely a means of methodically beginning discussion in a businesslike manner-a place to begin.

Here's the breakdown:

- Win/lose outcomes-one winner, one loser. Competitive.
- Impasse outcomes-no agreement or resolution.
- Compromise outcomes-some parties give up some of their goals to obtain others. Accommodation.
- Win/win outcomes-all parties feel their interests have been satisfied

By way of illustration, here's how a position can be articulated in terms of the underlying goal:

Position	Interest
"I want Wednesday night overnights"	I want to be involved in parenting my child during school time as well as vacation time. I don't want to be stuck being a "Disneyland Dad."
"I don't want to pay spousal support"	I want to be financially secure, and to be able to retire when I'm ready.

Positional bargaining vs. interest based bargaining is a fundamental shift in thinking which lets go of the labels in favor of the bigger picture. By way of example[8]:

Positional Bargaining	**Interest Based Bargaining**
Assumes: resources are limited, and solution will require compromise or someone giving up something	Assumes: resources not limited, look to "added value" as well as non-monetary solutions
Attitude: parties will come in firmly rooted in their position (think "label"), which they think is THE solution	Attitude: problem-solver, not winner/loser. Looks to win/win outcome
How do they reach agreement? When they meet enough of an opponent's interests to induce settlement. Often, parties leave with an agreement, but are still dissatisfied. Represents compromise or giving up rather than working out a joint solution.	How do they reach agreement? By identifying the issues and goals of each party, and working through them. 3 types: 1) Substantive: issues such as money and time are often central 2) Procedural: behavior & session are civil and organized. Focuses on mutual interests and a plan for implementing 3) Psychological: emotional and relationship needs – respect, mutual positive regard

Can you see the inherent problems in positional bargaining? It's typically positional bargaining that brings people to impasse and litigation.

[8] Adapted from *The Mediation Process*, Christopher Moore (2002), Wiley/Jossey-Bass. 2 See examples on 72 of The Mediation Process, Christopher Moore (2002), Wiley/Jossey-Bass.

INTEREST-BASED NEGOTIATIONS

During a conflict, many people become very "position-based", articulating their settlement proposals in terms of labels, and lose sight of the goals that they hope these positions will achieve. Because I'm a family law mediator, I'm using family law examples, but interest-based negotiations are key to resolving all kinds of conflicts, both professional and personal.

Interest based negotiations help divorcing spouses to identify their goals, i.e., to remain a meaningful part of their children's school life as well as weekend life, or to be able to have financial security at the end of the divorce, as opposed to the single option that would traditionally be set forth in a settlement offer. There may be many ways to accomplish the underlying goals, not just one single way.

Expanding the Options: By having each divorcing spouse define his or her goals, mediators can begin to generate multiple settlement options that could accomplish the goal. This helps the divorcing spouses see that there isn't just one way to settle, and gives everyone more bargaining room at the table.

Many people think that mediation is all about compromise. This is only partly true. A true "win/win" situation occurs when both parties accomplish their most important goals with fewer compromises, and compromising more on their less important goals.

As a result, it helps if each person can prioritize his or her goals. It may be that each spouse needs to compromise on some of his or her less important goals (which may be more important to the opposing party) in order to make sure the most important goals are accomplished.

Interest-Based Negotiation seeks to enlarge the range of alternatives so that the needs of all parties are addressed and met to the greatest extent possible. This is the basis of most mediation. It also works best when:

- Parties have at least a minimal level of trust in each other;
- Parties have some mutually interdependent interests;
- Equal, but not necessarily similar, means of influence exist, or the party with the superior power is willing to curtail the exercise of power and work toward a cooperative solution;
- Parties have a high investment in a mutually satisfactory outcome; because of mutual fear of potential costs that might result from impasse
- Parties desire a positive future relationship.

When parties cannot identify their issues:

- They may not know what their genuine interests are;

- Are hiding their interests in favor of "strategy";
- Are so set in their "position" that the interest itself is obscured;
- Are unaware of procedures for exploring interests.

It's up to the mediator to convey a positive attitude toward interest exploration:

- It is in each party's enlightened self-interest that the other party is also satisfied with the ultimate agreement (opposing party will be more cooperative in the future, and more likely to abide by agreement, for example);
- In order to settle, both parties must sign the agreement, so both must be satisfied. Divorcing spouses needs to have an agreement the other party will sign;
- All parties have interests and needs that are important and valid to them;
- A solution to the problem should meet the maximum number of interests of each party;
- Interests can be traded to achieve the most satisfactory combination;
- There is probably more than one acceptable solution to a problem;
- Any conflict involves compatible interests as well as conflicting interests.

The key to resolution is to link the solution to the underlying issue to be solved.

Here's an intervention to generate options for settlement in individual meetings with divorcing spouses (first) and in a 4-way conference (second):

Step 1: Convince them that they have options-many spouses will come into the room completely entrenched in their positions

- Make sure they feel heard;
- Get them to commit to listening to other options-not to agree, but to explore. Remind them that listening is not the same as obeying
- BATNA (best alternative to a negotiated agreement);
- Detach parties from unacceptable positions.

Step 2: Help parties develop options: strategies and procedures

- Building block approach, "baby steps"-small components are easier to deal with than big issues. Keep breaking impasses down into smaller components that are easier to settle.
- Agree on formula for settlement-agree on how to approach

Types of settlement options

- Collaboration-interest-based negotiations & option generating

- "logrolling"-trading off issues which are more important to the other party
- "alternation"—trading off times for privileges
- designing a new way -orange argument (one wants the peel, the other wants the fruit)

- Bargaining on positions-proposals and counter proposals

How to generate options:

- Begin with what's already agreed or working
- Develop objective standards for an acceptable agreement
- Open discussion
- Brainstorming
- Nominal group process-brainstorming, but each makes own list, then discuss in subgroups
- Plausible hypothetical scenarios
- Model agreements-how did somebody else do it?
- Linked trades-trading one issue for another since parties value issues differently
- Deciding a procedural solution to a substantive agreement (e.g., posting a bond)
- Package agreement
- Using outside experts or resources

Help them assess options for settlement:

- Reviewing their interests
- Assessing how these interest are met by solutions developed in session
- Determining costs/benefits of selecting or rejecting the solutions
- Determining BATNA (best alternative to a negotiated settlement)
- "tweaking": Beginning process of modifying/trading (etc.) options to reach a final settlement

Part of being a good mediator, especially for parties that are not represented is helping people understand the settlement range. As the mediator you're not setting the settlement range, but helping clients explore win/win options within the range established by the mediation participants.

Recognition of settlement range

- Moderation of inflated expectations:
- If you were in the other party's situation, would you accept the proposals?
- Is the offer fair? Would other people perceive it as such?

- Is the demand you're making in line with other court decisions or settlements?
- Do you have the power to force this issue?
- What are the benefits to you of pursuing your present course? Are there any risks?

BATNA-examples of what happens if you win/lose or give up a specific issue?[9]

The danger of adopting this as a mantra: never forget that the "interests" described in the techniques above are merely a rational, logical, sensible set of interests, and that people involved in conflict, particularly divorce conflict, may have non-rational "interests" as well. Revenge, reparations for hurt feelings, apologies, shame, guilt, embarrassment, public perceptions.... the list goes on indefinitely. Simply appealing to the logical component often won't be sufficient to complete a settlement or overcome impasse. It may be that the parties are not yet ready to contemplate a true resolution of the conflicts at hand, or it may be that you need to explore these other non-monetary, non-rational benefits.

Example:

Position: "I don't want to pay spousal support."

Intervention: ask why, and what they're feeling about it

Response: "I am really angry at my spouse. He/she has betrayed me, refused to work [every bad thing divorcing spouses can think of]

Intervention: reframe and rephrase what divorcing spouses have said, making divorcing spouses feel heard before making suggestions of any kind. Then address the emotional interest (fear about financial security, not wanting to be taken advantage of, anger) and attempt to get to underlying emotion, "so you are afraid of ____ happening". Get a "yes, you understand" indication from the spouse, and then go to the interest-based negotiations intervention: "Would you be open to exploring options that would satisfy your need for safety [security, whatever the concern is] and at the same time would allow you the possibility of an ongoing relationship with your ex-spouse?"

Address the fear, offer to come up with a solution that addresses fear and which also creates the possibility for settlement and ongoing cordial relationship.

By going beyond a party's stated goal, and uncovering the interest behind the goal, you can help open up the range of settlement possibilities and help the parties to reach a mutually acceptable agreement with the fewest possible compromises.

---

[9] Source: adapted from Christopher Moore, The Mediation Process, 2nd Edition, Wiley/Jossey-Bass (2002)

Mediator Intervention: De-Positioning: In caucus, you can work on de-positioning the most entrenched party by:

- Accurately restating the party's position;
- Ask the party: imagine if a judge accepted your position: how would that benefit you?
- Squeeze those benefits dry-keep asking that question until the client is all out of ideas. Add a few of your own if the client runs out. The idea is to exhaust the concept of the benefits of the client's position;
- Restate and summarize all the benefits of the client's stated position—then ask "if an ultimate settlement dealt with each of these concerns, would you consider settling on that basis?"

The idea behind this intervention is that parties must feel heard before they're ready to change.

The keys for success in this intervention are:

- Be accurate in restating the party's position;
- Lean over backwards to accept the party's stated goals, even if you don't agree;
- Go for the baby-step toward an agreement, and don't rush the agreement itself. What you're doing here is creating a readiness for an agreement, not the agreement itself.

You can use this technique with just one goal or issue or the overall settlement. What you're doing is helping the party to create his or her priorities. You're also helping them to truly examine whether they really want to do what they say they want to do. It's a very gentle version of a reality test coupled with goal setting and goal prioritization. Let the party come to their own realization that they want to change-they don't want to hear from you or their spouse that they need to change. This is a realization they need to come to on their own....but you can nudge it along.

The next step is for the party to realize that in order for that party to get an agreement, it must also be an agreement the other party will sign. Again, we're back to hanging the ham low enough to where the dog can get at it. The idea is to:

- Create an openness to the other's needs; and
- Pointing out that there's a low cost and just a little time invested in exploring the other party's needs; and
- Listening to needs is not the same thing as obeying, or doing what the other party asks.

And, just like it was necessary for the client to feel heard before he or she was ready to change, it will be necessary for the other client to feel heard before he or she will be ready to change. It all comes back to baby steps toward and agreement.

Changing the Perception of Gap

You'll probably use this intervention we learned from Forrest Mosten in his May 2004 advanced family mediation class in caucus, but it's also possible to use it in joint sessions. This is a more sophisticated way of going over the costs of litigation with a client because it also includes some non-monetary factors. You'll start by using a flip chart to:

- Delineate the gap;
- Assess the probable outcome (get the lawyers to help with this step if they're available);
- Assess the soft costs and emotional costs;
- Talk about the financial benefits of settling;
- Examine the transaction costs of not settling;
- Do the math to delineate the remaining gap;
- Set strategies for closure.

When the client makes an estimate as to costs of litigation or other expenses, encourage them to over-estimate. Anyone who's been to a timeshare presentation will recognize this as a sales technique. Also over-assess the client's chances of success at trial-if the client sees it as 50/50, encourage him or her to assume 60% for the sake of this discussion. By being overly optimistic and encouraging in this part of the exercise, the math works such that the gap seems even smaller.

After you've done the steps above, then ask the client to:

- Assess the probability of winning his or her position in a percentage;
- Define the amount of money it would take to make him or her feel better
- Assume the cost of trial;
- Assess any financial benefit to keeping the relationship (e.g., not polarize friends, being able to stay on medical insurance, etc.);
- Agree that estimates have been conservative.

Remember, you're taking baby steps here:

- Be modest in your strategy goal;
- Stop before you're pushing the client too much or too fast;
- Do this exercise in the light most favorable to the client;

- No hammering the client to accept any of this.

Party Presentation of Offers

The key to the party presentation of offers is that once the offer is presented, there is no discussion except to ask clarifying questions before the presenter leaves the room.

The scenario: you are already in caucus and one party would like to make a settlement offer. If there's a lawyer helping the party, the lawyer will make the presentation. If there's no lawyer helping the party, or the lawyer isn't at the mediation session, the party will present the offer.

Generally, the party will have formulated the proposal in caucus with the mediator and/or his or her lawyer. When the offer is ready to be presented, the party will present the offer himself to the other side.

The mediator accompanies the party to present the offer in the other caucus room to the adverse party and his or her lawyer (if a lawyer is involved). The recipient of the offer may ask clarifying questions but may not respond or otherwise react to the offer when it is made. When the presenting party is done, he or she returns to their original caucus room. The mediator stays with the party receiving the offer to discuss the pros and cons and perhaps formulate a counter-offer which will be presented by that party.

Why this move works: If lawyers are involved in the case, they typically love being able to make their own pitch of the offer. As the mediator, you facilitate the discussion but you remove the risk that you've interpreted the offer incorrectly as you move from room to room. By not allowing an immediate reaction, you give the recipient of the offer a chance to think about it before making a knee-jerk response. Since you'll stay in the room after the offer is made, you give the offer a chance by sorting it out with the recipient and giving him or her a chance to make a reasonable, thoughtful response.

Developing Your Signature Style and the New - New Riskin Grid

Developing your signature style is a component of your internal case management, and an important part of your maturation as a mediator. Learning who you are, defining your strengths as a mediator, and understanding why you do what you do in the mediation room helps you to focus and build on your best qualities as a mediator. This in turn helps you to define your practice. In addition to the positive attributes, it also helps you to identify where you may need more training, to keep your personal biases in check, and to find ways to expand your range of skills. Understanding what you offer to clients, and what you do not offer to clients, is also an integral part of self-identification and defining the scope of your services.

We spend a huge amount of time assessing and re-assessing what works and what doesn't work in our practice and in our mediation styles. Developing your own style is what makes you unique as a mediator. Clients take some comfort in knowing that you will and won't do in a mediation session, your basic outlook on the evaluative vs. facilitative continuum, and in knowing that you know yourself well enough to convey who you are in the mediation room. Mediation is a very personal process, and you're not going to be the perfect mediator for every potential mediation case.

In hearing Professor Leonard L. Riskin speak at the 2004 Spring ABA DRS conference in New York City about his Grid System, and "New New Grid System" Diana realized that Professor Riskin's grids and self-evaluation system was actually a way to quantify where you place yourself in terms of a signature style. It's a component of internal case management.

Some of you may be familiar with Leonard L. Riskin's work with the "Riskin Grid". Prof. Riskin has revised his grid to go from being one-dimensional to becoming two-dimensional in his recent Notre Dame Law Review article (79 Notre Dame Law Review 1-53 (2003). For more than just this brief overview, take a look at the full article. Taking the time to do the self-evaluation as part of developing your signature style is certainly worthwhile. In addition, you can plot out where you felt the participants in a recent case landed on the grids to help you to de-brief after a mediation and to plan for the next session.

The basic premise of Professor Riskin's grid system is to provide the ADR practitioner with a set of measuring tools to make a private assessment of his or her orientation in different facets of mediation: e.g., evaluative vs. facilitative, narrow problem definition vs. broad problem definition. Figuring out where you fall on the continuum between these problem-solving approaches helps you to understand who you are as a mediator and to develop your signature style.

Just as mediators work to find the parties' underlying interests, rather than relying on labels, Professor Riskin found that affixing the labels of "evaluative" and "facilitative" was problematic in determining mediators' signature styles, and that the labels had unintended interpretations. As in mediation, the labels in the old grid system became too confining. It was time to get to the underlying interests involved, and hence the new grid system.

The New-New Grid developed by Professor Riskin adds new dimensions: more mediator orientations, influence continuums, expanded types of decision making grids, recognition that the procedures in place in the mediator's office can influence the outcome, and it also includes more ways to define of the types of problems experienced by the participants. One purpose of the New New Grid is to point out that each of these elements can be issues.

Using Professor Riskin's grid systems can be helpful in understanding where you are in terms of cultivating your skills and orientation as a mediator, in defining your services through your signature style, and determining where the next expansion in your skills should begin. In The Reflective Practitioner, Donald Schoen outlines the continuum of becoming a mediator: unconscious incompetence, unconscious competence, conscious competence, and artistry. (The Reflective Practitioner, Perseus/Basic Books, 1983). As we move along Dr. Schoen's spectrum, Professor Riskin's grid system provides measuring tools for self-assessment.

Turning Business Away

When in doubt, don't take the case. Trust your intuition. Or, if you're hungry enough for new business, take the cases you're not sure you should take and do your own trialand-error. We learn more from the cases which fall out of mediation and from the cases we have to work too hard to keep in mediation than we do from the successful cases, after all.

Keep a good list of referrals for other mediators and related divorce and family professionals. What goes around comes around. Make referrals out, and referrals will come back in. By choosing only cases that seem like a good fit for your signature style, you have a better chance for success as a mediator, and the parties have a better chance at success for their agreement.

When to Let Clients Go, Both Temporarily and Permanently

Not every client is worth working with. Seasoned practitioners have their own boundaries (and horror stories) about what clients are worth working with and which are best refused. Our rule of thumb is that the cases which are too difficult to convene are that way for a reason; we could spend as much time trying to get some parties to agree to mediate as they spend mediating their case. We call those clients "suspects" rather than "prospects" (borrowed from the book Selling the Invisible). Is that client on the phone really a potential client, ready to mediate, with a spouse or partner who's ready to mediate, and who can afford your services? As the demand for mediation grows, and our practices grow, it's natural to stop trying to convene these more reluctant cases sooner and sooner into the convening process.

Ironically, when we recently told a very unpleasant couple who were both entrenched in telling us how awful the other parent was before they'd even signed the fee agreement that we didn't think we could help them, it seemed to shock them back to reality and they agreed to call their Rabbi to work with him to get prepared to mediate before attempting to reach a resolution. With our refusal to work with them, they realized that they weren't ready to mediate. To have taken that case would have resulted in impasse or nonstop bickering in the mediation room, leaving the clients with the message that mediation doesn't work or that we're unskilled mediators. By turning down their business, we did both the clients and ourselves a favor.

By setting limits on how hard you'll work at convening cases, you also regulate your office workflow. Resources are dedicated to convening cases. Could they be better allocated toward providing better, speedier, more thorough service to existing clients, or in cultivating new clients or referral sources?

Setting limits on the types of cases you'll take is also important: will attorney-mediators handle any litigation cases in the "non-mediation" portion of their practices? Will therapist-mediators have any individual therapy clients?

You may also put limits on the types of mediation cases you will take. For example, if you're a family law mediator, will you handle cases that have domestic violence issues, or emotional abuse claims? Will you handle same-sex union cases, or just divorces? As an attorney-mediator, how deeply will you delve into hotly contested custody disputes? As a therapist-mediator, how deeply will delve into the financial issues?

And, at what point will you give up on cases that seem to be falling out of mediation? How hard will you-or should you--push clients to come back into mediation? What are some of the strategies you will use to encourage clients to come back?

As we work our way through this particular issue in our own practice, we use varying degrees of follow up with clients whose cases are becoming more contentious rather than moving toward resolution. Much of our effort depends on the mindset of the clients themselves, and our own assessment of the likelihood of success in mediation if the clients are convinced to come back to mediation. At what point are you wasting a client's time and money mediating a case that the client swears cannot be resolved? How do you promote mediation, when resolution looks very far away to the client, in way that doesn't make you look like you're simply a fee-hungry professional?

PRACTICE HINTS: PROPERTY DIVISION

ORGANIZATION AND APPROACH

The most critical mediative skill and strategy in approaching property division and financial responsibilities issues are structure and organization. Don't let the parties "fight" before they are ready, so that the substantive conflicts, not peripheral conflicts are kept in focus. The parties need (1) to have all necessary information, (2) know the issues, (3) know the options, and (4) know the pros and cons of each option before they can effectively negotiate. There are four basic steps that should be done in order:

1. inventory of all assets (marital, nonmarital and children's)
2. understanding of the assets
3. valuation of the assets
4. division of the assets

In property division, the mediator has a responsibility to give legal and business information (not advice) and/or make sure parties have that information from attorneys or other experts (e.g., marital/non-marital property, real/personal property, whole/term life insurance, etc.). However, the standards of fairness the parties apply for the division of assets should be their own. Reframe issues from legal to equitable division standards.

DIFFERENTIATE BETWEEN QUANTITATIVE AND QUALITATIVE DIVISION

Many parties (and lawyers) become preoccupied with the quantitative ("bottom line-who gets how much" division. Remember that the qualitative dimension, (who takes which asset) may be as or more important in terms of future financial security. A quantitative (value for value) division of assets is often too simplistic: "she takes the house, he takes the pension."

Before the parties begin property division asset by asset, make sure they see the whole picture; complete the Property Division Summary, (8.6.6).

NOTES ON FORMS:

Financial Profile: Statement of Property

This form was given to the parties as an initial homework assignment in the first working session.

Property Inventory and Valuation of Assets

This exercise/form is generally done in the second session from parties' statements of property. The subtotals for each asset are entered into the Summary of Property Division.

This form allows both parties to confirm the inventory of assets and values and provides a checklist of what further information/values need to be obtained (e.g., car "blue book" values, appraisals of real estate/business, etc.).

Summary of Property Division

This form will allow parties to see the whole picture of assets and possible options for distribution. Also, when finally agreed upon, it becomes the final exhibit (see Agreement form, 8.10.4, Exhibit III). Generally, the form is redone two times or more as values, options and tradeoffs are considered and refined by the parties.

PRACTICE HINTS: MANAGING PROPERTY DIVISION AND FINANCIAL RESPONSIBILITY ISSUES

1. In approaching both financial and property division issues, assess the "exchange environment" - how the parties deal with money and property. Who controls? How do they discuss topics? Remember money/property issues are only personal issues "in drag." There are few personal issues that do not have a business aspect and few business issues that do not have a significant personal dimension.
2. Make sure to conceptually distinguish financial responsibility issues from property division issues. Most parties will confuse the two. While there is overlap, dealing with each issue separately and then integrating them is important to minimize confusion. This allows the parties to "grasp" the "whole picture," while at the same time separating it into manageable parts.
3. Money and property issues are not synonymous with legal issues. Lawyers do not necessarily know better about these issues because of their professional training. Encourage the parties to read and to consult with accountants and qualified financial planners.
4. In approaching property division and financial responsibility issues, use the method scientists call the "theory of successive approximation" - obtain rough ideas about what makes sense and then refine the numbers in future reviews. Do not let the parties try to do it all at one sitting.
5. The order and approach to property division and financial responsibility issues in the course of mediation needs to be thoughtfully and strategically planned so that the parties are not overwhelmed. A suggested order is as follows:

- A. Arrive at tentative understandings about the division of property; complete the Summary of Property Division.
- B. Develop tentative understandings with regard to financial responsibilities; complete the Distribution of Financial Responsibility. (Generally the parties should have developed the parenting plan before beginning financial responsibility.)
- C. With the proposal format, have the parties complete the bargaining process, considering overlaps and tradeoffs between property division and financial responsibilities.
- D. The final level of refinement will include tax planning and ramifications and allocation of professional fees.

PRACTICE HINTS: FINANCIAL RESPONSIBILITY ISSUES

6. The most critical mediative skill and strategy in approaching financial responsibility issues is structure and organization. Remember that the mediator should not be the expert so that it is less important what the mediator knows than how effectively he or she presents and frames the issues for discussion.
7. Financial issues overwhelm many people and they are some of the most stressful in both marriage and business relationships and even more so in the restructuring of those relationships. Money issues - scarce resources - are also most likely to be the source of "real" or substantive conflict. Use that information; let people know that as you begin the discussion, to normalize the circumstance.
8. Observe and assess the parties presumptions about fairness. Often they will unwittingly or implicitly, if not explicitly, attempt to use the legal standard (what the court would do vis a vis child support, property division) or a facile mathematical standard (50/50 is fair). Recall discussions of fairness in the first working session and frame the discussion in terms of the parties' personal standard of fairness. (See 8.3(4).) The legal or mathematical standards are mere "buoys" or markers - not determinants of fairness. Review the Court Guidelines in mediation for the purposes of comparison after doing the budgeting exercise. This will tend to discourage the parties from assuming the Child Support Guidelines are "set in stone." However, it is important to consider the Guidelines in the mediation process to fully inform the parties before the agreement is reviewed by attorneys ("No surprises" mediation). If parties are made aware of Child Support Guidelines for the first time by their attorneys, the credibility of the mediation process and mediator are justifiably open to question.
9. The primary task in financial responsibility is typically best framed as how both households or parties can maintain an adequate level of financial security or lifestyle, or conversely, how both can avoid feeling exploited or taken advantage of by gross disparity. Avoid confusing equality or parity with equitability. Specifically, if one party is to subsidize another, the issues will be how much and how long.

USING CAUCUSES AND SEPARATE APPOINTMENTS

There are pros and cons to using caucuses and separate appointments as part of your case management.

Whether and when to use caucuses is the subject of much discussion among mediators. Some mediators use only joint sessions, some begin in joint session but leave the option of caucusing open, and other mediators begin mediations with individual sessions/separate appointments (like a caucus) and only after the mediator has met with all parties individually will the parties and mediator meet in joint sessions.

The civil mediation model typically uses caucuses either from the beginning, with the parties always separated, or after a very short joint session that simply outlines the facts of the case. Family mediations often minimize the use of caucuses, yet caucuses can be a very useful part of the family mediation process as well.

For the purposes of this section, we'll use the word "caucus" to mean both an individual session within a joint mediation session as well as an individual appointment scheduled by a client when no joint session is scheduled.

Our typical mediation model uses joint sessions as much as possible. We start in joint sessions if we can so that we can observe the dynamic between the parties. Of course, there are situations where joint sessions won't work or aren't desired by the parties, and we've set up our office to accommodate separate sessions and caucuses. Once in awhile, parties ask for individual sessions before the first joint session, or during the mediation orientation we've learned of domestic violence or an apparent addiction to arguing that would be counter-productive in a joint session. That said, we believe that the most efficient, transformative progress is made in joint sessions.

There are times when caucuses are absolutely necessary, however. If you observe a client becoming more and more disregulated (i.e., agitated or out of control), it may be

time to caucus. Pay attention to the clients' behavior, and their apparent physiological state. You cannot rely on clients to be accurate reporters of what should happen next. They may or may not realize how out of control they are (or are becoming). A common example of this is the client who is crying but who protests "I'm fine, let's keep going." Any kind of agitated behavior is a sign to the mediator that a caucus may be the next best move. If not a caucus, at least take a short break.

Caucuses can be a great tool for making clients take the break from each other that will allow them to calm down. We use them for a variety of reasons, typically to good effect:

- Self-soothing;
- Trust building with the mediator(s);
- Helping clients reality test;

- Helping clients prioritize their goals;
- Letting clients articulate their potentially unmanageable emotions and vent

In our eyes, the three drawbacks of caucuses are (1) the increased cost because it slows the process down, (2) because caucuses slow things down, they make it harder for clients to see progress and success in the mediation session and (3) the clients are the ones who really need to hear each other and learn to listen to each other, and the caucus doesn't permit them to do that. In a situation where no progress is being made because of persistent low road behavior, and where it's apparent that clients are not listening to each other and cannot be persuaded to do so, then the two drawbacks of caucuses are overcome because it helps prepare them to return to mediation.

We've overcome what would have been a fourth drawback to caucuses by using a comediation method that is a little unconventional: when we caucus, the mediators split up and one mediator goes with one client and the other mediator goes with the other client. We've worked together long enough to trust what the other is doing in the other room and to anticipate what that might be. No one sits alone in our practice. We've simply found that no matter what clients tell us, i.e., "I'm fine sitting here by myself. I have work to do and calls to return," that they are not comfortable sitting alone. The exceptions are rare.

If one client really needs both mediators' attention, then we ask our Dispute Resolution Associate to sit with the other client. This gives her an opportunity to make sure that the client has completed his or her financial disclosures or to review other paperwork. At the very least, she'll sit down with the client and watch a video or make small talk. It's the rare client who is truly comfortable sitting alone with the mediators in the other room with the spouse.

This is our take on the use of caucuses in our practice. As your role model or guide, you may also want to consider Christopher Moore's analysis on some of the reasons and benefits of using caucuses as outlined in his book, *The Mediation Process* (Wiley/Jossey-Bass, 2003):

Caucuses[10]

In mediation you may encounter some internal dynamics between the parties and their lawyers which may make caucuses helpful:

- Problems with the relationships between the parties or within a team
- Problems with the negotiation process
- Problems with the substantive issues under discussion

10 Adapted from Christopher Moore's The Mediation Process (Wiley-Jossey Bass 2003)

Other useful features of caucusing:

- Provides parties with a break if the joint session is too intense
- Refocus the motivation of the parties on why a settlement is important and the alternatives to a negotiated settlement (e.g., you can ask a lawyer in front of the client what the weak parts of the case are)
- Reality testing and acting as a sounding board
- Gives parties a chance to review BATNA (best alternatives to a negotiated agreement)
- Uncover confidential information that may not be revealed in joint sessions
- Control communications of parties and help them focus, helps eliminate emotions when you separate them
- Educate an inexperienced disputant about negotiation procedures or dynamics
- Prevent a party from making premature concessions or commitments
- Moving a party off an untenable or hard-line position
- Develop a single-text negotiating document when parties too numerous, issues too complex, or emotions too heated for face-to-face encounters
- Develop settlement alternatives in an environment that separates the process of generating options from that of evaluation
- Determine if an acceptable bargaining range has been established (or create one)
- Design proposals or offers that will be later brought to joint session
- Test the acceptability of one party's proposal by presenting the offer to the other party as an option generated by the mediator rather than opposing party
- Make appeals to common principles or goals
- Express your own perceptions of the situation and maybe make settlement suggestions

Timing and location are both important. Explain at beginning of mediation whether you may use a caucus, and under what circumstances. Also be clear about whether the content of the caucus is confidential, and what information will or will not be shared with the other side.

If you caucus with one party, always caucus with the other party, too, even if it's short.

Protocol-up to the mediator to do:

- Educating the parties about caucuses and why they're useful
- Overcoming resistance of the parties to separate meetings

- Making the transition to the caucus
- Deciding who to caucus with first
- Determining the duration of the caucus
- Determining what is said in the caucus
- Facilitating the return to the joint session

Despite the benefits to be gained from a caucus, however, many family mediators prefer to work without them, or mostly without them. As a family mediator, it's easy for parties to develop a "conspiracy theory" about what is happening in a room from which they've been excluded. Using or not using caucuses is not only a matter of the mediator's preference, but also the perceived needs of the parties, and the parties' tolerance for individual appointments, knowing that there will be a time when the mediator is meeting alone with the other party.

Deciding when and how to use caucuses is part of good case management and a way to move toward artistry in your mediation practice. To always handle every mediation in exactly the same way with the same format may or may not serve the clients' best interests.

Caucus Tips for clients

1. when mediator asks to speak with one of you alone, leave quickly and without attitude, and don't try to get in the last word
2. when alone, do not obsess. Try to relax, shake anger and tension
3. if conference takes longer than anticipated, sit tight. Don't knock. You could be befitting from this conference. If you have a question about the direction of the mediation, use the time to call your lawyer
4. if you're asked to caucus, don't refuse. Let mediator direct conversation. Exception: if you're bursting, it's okay to vent
5. be candid with the mediator. If the caucus is confidential, trust the mediator to keep your secret. If the caucus is not confidential, trust the mediator to use best discretion in handling your confidences. If the mediator asks you to reveal your secret to the other party, do so. If you're unsure of how to do so, ask the mediator to help
6. if you are ever uncomfortable with what the mediator says or does, bring it up to the mediator
7. if you feel you're getting out of control, as for a break
8. if you have a settlement proposal but are unsure about certain aspects or don't know how to present it, ask for a caucus and run it by the mediator

WORKING WITH AMBIVALENCE

What is ambivalence? Ambivalence is the simultaneous back-and-forth conflicted feelings that most divorcing clients seem to experience. One moment, the divorce is necessary and must be completed as soon as possible, and the next moment the client waivers, not sure if the divorce is a good idea or not. One moment, clients are working well on an agreement, and the next moment they are fighting over what was just settled. Ambivalence is evidence of unfinished emotional business, either for the parties as individuals or as a couple.

How will you know you're confronted with ambivalent clients? Look for clients who come in to their appointments still wearing their wedding rings, or clients who cry easily when discussing the issues and are hard to console. Does the date of the appointment coincide with an important milestone in the relationship? This is yet another clue. Some other examples of ambivalent behavior in the mediation room include clients who say that they're ready to mediate, and then immediately express love for the other party or pick a fight. Other clients say they're ready to divorce and then never return the necessary paperwork.

We have come to believe that ambivalence is the underlying force at work in our toughest cases. When impasse occurs, look for ambivalence, and the shame and trauma around it, at the root of the issue. Ambivalence isn't the only reason impasse happens, but where you have ambivalence you'll almost certainly confront an impasse at some point. By paying attention to and addressing the client's ambivalence, as uncomfortable as it may make you feel, you are proactively working to prevent impasse. Here are some examples of how you can take notice of and then address a client's ambivalence.

Making the Hidden Transparent

In making the hidden transparent, you're naming the unspoken, acknowledging the taboo material, and attending to body language. Here are some examples:

Client Says or Does	Mediator Intervention
Client displays frustration	Acknowledge their frustration. Encourage the client to name what it is in words that is so unnerving. Explore what this means to them.
One or both are showing emotional	Ask the client who's not crying or visibly upset if they know what distress. the other's tears or anger is about.
One or both are wearing wedding rings.	Acknowledge it out loud. Ask what this means to them.

One or both has a glazed over and/or far Acknowledge this.	Try to understand away look in their eyes and appears not to what it is you can do to help. Changing the seating arrangement be taking in the information can help.

We know divorce is never easy for the divorcing couple. Even the couples that seem to be in agreement that divorce is the right decision are susceptible to ambivalence, if for nothing else but that the divorce represents the death of a dream that was once important.

There are several components to ambivalence, including the grieving that takes place in mourning the relationship. Another component is unfinished emotional business, which is a clue that there's likely traumatic material from earlier in the participant's life which is being re-activated as part of the divorce and which probably needs to be explored in therapy. As mediators, we can acknowledge it and help the clients put these feelings into words, and to help them understand it in the context of the divorce, but to take it beyond this articulation phase would be outside of our role as mediators. To begin to understand how to address ambivalence in the mediation room, it makes sense to understand the basic stages of grief and loss.

Mourning the Relationship

When humans suffer grief and loss, current conventional wisdom is that they go through 5 basic stages of grief and loss. These are defined by Elisabeth Kubler-Ross in her 1969 book, On Death and Dying[11] as:

- Denial
- Anger
- Bargaining
- Depression
- Acceptance

DABDA is an acronym to describe this 5-step mourning process. Kubler-Ross's thinking grew out of her work in the hospice movement in the 1960s and has now been applied to many different mourning processes, like divorce. As much as DABDA appears to be linear, at any given moment, a grieving person may be experiencing one or more of these emotional states, and may jump back and forth between several.

The grieving process may also be complicated by unresolved trauma that is reactivated by the divorce.

[11] The most recent reprint is by Touchstone Press, 2005.

The Buy-In

The idea of attending to clients within the optimal range of responsiveness is easier said than done. One way to do this is to narrate what you have in mind, e.g., "I know that this discussion is painful, but I think it will lead to clues as to how to get this matter resolved. With your permission, we're going to talk about this for a few minutes in order to put this to rest once, if not for all time, then for now. And then we're going to ....." Tell clients what you're going to do, and get their permission to do it first. We call this the "buy-in" and when clients know exactly what we're going to do, give their permission, and then we do what we said we'd do, we're building trust into the process.

Oftentimes clients profess that they want to work quickly through the agreement without getting into the underlying ambivalence. This may work with some clients who simply need a few ideas to work out some details of their case, but it won't work for higher conflict cases. And, as the field of mediation matures, we see more challenging cases all the time. Five years ago mediators got away with ignoring ambivalence, but that doesn't work in contemporary practice.

Working as superficially as clients request can be counter-productive. Some clients are uncomfortable if they reach an agreement more quickly than they'd anticipated. Or, more commonly, it becomes obvious that the impasses are generated precisely by the unexpressed, awkward and painful material that is imbued with unresolved dramatic, often traumatized, feelings. By ignoring the clients' ambivalent feelings, and skimming over the trauma points, we as mediators do clients a disservice.

While the application of rational vs. emotional, "product vs. process" and "left brain vs. right brain", is most obvious in a family law case, ambivalence isn't limited to family law. Accident cases involving severe, lasting injuries or financial hardship, dissolution of business partnerships, neighbor disputes, malpractice claims, criminal victim/offender matters, and even the shame of being involved in a collections lawsuit can stir complicated feelings in even the most stoic individual.

How to Address Ambivalence?

Often it helps to make the mediator's quandary transparent by addressing ambivalence indirectly rather than directly. Would you believe that this hypothesis of ours is based on how to handle babies? Mary Main, Ph.D.'s and Mary Ainsworth, Ph.D.'s infant attachment research on wooing back infants in distress suggests that caregivers turn their head to the side while looking up at the baby rather than a full frontal approach. We suspect the same is true of mediation participants experiencing ambivalence.

For example, the mediator might say, "You've told me that there are only 3 hours to spend in this session, and that you want to leave with an agreement on every issue. I want to help you accomplish what you've set as your goal, yet here we are spending time talking about past arguments. I think it might be helpful if we dedicated some time to talking about what it is that's making it hard to get to the business you've told me is important to resolve. What do you think?"

While you're saying this, make eye contact to the left side of your client's face, which is where the client's right-brain (i.e., rational) processes show up. Making left side eye contact is more effective than looking at clients straight on, which can be perceived as aggressive. The left side of the face tends to hold more emotion than the right side of the face. If you want to read the cues behind the words, look to the left side of the client's face.

In a counter-intuitive fashion, slowing the discussion down to talk about these "nonbusiness" issues actually speeds up the process, eliminating some of the checkmates and standoffs, arguments and outbursts and the more subtle forms of sabotage that can derail a mediation session. It's a version of taking the temperature in the mediation room. Being transparent about the mediation process, checking the meta-level of communication as well as being clear-cut with each of the clients (and representatives) about the pacing of the case, and articulating their deadlines (both real and self-imposed) can help keep the psychological agreement process from being de-railed by the legal agreement process, and vice versa.

A Meta-Communication Technique for Tuning into the Right Brain:

To help yourself to remember to make eye contact with the client's left side, here's an easy way to remember: put your hand over your heart as if you were going to take a pledge of allegiance. Take a breath. Feel your heartbeat. If you are sitting diagonally across from your subject look reciprocally across at your subject's face and body. That is his or her left side. If your subject is to your right, their left is adjacent to you. If your subject is to your left, the left side is away from you and not always easy to see. That's when it's advantageous to have your co-mediator cover the client on your left. When there are two mediators everyone's left side is 'covered' where the right brain is expressed.

Conclusion

Knowing that ambivalence is at work in the toughest cases makes it easier to tune into the clients' behaviors and to hypothesize about what might be making it difficult to negotiate or reach agreement. Acknowledging the client's mixed feelings and the challenges of overcoming the grief associated with the end of a marital relationship can go a long way toward helping ready the clients for resolution.

IMPASSE IN NEGOTIATIONS

As a therapist and a mediator, I often see things in negotiations a little differently than the attorneys I know. Using a little of your intuition and some of the psychology behind deal-making, you can improve your negotiation skills in the room and in selling your clients on what you know is a good deal.

Here are my top 10 tips for breaking impasse in negotiations:

1. Determine how the pecking order in the relationship is maintained.

Regardless of who technically has more or less power in the hierarchy of the relationship. Then shift the oneup/one-down zero-sum competition to one of power-sharing in the spirit of enlightened self-interest.

Like it or not, there's usually an underlying psychodynamic basis to every conflict. Some old unresolved familial drama is being played out in the workplace, in a marriage, or wherever the conflict exists. Top negotiators can quickly spot personality types that are particularly likely to engage in conflict and the pecking order in relationships even if it's unspoken as to who is "the boss."

For example, a boss might be domineering and controlling and the subordinate may be indecisive and dependent. This pairing of personalities creates perfect conditions for conflict when the latter starts to feel more powerful as a result of having been mentored by the former. Not any longer the worshipped mentor, trouble starts when the dominant one will not promote a more equitable relationship with the subordinate one or adequately acknowledge the contribution of the subordinate one. Without using jargon, speak to the dynamics that lead to this 'deadly dance' in which there is a request, usually not for a complete role reversal, but usually a renegotiation of roles that is perceived as threatening to the one normally in power and a scenario for sabotage for the one seemingly less powerful. The request may be a case of role-sharing or to reframe the conflict, a renegotiation of the division of labor, or even a change of title or labeling of work responsibilities that can be accommodated within the relationship.

One way you might handle this dynamic would be to first acknowledge the two-way street nature of relationships. Ultimately one party is only as content as the other, because if one party has a complaint, the other will hear about it. The conflict will be ongoing until the underlying complaint is resolved. Being heard and having your concerns taken seriously is another reframe of the win/lose conflict in that there are never clear-cut winners and losers when you look at the long-term perspective if the relationship is overall a productive one.

Another more basic reason people get into conflict because they care about the other person or about the situation. The opposite of love is not hate-it's "I don't care". The fact that these people are in conflict tells you that they care about something in this relationship. If you can figure out their connection, or what it is that they care about, then you've got an important clue to the solution. When you can point out common interests, you can begin to develop some common ground for settlement. Often, the parties' interests are intertwined and ongoing, e.g., a manufacturer and a supplier of raw goods, professional colleagues in the same community, business partners or relatives. It's in their best interests to satisfy the other person almost as much as it is to satisfy their own needs. Here's the rationale: if the other party is happy (or at least happier), then he or she will be less likely to cause trouble in the future. So by definition, in any ongoing relationship, if one party has a complaint the other will have a problem. If both parties are satisfied with the result of the negotiations, it will be easier to work together, or at least be cordial, in the future.

2. Explore the payoffs and secondary gains from being in conflict.

No one gets into conflict by himself and it takes two people (at least) to fight. Knowingly or not, each party contributes to the cause and/or maintenance of the problem. One or both parties may even be protective about maintaining a 'perfected' complaint. Although one party may point a finger decisively at the other for having started the conflict, the finger-pointer is also a participant. He could, after all, simply choose to stop fighting.

Despite their protestations to the contrary, many people become embroiled in conflict as a way of avoiding something else. For example, if they can focus on the problem at work, they can ignore their failing marriage. If the conflict at work ends, they might have to face the bigger conflict at home. So the conflict is maintained and continues needlessly, even if it could be easily solved. If litigants understand that one way of staying in touch, or avoiding something else, is through conflict they might understand the real issue and be ready to deal with the conflict on its own merit. Once they see their own role in the conflict, and the secondary gains for continuing the conflict, they can begin to see their role in negotiating the solution.

3. Take turns putting the parties on the 'hot seat.'

Becoming an agent of reality for each party in turn can be very effective. It works best when you can cite a prior case, anecdotal example, statistic or study and therefore frame the information as neutral and objective even though it is likely to be more acceptable to one party than the other. Pre-empt the score-keeping by acknowledging to the party who won't like what you're saying that they might not want to hear this, and then be prepared to warn the gloating party not to use this as ammunition as their turn is next. Make sure that you use this technique equally with both parties, or do it in private caucus. Follow through on your promise to make the process equal no matter how difficult it is to find a neutral angle on the dispute. Remember that one party's best case scenario is the other party's worst-case scenario, after all.

4. Distinguish between stylistic differences that are negotiable and personality differences that are not.

Sometimes something as simple as a personal style or use of language can exacerbate a complaint to the point of conflict that never actually represented a disagreement in the first place. In a recent case I mediated, one party was a New Yorker and one party was a Southerner. The New Yorker called the Southerner an "SOB", which was acceptable everyday parlance for the New Yorker. The Southerner took great offense, and couldn't hear what the New Yorker was saying after hearing himself being referred to as an SOB.

If the New Yorker had a point to make, the Southerner was not going to hear it until he got past the language. Were the parties hearing each other? Is their disagreement as deep as they believe, or has an intervening event, such as the abuse of language, either irritated a problem or caused one where none existed?

5. Express needs in language that the other can hear and accept.

There are certain phrases used over and over when people are in conflict that rub the other party the wrong way. Take time to note what those 'fighting words' are and request

that each side refrain from using them in the spirit of resolving the conflict. Help them to create a new phrase to describe their concerns, and avoid these triggers that the other party has heard over and over again. Remind them that they've probably had this same argument before, and since it's not working, it's time to try a different approach.

Like the New Yorker and Southerner described above, until Mr. New York could stop cursing and use more business-like language, the Southerner was unable to hear him. Every time Mr. Southerner heard "SOB" or a similar curse, he tuned out of the conversation because he was angry over what he considered to be disrespectful and belittling remarks. Clearly, if Mr. New York wanted to be taken seriously it was in his enlightened self-interest to use language that would not make Mr. Southerner less open to his concerns. Once this was brought to his attention, Mr. New York was able to adopt a more conventional tone, and Mr. Southerner was much more open to Mr. New York's ideas.

6. Frame the disagreement as something they have in common and point out the irony of the situation.

This is particularly helpful in having otherwise competent and rational people who have gotten out of control with their conflict realize this and be embarrassed enough to reach resolution. If people develop an 'observing mind' and can see themselves being seen, this might also help. All too often people in conflict forget that they are not the first people with a similar conflict and that with variation their story has been told before and lived through by others. The various professionals who work in the law and courts have seen hundreds of similar cases. It helps for clients to know this and to begin to see their case from the outside perspective when thinking about how to present themselves to others to asses the rationality of their arguments and complaints.

7. Address the physical and mental toll paid from the stress of being in conflict.

Sometimes after being involved in conflict for an extended period of time, people forget that they might have better things to do than continue fighting. The sheer exhaustion conflict creates and the resulting inability to be truly productive in other areas of life may need to be pointed out. A simple question like, "what will you do when this lawsuit is resolved?" may do the trick, reminding people of vacation plans, family responsibilities, and new business ventures may bring them back to reasonableness.

8. Discuss the basics of compromise and the difference between listening and obeying.

No one gets everything that they want in conflict resolution, but each should at least have their concerns and goals heard. Sometimes people confuse listening with having to obey. Hearing and acknowledging another's position is not the same as agreeing with it. Everyone has the right to be heard and listened to, without the commitment to agreement or to being obeyed. If you can stop this part of the dynamic, you can start to make real progress on the resolution of the case.

9. Distinguish between perception and reality as a method for beginning to take responsibility for the consequences of one's actions without admitting one is wrong.

This technique is lifted from Alcoholics Anonymous. Though it can be particularly effective when one party makes allegations that the other denies it must also be used judiciously.

There is the valid point of view that establishing guilt does matter as much or more than the perception of guilt and no one wants the reputation of being insensitive to such issues.

Nevertheless, in this impasse-busting scenario validity of the allegation is not the problem; rather it's the consequence, or appearance or claim that the allegation is true that is cause for concern. For instance, in the case of domestic violence, whether or not the alleged perpetrator committed the act of violence is separate from the idea that the person making the allegations is afraid or of the alleged perpetrator. In addressing the alleging person's fears, the 'crime' takes a back seat. In negotiation, you can point out that the truth matters as much as the perception of truth to the other party, and you can begin to structure ways in which the settlement, including reparations, might be reached without having to determine whether one party is "wrong" or not.

10. Determine how to give the parties what they need and not only what they ask for.

Quite frequently I have clients who come in and are adamant about only wanting to work on an agreement and not use their precious billable hour to address problems in the relationship that has lead to the conflict. I naively proceed as requested, oftentimes getting to a pretty sound agreement, or at least a first proposal is made. Then I get the feedback that one, less often both, parties feel we moved too quickly into a settled agreement. Clinically, I know it is because we did not address the dynamics of the relationship. I grapple with how to 'slow down' the negotiation just enough that clients do not feel they are wasting their time in the room but enough so that the agreements stick or at least are not sabotaged for other reasons.

Taking a semi-psychological approach to negotiations can help your client-and the other litigants-get past what seem to be impossible sticking points. When you're stumped, try and look at the situation a different way and perhaps you can help the litigants see past the basic dollars and cents of the situation.

THE THREATENED WALK OUT

Peace Talks® Mediation Services

8055 W. Manchester Ave., Suite 201

Playa del Rey, CA 90293

(310) 301-2100

Diana Mercer, Attorney-Mediator, is the founder of Peace Talks® Mediation Services in Los Angeles (www.peace-talks.com) and the co-author of *Your Divorce Advisor: A Lawyer and a Psychologist Guide You Through the Legal and Emotional Landscape of Divorce*, (Fireside, 2001).

The threatened walk out is a beginning mediator's worst fear. After all, how can you continue a mediation session if one party walks out? Admittedly, it's tougher if you're the sole mediator with two unrepresented parties because you're torn between chasing the walk-out and calming down the remaining party. The good news is that the threatened walk out is generally more of a cry for help than it is an actual desire to leave the mediation session. Once you understand what the threatened walk out is about, there are things you can do to help make sure it doesn't happen.

Why do participants threaten to walk out? Threatening to walk out is an example of a party's disregulated state. Walking out could also be a defense against dissociating (i.e., it's a last-ditch effort to calm down). It may also be sadness energized or a sign of agitated depression, both of which should be taken very seriously.

You're most likely to see this kind of behavior at the beginning and end of the mediation. The beginning of the mediation is when tough material first surfaces and as the agreement comes into focus, it becomes clear that closure is near. As much as people may say that they want the conflict to be over, many may fear the future, post-conflict life. When the conflict is gone, what will be left? It may be a housewife who is fearful of rejoining the workforce, or a businessperson who will have to confront an uncertain financial future. Without the conflict to take up his or her time, he or she will have to face reality, which is sometimes an incentive to stay in the conflict.

By threatening to walk out, the party may believe that stepping out of the room also means stepping away from the problem, either avoiding the conflict or garnering all of the attention in the group. When clients threaten to walk it, it's important for the mediator to help the client calm down. As a mediator, you'll be both physically and emotionally with the client, following the client physically out of the room as well as not allowing the client to be alone.

Prevention can go a long way to avoiding walkouts. Although the mediator may be taking the temperature in the room, calling breaks and working every mediator move in the book to avoid having one party walk out, walk outs and threats of walk outs happen. In a perfect world, you'd never deal with a walk out, but it happens to every mediator once in awhile.

Symptoms that a client is too agitated to continue may include (but not be limited to) such behaviors as crying, slamming the table, twitching, incessant sniping, and other clearly agitated behaviors.

The first, and most basic, move, is to call a caucus. A caucus allows you to follow the person walking out and to help him or her calm down before leaving the premises. Even if you can't get the participant back into the mediation room, you don't want him or her getting into a car and unleashing frustrations in rush-hour traffic. The caucus will give him or her a chance to calm down, and it gives the mediator a chance to find out what triggered the walk out reaction. If the participant wants to be left alone, you can talk about what might help him or her regain composure.

In caucus, you'll ask the upset party, "what can you do to make yourself feel better?" Your first focus is on helping the agitated party calm down. Acknowledge his or her pain or fear in the underlying conflict. Get the client to make a commitment to get a grip in him or herself. Ask them what has worked in the past, and let them choose what they think might work. Don't suggest a method for self-soothing until after the client has made his or her own suggestions and decided that they won't work. Make sure the client is out of ideas before you make your first suggestion. Suspend the negotiations until the party has calmed down and self-soothed. Expect a relapse, but hope for progress.[12]

When caucusing with a client who is threatening to walk out, you can point out that the client is free to walk out of the mediation session, but that in making the choice to walk out, the client is making an affirmative choice to proceed in a different way. The client needs to consider what the next choice of how to proceed will be before walking out of mediation, because rejecting mediation means choosing litigation or anther path. Encourage clients to gather all the facts about how next to proceed before actually walking out of the mediation: know what you're choosing, not just what you're rejecting.

The second problem a walk-out causes is that you've left the other client in the room alone while you've been dealing with the party threatening to walk out. If you've got a co-mediator or the remaining party is represented by counsel, they haven't physically been

---

[12] 1 While we'd been practicing something similar without a formal name, Diana first learned about the technique called Self Soothing from Forrest S. Mosten in his Advanced Family Law Mediation training at the Los Angeles County Bar Association Dispute Resolution Section seminar in May 2004.

alone, but be mindful that spending too much time with one party without checking in with the second party can derail the mediation process as much, or more, than the walk out itself.

The client who has not threatened to walk out is typically very understanding of the need to caucus and that [at least at the moment] most of the office's resources may be devoted to keeping the other party in mediation. The threatened walk out is not limited to just one client at a time, however. It's not unusual for the threatened walk out to spark a competition of who can walk out first. This is another instance where the comediation model works in a way that other single-mediator models can prove more challenging, particularly when parties are unrepresented.

When you're not co-mediating and there's a threatened walk out, you may also be able to call upon another office employee, ideally a Dispute Resolution Associate (DRS). A Dispute Resolution Associate has attended a 40-hour beginning mediation class, and so he or she can also help in this situation. For a DRS to step in without having been part of a session is difficult, but at least as a trained mediator the DRS has an idea of what might be going on and what to do next. At the very least, he or she can keep the waiting party company while the mediator attends to the party threatening to walk out.

Throwing the Hail Mary Pass: If the client can't be talked into finishing the mediation session or returning to mediation at all, there is still a chance to help him or her through this low point in the process. It's at this point you could suggest that the client consider Collaborative Law, arbitration, private judging or anther ADR process. You can reality test as to what the next legal step will entail. You can refer the client to an accountant or mediation friendly attorney. You can even suggest a different mediator who might be more suited to the case. Remind the client that many, many couples start mediation, find it's premature or not working, and several months later decide to come back. Reassure the client that the mediation door is always open. The walk out caucus gives you a chance to salvage some or all of the client's ability to resolve the case without litigation, even if that resolution doesn't include your services.

Clients threatening to walk out of a mediation session are always challenging. There's no substitute for taking the temperature continually in the mediation process, but threats of walking out still happen. Knowing what's behind the threat and how to help the client calm down enough to rejoin the mediation while considering how to continue to engage the client who didn't threaten to walk out will help you the next time you're confronted with the walk-out scenario.

"WHAT TO DO IF" INTERVENTIONS

Peace Talks® Mediation Services

8055 W. Manchester Ave., Suite 201

Playa del Rey, CA 90293

(310) 301-2100

Diana Mercer, Attorney-Mediator, is the founder of Peace Talks® Mediation Services in Los Angeles (www.peace-talks.com) and the co-author of *Your Divorce Advisor: A Lawyer and a Psychologist Guide You Through the Legal and Emotional Landscape of Divorce*, (Fireside, 2001).

Mediation relies heavily on intuition mixed with underlying skills. As much as mediation involves feeling your way along given the tone of the mediation session, it's also helpful to have a mediator's toolbox of moves and interventions to call upon when you're out of intuitive ideas.

What to do when parties don't see the progress they've made in mediation:

From a therapist's perspective:

- Acknowledge their frustration;
- Ask clients to articulate more clearly what is 'a lack of progress;'
- Identify what progress they do see;
- Explore what this means to them;
- Ask what they think stands in the way of their progress;
- Ask what could be done to clear the path to progress;
- Explore what progress would look like;
- Explore what progress would feel like.

From a lawyer's perspective:

- Reiterate all that they have accomplished;
- Reiterate it in writing in the summary letter;
- Be transparent about the lack of progress at the time, e.g.,"You've said you only have 15 minutes to talk about this, but you keep going off the topic. We can't finish unless we stay with the agenda." Straying frequently from the agenda can be a sign of ambivalence, so be sure to address this issue soon enough for the

clients to be able to change their behavior and still make progress. It's okay to deviate from the agenda, but do it with everyone's agreement that you're switching topics;

- Suggest a caucus if the clients can't stop fighting;
- Ask what they'd hoped to accomplish and how best to get to their goals;
- Ask if there's another way to go about things that might show them more progress more concretely;
- Point out how much faster mediation has been than litigation.

What to do when parties seem to want to stay in a joint session but you think it's counter-productive

- Talk about your own physical or emotional discomfort. Where and how are you as the mediator feeling it?
- Ask each one of them if they're uncomfortable. You'd be surprised how normal extreme discomfort can feel for some people. If you're uncomfortable, say so.
- Make the hidden transparent: e.g.,"You've said you only have 15 minutes to talk about this, but you keep going off the topic. We can't finish unless we stay with the agenda. I'm concerned that you won't reach your goal for today's session if this fighting keeps up."
- If none of this helps, you may have to insist upon a caucus.

What to do when it appears that one party has chosen mediation to bamboozle the other spouse under the guise of the mediator's legitimacy

- Make it clear that full disclosure of assets is mandatory, not optional, and explain the unpleasant consequences of untruthful or less than full disclosure of financial information if the matter goes to court.
- Explain your office policy about legal information and consultation with attorneys. Make it your policy is that clients may make an unconventional decision in mediation but it must be an informed decision. To preserve the integrity of the process, mediation participants can choose to give up their legal rights in a mediated agreement, but only after they have an understanding of what their rights might have been.
- Articulate your concern in the session, summary letter or in subsequent sessions by talking about each party's distress. There are typically behavioral clues related to this problem, and if you notice them during the session you can bring it up at that time. If you notice it afterwards, you could bring it up in the

summary or next session. If it's too risky to do it in joint session, you could do it in a caucus.

- Explore with the bamboozling spouse what is going on. Although it may appear to you that there's an attempt to curtail the other participant's power or rights the parties may not see it the same way. Check your own biases or discomfort and make sure it's truly about the parties and not about your own agenda. For some bamboozlers, the attempt to unduly sway the other party stems from the sense of having done everything right in the marriage and now having to pay when the divorce wasn't his or her idea or fault.
- Explore with the other party about any perceived lack of contribution to the marital team's successes.
- Re-screen for domestic violence, controlling behavior or severe power imbalance in the relationship.
- Be prepared to let go of the case.

What to do when a client is out of control

- Caucus, or end the session early;
- Take a break that's long enough for everyone to calm down;
- In caucus, help the client self-soothe, and don't try to cover any more ground on the agenda until the client has completely calmed down;
- Reiterate that for mediation to work, the timing must be right. Give the client the opportunity to stop the mediation, and the option to return when he or she is more ready to reach an agreement;
- Separate the behavior from the person, not to establish guilt or blame, but to emphasize how the behavior is perceived or perhaps even misinterpreted as scary, manipulative or odd;
- Talk about your own discomfort even if the parties cannot;
- Consider more drastic security measures like installing a panic button.

What to do if the session is moving too fast: signs you should slow things down

- Ask. If you suspect you should slow down, you probably should. Take the temperature.
- One or both clients are showing emotional distress. For example, if one party starts to cry, ask the one who's not crying if they know why the other party is crying and if they know what the tears are about.

- If one or both parties are wearing their wedding bands. This unspoken gesture speaks volumes and is usually an outward sign of ambivalence about the breakup.
- One or both clients have a glazed over or far away look in their eyes and don't appear to be taking in the information.
- By paying attention to clients' right hand side of their face and eyes, you are beginning to tune into your client's internal world. This makes them feel more attended to, thereby slowing things down to a more manageable pace.
- Acknowledge agitated behaviors such as a client pounding the table or clenching their hands by talking about them directly in the session. For example, "I couldn't help but notice that when she said XYZ that your face flushed and you clenched your teeth. Can we talk about that for a minute?"
- If you notice from the intake that the date of the appointment coincides with an important time in the relationship, or that one or both parties tell you about a recent death in their respective families. Remind them of the anniversary, acknowledge that it can be difficult to reach an agreement when they're remembering an important milestone, and invite them to either slow down or come back another day.
- You know one client is giving up much more of the marital assets than is provided under the law without having the opportunity to fully explore the issues. It's time to do some reality testing, to check for bamboozling, or to discuss the reasons he or she might want to give up too much.

What to do if the mediation is meandering: Signs you should speed things up

- You should probably never speed up a mediation session. It's not your job to make the clients go any faster than clients are inclined to go. A nice, slow pace may be exactly what the clients need. Part of your job is to keep clients on the agenda, or to mutually agree when to stray from the agenda. Your job is never to race through the issues.
- Our policy is never to work harder at reaching an agreement than the clients are willing to work themselves. Check your own discomfort at the slow pace of the mediation. Are you truly at fault? If you're still uncomfortable a few minutes later, take the temperature and ask the clients how you can best help them.
- For clients who aren't talking at all, ask why they're not talking or engaging in the process.
- If clients are going round and round on a subject starting to repeat themselves, not adding new information, and getting emotionally distraught, suggest that the

issue should be tabled for the moment, that it will be an issue to return to and that by addressing other issues, the solution to this one may become clearer.

- When you return to the issue and there is still no resolution, start offering some suggestions for resolution, or make a referral to an attorney or accountant who might be able to make suggestions.
- Clients should never feel rushed in their progress. Remember that mediation is a very thoughtful process and bound to bring up highly volatile material that takes time to take in satisfactorily. Relax. They will reach an agreement when they're ready.

A full mediators' toolbox can help you get over some rough moments in tough mediation sessions. One of the best perks of being a mediator is sharing techniques with other mediators and mediators' commitment to lifetime learning.

ADVANCED SKILLS

- Mediator's choice;
- Promoting self soothing and self-regulation;
- Content to process shift;
- De-positioning through self interest;

Mediator's Choice

Mediator's choice is a technique to use when you're all out of other ideas and time is running short. It was taught to Diana by Nancy Spero, and we've used it more in civil mediations than in family mediation situations, but it's useful to discuss because it's an interesting jumping off point for how it might be adapted in family law mediations.

The mediator silently formulates a proposal that he or she thinks will be barely palatable to each side—hanging the ham low enough to where the dog can get at it, so to speak. After spending several hours with both sides, if the mediator has an idea of each side's breaking point, he or she can formulate the "mediator's choice" proposal. The idea is that it's the last dollar that each side may be willing to concede.

The mediator then presents the proposal to each side in caucus clearly indicating that it's the mediator's proposal, not a proposal made by either side. In the first round there's no "yes" or "no" answer, but simply an opportunity to think about the mediator's proposal. Some mediators put the proposal in a basic stipulation form so that a written agreement can be left with the parties and signed if there is indeed an agreement.

Once the proposal has been made to both sides, the mediator clearly explains the rules: the mediator will not reveal either side's answer to the proposal unless the answer by both sides is "yes" and the parties have an agreement. If they have an agreement, the stipulation is signed. There is no re-negotiation of any terms of the agreement-it's mediator's choice or no agreement.

If either side says "no", the answer from both sides is kept confidential. That way, if one side says "yes" and the other side says "no", the rejecting side doesn't know the agreeable side would settle for the mediator's proposal. By revealing only mutual "yes" answers, the mediator preserves confidentiality for the ongoing negotiations.

Adapted from Forrest S. Mosten's *Advanced Family Mediation Training*

This is a last-ditch attempt to help the parties reach an agreement, and is generally only suggested 15 minutes before the mediation is scheduled to end. It's very evaluative in nature, and is simply one last mediation intervention to try before sending the parties on their way without an agreement.

Self Soothing and Self Confrontation

At times in the mediation process, some clients will become agitated such that they cannot continue to mediate. If you're already in caucus, it may be time for a break or even a postponement of the rest of the mediation session. If you're in joint session, however, there's a technique which can help clients self-soothe and self-regulate before the entire mediation is derailed. We first learned of this technique from Forrest Mosten in his advanced family mediation class held in Los Angeles in May 2004.

When you note that a client is too agitated to continue to make progress in a joint session, to use this technique you'll call a caucus. We'd suggest that your client is too agitated to continue when you observe such behaviors as crying, slamming the table, twitching, incessant sniping, and other clearly agitated behaviors.

In caucus, you'll ask the upset party, "what can you do to make yourself feel better?" Your first focus is just on helping the agitated party calm down. Acknowledge his or her pain or fear in the underlying conflict. Get the client to make a commitment to get a grip in him or herself. Ask them what has worked in the past, and let them choose what they think might work. Don't suggest a method for self-soothing until after the client has made his or her own suggestions and decided that they won't work. Make sure the client is out of ideas before you make your first suggestion.

Suspend the negotiations until the party has calmed down and self-soothed. Expect a relapse, but hope for progress! Once the party has self-soothed, you may wish to move onto self confrontation before going back into joint session.

Self Confrontation

In caucus, after self-soothing, you'll ask your client, "what can you do to take responsibility for improving your (or your spouse's) willingness to negotiate?"

Explore the possibilities with him or her. Acknowledge the progress he or she has made from self-soothing. Before asking your question, confirm that the client is ready to

go on and if they're ready for a bigger challenge. Ask what they can do to move the negotiations along. Use this caucus time in a focused way to discuss the client's options and select an acceptable proposal for the client to make in joint session or as part of your shuttle diplomacy.

Content-to-Process Shift

When things get too heated or counter-productive in the mediation room, you can borrow a therapists' intervention called content-to-process shift. Diana first learned of this intervention from Carol Hirshfield, Ph.D. at the Los Angeles Collaborative Family Law Association in 2004.

The premise is pretty basic: when the content of the session, e.g., the current discussion topic, is too controversial or generating too much conflict, step back a little in the session and think about what mediation process tools you could use to diffuse the tension. You're switching from the discussion itself to the mediation process, hence content-to-process shift. Do you need to take a break? Call a caucus? Help a party self-soothe? What mediation intervention can you use to lower the temperature in the room and make the discussion possible again?

De-Positioning Through Self Interest: Interest-based negotiations

Labels vs. Goals: During a divorce, many people become very "position-based", articulating their settlement proposals in terms of labels, and lose sight of the goals that they hope these positions will achieve.

Interest based negotiations help clients to identify their goals, i.e., to remain a meaningful part of their children's school life as well as weekend life, or to be able to have financial security at the end of the divorce, as opposed to the single option that would traditionally be set forth in a settlement offer. There may be many ways to accomplish the underlying goals, not just one single way.

Expanding the Options: By having the client define his or her goals, you can begin to generate multiple settlement options that could accomplish the goal. This helps the client see that there isn't just one way to settle, and gives you more bargaining room at the table.

Prioritize: Also have the client prioritize his or her goals. It may be that the client needs to compromise on some of his or her less important goals (which may be more important to the opposing party) in order to make sure the client gets the most important goals accomplished. A true "win/win" situation occurs when both parties accomplishing their most important goals with fewer compromises, and compromising more on their less important goals.

Win/lose outcomes-one winner, one loser. Competitive.

Some examples:

Position	Interest
"I want Wednesday night overnights"	I want to be involved in parenting my child during school time as well as vacation time. I don't want to be stuck being a "Disneyland Dad".
"I don't want to pay spousal support"	I want to be financially secure, and to be able to retire when I'm ready.
"I don't want to share the marital assets"	I shouldn't have to pay for having done nothing wrong.

Positional bargaining vs. interest based bargaining

Positional Bargaining	**Interest Based Bargaining**
Assumes: resources are limited, and solution will require compromise or someone giving up something	Assumes: resources not limited, look to "added value" as well as non-monetary solutions
Attitude: parties will come in firmly rooted in their position (think "label"), which they think is THE solution	Attitude: problem-solver, not winner/loser. Looks to win/win outcome
How do they reach agreement? When they meet enough of an opponent's interests to induce settlement. Often, parties leave with an agreement, but are still dissatisfied. Represents compromise or giving up rather than working out a joint solution. See examples on p. 72 of The Mediation Process, Christopher Moore (2002), Wiley/Jossey-Bass.	How do they reach agreement? By identifying the issues and goals of each party, and working through them. 3 types: 1) Substantive: issues such as money and time are often central 2) Procedural: behavior & session are civil and organized. Focuses on mutual interests and a plan for implementing 3) Psychological: emotional and relationship needs – respect, mutual positive regard

PHRASES FOR ACTIVE LISTENING

Phrases for Active Listening[13]

ENCOURAGING: "Can you tell me more?"

CLARIFYING: "When did this happen?"

SUMMARIZING: "Let me see if I understand what you just said...."

AKNOWLEDGING: "I can see you are feeling angry right now."

OPEN QUESTIONING: "Why?....What would you like to see happen?"

RESPONDING: "What would you like to see happen?"

SOLICITING: "I would like your advice about how we can resolve this."

ENCOURAGING: "How would you feel if it were you?"

NORMALIZING: "Many people feel the way you do."

EMPATHIZING: "I can appreciate why you feel that way."

REFRAMING: "I understand that you feel ___ when she/he ____."

VALIDATING: "I appreciate your willingness to be here.... "

Phrases for Miscommunication-AVOID!

ORDERING: "You must...." "You have to...." "You will...."

THREATENING: "If you don't, then...." "You'd better or else..."

PREACHING: "You should...." "You ought..." "It's your duty..."

LECTURING: "Here is why you are wrong...." "Do you realize...."

GIVING ANSWERS: "What I would do is..." "It would be best if you..."

JUDGING: "You are lazy....you are ___ " "You'll never change"

EXCUSING: "It's not so bad..." "You'll feel better..."

DIAGNOSING: "You're just trying to get attention." "What you need is..."

PRYING: "When? How? What? Where? Who?"

LABELING: "You're being unrealistic....emotional...angry...."

---

13 Reprinted with permission from Ken Cloke, "Mediation: Revenge and the Magic of Forgiveness"

MANIPULATING: "Don't you think you should..."

Active listening is a way of listening and responding to another person that improves mutual understanding. Often when people talk to each other, they don't listen attentively. They are often distracted, half listening, half thinking about something else. When people are engaged in a conflict, they are often busy formulating a response to what is being said. Parties in conflict assume that they have heard what their opponent is saying many times before, so rather than paying attention; they focus on how they can respond to win the argument.

Active listening is a structured form of listening and responding that focuses the attention on the speaker. The listener must take care to attend to the speaker fully, and then repeats, in the listener's own words, what he or she thinks the speaker has said. The listener does not have to agree with the speaker--he or she must simply state what they think the speaker said. This enables the speaker to find out whether the listener really understood. If the listener did not, the speaker can explain some more.

Active listening has several benefits. First, it forces people to listen attentively to others. Second, it avoids misunderstandings, as people have to confirm that they do really understand what another person has said. Third, it tends to open people up, to get them to say more. When people are in conflict, they often contradict each other, denying the opponent's description of a situation. This tends to make people defensive, and they will either lash out, or withdraw and say nothing more. However, if they feel that their opponent is really attuned to their concerns and wants to listen, they are likely to explain in detail what they feel and why. If both parties to a conflict do this, the chances of being able to develop a solution to their mutual problem becomes much greater.

The mediator, serving as the facilitator of communication, has a duty to actively listen so that he/she can correctly communicate one party's statements to the other party if they are using the caucus format. Repeat what you think you heard from the presenting party before transmitting the information to the other party. It will not be uncommon to be corrected as you repeat what think you heard, as this may be the first time that party has heard their own argument recited.

REFRAMING

Instructions: Reframe the following statements.

1. I'm not going to spend another minute trying to negotiate with that SOB. I've told him again and again that this computer equipment needs updating. He's just too darn stupid to realize that sometimes you've got to spend money to make money.

2. This is another example of the Feds grandstanding and trying to take all the credit. We put a lot of time into this program. Just because there were a few glitches that needed to be ironed out, that doesn't make us idiots.

3. Senator Whiney is making my job so difficult. He did me a favor three years ago and he acts like I owe him something. Now he wants me to find a job for his idiot nephew. This situation must look really bad to my colleagues.

4. "Sam's always trying to tell me how to run my projects. I trust him to do his job. I wish he would trust me to do mine."

5. "You'd have to have a Ph.D. to use that software. Marva's the only one who's familiar with it. None of the rest of us can get the data we need. It may be cheaper, but it's not worth it."

6. "Her negotiating style is as subtle as Sherman marching to sea. We can't get agreement on anything."

Conflict Resolution Styles

- Avoid
- Accommodate
- Compete
- Compromise
- Collaborate

Listing Skills

Overview & objectives:

- Good listening in general
- What we mean by "active listening"
- Demo and exercises - clarify some skills
- Listening Skills Self-Assessment - work on skills during roleplays
- Role of listening in mediation

Listening is Important and Powerful

- Good listening is helpful in and of itself--if you do nothing else in mediation...
- Builds trust and rapport
- Deescalates/calms
- Creates clarity
- Listening is a precursor to problem-solving
- Feels like a "gift"-everyone wants to be heard

What's "Active About It?

- Requires work and concentration
- Two-way
- Three ways of looking at Active Listening
- Set of skills (e.g. open-ended questions)
- Ability to focus/concentrate - focused on all aspects of speaker's communication, setting aside my own issues for the moment.
- Attitudes (ideally):
- I care what this person has to say
- I'm sincerely curious about how this person sees things
- I'm willing to withhold judgment and accept this person's reactions, perceptions, feelings as legitimate.

Active Listening Skills

- Get the Story
  - Encourage the speaker
  - Ask open-ended questions
  - Draw out background/context

- Clarify and check understanding

- Probe / Clarify Meanings
  - Use questions that take the speaker's understanding a step deeper, or bring out the meaning or significance of the situation for the speaker.
  - Examples: "By 'disrespect'? What about that felt disrespectful?" "Why do you think she did that? "How do you think he sees the issue?" Are you more upset about money, or sentimental value? "What is your concern about that?" "What do you mean?"

- Listen for Emotions
  - Be aware of non-verbal cues Hesitation, change in tone, body language
  - Name the emotion, in a way that validates it. - When in doubt, stay general ("upset", "frustrated")
  - Allow venting

- Summarize
  - Make a "story" out of what you've heard
  - Capture what's most important to the speaker
  - Include main facts, issues, concerns, feelings, perception
  - Check accuracy: "You've said a lot. Let me see if I understand..." "So the issues you're concerned about are X, Y, Z, and it sounds like the biggest one for you is Z. is that right?"

- Value Silence
  - Shows concern, empathy, respect
  - Allows people to hear themselves, and each other
  - Watch non-verbal cues
  - Let people answer questions

Uses of Active Listening in Mediation

- Getting information
- Building trust
- Modeling constructive communication
- Helping people hear themselves
- Defusing emotions, de-escalating
- Increasing clarity about issues, feelings, goals
- Bringing out underlying interests and concerns

- (positions ? interests)
- Translating, building bridges

Example

Elaborate on the facts here and make up additional information as needed.

You are working on a major group project for a physics lab. You feel that one of your team members is really not pulling his weight. He does not seem to take it very seriously. At a meeting last week, you thought the piece he was working on was really sub-standard. You made what you thought was a subtle comment about the quality of work (but maybe it came off as snide). He got defensive and the subject got dropped, though tension remained. You are angry with him, but think perhaps you could have approached it differently. You talk with you GRT about the situation.

Elaborate on the facts here and make up additional information as needed.

Your boss gave you a dressing down because there were some errors in a major report you worked on that just went out. You were incensed, because you had worked tremendously hard, long hours to get the report done. You would have caught most of the problems if the boss hadn't thrown in so many last minute changes and additions at you. After your boss finished her tirade, you shot back "You're impossible! I'm not going to deal with this!" and left the room. You have come to [mediator] to vent and figure out what to do.

REFRAMING

Using the Language of Diplomacy

- Reframing means choosing your words carefully in order to
- De-escalate hostility and calm emotions,
- Move from positions to interests,
- Describe issues as solvable problems, and
- Develop shared goals, when possible, or trade-offs.

De-escalate and calm.

- Let the speaker feel heard, by reflecting back facts and emotions.
- Use neutral language.
- Describe the speaker's feelings, not the other person's character.

Move from positions to interests

- Ask, gently what the critical elements are in the speaker's position.
- Explore what the speaker wants to avoid.
- Consider alternatives through "What if..." questions.

Turn concerns into solvable problems.

- Change an attack on a person to a description of a problematic behavior.
- Change a list of past wrongs into future goals.

- Divide broad / global demands into components, which can be, approached one at a time.

Develop shared goals or trade-offs.

- Point out common or joint interests.
- Explore relative priorities of issues, to locate willingness to trade something one considers minor and the other considers important.

REFRAMING BATTING PRACTICE

- P & Q work in the same office. Each accuses the other of monopolizing the copier. P says to a friend: How can I try to resolve this when he refuses to talk about it?!
- A & B are working on a joint lab project. A complains to the TA: B is so lazy! I've been asking her to finish this for ages. She says she will but never does.
- A complains to the RA about noise from B's room next door: Whenever I ask him not to do that, he always yells at me and slams the door.
- X & Y, grad students, share an apartment and a car: X says, "She takes the car on Saturday to go hiking, when she knows I have to have it to do the grocery shopping." Y says, "That's ridiculous. I go hiking when my hiking club goes. He can go shopping any time."

THE FLOW OF A MEDIATION

Where You Are	What You Are Doing
Mediator's Introduction	Explain process Being building trust
First Joint Session	Hear parties' stories Distill issues Identify positives Ask for desired outcomes
Early in Private Sessions	Allow venting Probe for understanding Focus on interests under positions --fantasy outcome
Late in Private Sessions	Look for similarities in interests Discuss priorities & trade-offs Brainstorm Discuss effect of not resolving Name areas of agreement Review possible final agreement
Final Joint Session	Write agreement

PRONOUNS

Pronoun	Form of Language	Likely Result
They	Stereotype	Prejudice
You	Accusation	Denial and counter attack
He/she	Demonization or Victimization	Hostility or disempowerment
It	Obejectification	Problem solving

I	Confession/request	Taking responsibility/introspection
We	Collaboration	Commitment

PREPARING FOR DISTRIBUTIVE NEGOTIATION

- Figure out you own interests and reservation point as well as you can. Keep reviewing these points while you negotiate.
- Figure out the interests and reservation point of the Other (the other party or parties). Be alert to new data while you negotiate.
- Seek to move the reservation point of the Other to widen the bargaining range especially if there is a negative range. (This process is often begun by "sowing doubt.") However, if necessary for a settlement that you must achieve, move you own reservation point.
- Seek a settlement as close as possible to the reservation point of the Other so that you win the maximum profit.
- Do what you can to see that both you and the Other come to see this settlement as the best possible one under the circumstances.

PREPARING FOR INTEGRATIVE NEGOTIATION

- Figure out your own interests and reservation point as well as you can. Keep reviewing the points while you negotiate.
- Figure out the interests and reservation point of the Other. Be alert to new data while you negotiate.
- Through judiciously shared information and brainstorming, seek to expand the pie so that each side may get as much as possible of what it would like. Explore moving the reservation points of each side.
- Decide on fair principles to determine how to divide the pie.
- Do what you can to see that both you and the Other come to see this settlement as the best possible one under the circumstances.

PREPARING FOR MEDIATION

- Figure out the real interests - not the "positions" - and reservation point for each side as well as you can. Privately review these points with each side. If appropriate, keep reviewing these points during the mediation. Stay alert for new data.

- Through acquiring information and brainstorming, seek to expand the pie so that each side might get as much as possible of what it would like. Explore moving the reservation points of each.
- Help the parties decide on fair principles to determine how to decide the issues at hand.
- Do what you can to see that all parties come to see the settlement - any - as the best possible under the circumstances.

SOURCES OF POWER IN NEGOTIATION

- Positional power or the power of legitimate authority
- Rewards
- Sanctions
- Force
- Expertise
- Information
- An elegant solution
- Commitment
- Charisma - referent authority - moral authority
- BATNA - the best alternative
- Relationship - power gained or power lost

GROUND RULES - AVOIDING PITFALLS

Walking the tightrope:

- Becoming the "police" ———- Losing trust and credibility

Avoiding a fall:

- Get parties to "own" the ground rules
- Share responsibility with the parties
- Avoid "heavy-handed" responses

No applicable ground rule

- Use observation of effects
- Acknowledge emotion behind "violation", express concern

Existing ground rule

- Check violations with the parties

- Revisit buy-in to ground rule

Types of Agreement Agreeing to participate in the discussion

- Agreeing on agenda & ground rules
- Agreeing on a process for continuing
- Agreeing on how to collect more data
- Agreeing on shared values or principles
- Agreeing on shared goals or interests
- Agreeing on criteria or constraints
- Agreeing to disagree on specific issues
- Agreeing on a process for handling future disputes
- Agreeing on specific behavior or actions

THE MEDIATOR'S ROLE

What it is NOT:

- to be a detective - get information and stop
- to be an arbitrator - decide the best outcome

The Mediator structures the process to

- separate out emotions
- move from positions to interests,
- channel communication between the parties,
- provide a reality check,
- initiate brainstorming & generation of options,
- create opportunities to see the other side, and
- identify the signposts of agreement.

Channeling Communication

- In joint session, reflecting back one party's issues / concerns when the other party can hear it
- Choosing neutral language, especially phrasing unwelcome information in terms the party can hear
- Asking "What if...?" questions
- Asking one party what the other party's view is

Reality Check

- Pay attention to the little voice inside your head saying there's something not right here.
- Then ask a question to elucidate.
- Reflect back extreme statements.
- Challenge gently, "My experience has been different ..."
- Allow time for party to consider and re-visit it.
- Use with moving from positions to interests & discussion of the other person's views.

Brainstorming & Generating Options

- In joint session, if possible, initiate a process:
- List all conceivable options, even if they seem impossible;
- Review the list & eliminate real impossibilities;
- Rank the remaining options in order of preference;
- Add new options and rank again;
- Discuss strategies for achieving #1 option and ability to live with #2.

Creating Opportunities for Understanding

- Ask:
- What do you think he wants?
- How do you think she feels?
- What do you think is causing him to feel that way?
- How do you feel about [the way he feels]?
- Timing is critical. Do not try this too early. Be aware of where you are in the process.

Noticing the Signposts

- Ask, "What can I work with here?" and look for Misunderstanding due to indifferent meanings for the same word or to just not talking at all
- Positives in the relationship in the past, to build on
- Shared or parallel interests
- Desire / need to maintain the relationship
- Multiple issues and potential trade-offs
- Readiness to consider alternatives
- Contrition

- Acknowledging the other's view

Turning a Conflict Style into a Strategy

In Your Dispute	Then
Neither the outcome nor the relationship is important to you	Avoid
The relationship is much more important than the outcome	Accommodate
Both the relationship and the outcome are important to you	Collaborate
The outcome outweighs the relationship	Compete
The outcome and the relationship are both somewhat important (or external forces impinge)	Compromise

Transformative Mediation	Problem-Solving Mediation
Primary Goal: Empowerment and recognition Values: Individual growth, self determination Mediator Role: • Facilitator; helps parties make the most of opportunities for empowerment and recognition • Mediator attends to conflict dynamics • Less directive and structured • "Parties own both process and content" • Discuss past as a way to encourage recognition of others • "There are facts in the feelings" that lead to opportunities for empowerment and recognition	Primary Goal: Settlement Values: Satisfaction of parties' interests Mediator Role: • Conflict resolution "process expert"; helps parties analyze interests and maximize joint gains • Mediator attends to parties' interests • More directive and structured • "Parties own the content; mediator owns the process" • Focus on future, as talking about the past focuses the blame • Strong emotions are to be expected, but need to be managed in order to get to problem solving

MOVING BEYOND ARGUMENT TO DIALOGUE: "CREATING THE AMBIENCE FOR CONFLICT RESOLUTION"

Presented by: Tara Fass, Therapist-Mediator and Diana Mercer, Attorney-Mediator

Peace Talks® Mediation Servies

8055 W. Manchester Ave., Suite 201

Playa del Rey, CA 90293

Telephone (310) 301-2100

Website: www.peace-talks.com/ or www.yourdivorceadvisor.com/

e-mail: tarafass@aol.com and diana1159@aol.com

1. Start with the Listening Game with the help of Diana Mercer and two volunteers from the audience. (about 5-10 minutes)

2. Next do the Tuning into the Right Brain Exercise with the help of Tara Fass. (about 5 minutes)

3. What are you listening for? What are you hearing? How to tune into both parties evenhandedly. Communication is handled differently in mediation or collaborative law versus litigation. How?

   a. The Role of Questions

      i. Collaborative processes including mediation encourage open ended communication, exploration and sharing of ideas.

      ii. Lawyers are trained to ask closed end questions which they generally know the answers to.

      iii. Therapists are trained to ask open ended question which they shouldn't know the answers to.

4. Listening for Shame and Trauma:

   a. Complaints v. Crying Out In Pain

      i. complaints are unmet or unaddressed needs

      ii. crying out comes from the overwhelming and disregulating pain of having complaints

      iii. turning complaints into pleas for assistance that the other can hear and respond to reflectively (more about this later)

iv. how one manages this harkens back to attachments styles in adulthood formed in childhood and what is going on in the brain

b. Shame and Trauma is like a Boomeranging Echo.

i. Whatever the content you are likely hearing is a re-traumatization of an earlier unresolved, partly digested family of origin issue that is played out in the history of the relationship.

c. Exercise: Everyone has a Wound That Needs Healing, Everyone Has a Secret (5-10 minutes bring out the hankies)

5. Feeling Your Pain and Moving Beyond It: Re-directing the Vector of the Energy of the Dispute

Part 1: Raising the Sparks: Constriction, Release, Expansion, Embrace

Part 2: Moving from Reflex to Reflect: Reset, Pause, Return

Remembering what was forgotten in the agreement:

6. Moving Beyond Conflict as Contact.

a. Tools for Feeling and Releasing Pain without Remaining in Pain

i. Saying Out Loud and Naming of One's Pain

1. Taking turns for oneself and the other.

a. Example: One party calls the other a liar. Ask the accused to think back at what this could mean?

2. Using neutral two-way statements and proposals that address both parties though only one may have the 'problem' or 'complaint' at the moment.

a. Example: adding reciprocal (phrased neutrally, without finger-pointing) New Partner Protocols to parenting plans or protocols for lateness or drug/alcohol use as well as issues like watching R-rated movies with the children.

b. Tools for Promoting Reflection

i. Reframing and Rephrasing

1. Neutrally re-framing and re-phrasing concerns, especially when written on flip chart or white board (where others can see)

2. Turning Back the Hands of Time: Giving each other 'the benefit of doubt' with the goal to develop greater trust of one another.

While the lawyers and coaches may find this kind 'the depths are the heights' and 'the obstacle is the path' of communication generally helpful, for the parties it may still include the inclination to blame and shame (or the temptation to communicate through blame and shame).

Talking point: How can professionals encourage open communication without getting stuck and shutting down the dialogue.

7. Forgetting in Conflict/ Remembering in Agreement

Tools are: Repeating, Summarizing, Mirroring

To make sure each party is heard and felt to be taken seriously whether agreed with or not.

Makes people feel like you've really understood them.

Listening for new information: actually ask, "Is there any new information that has been shared that is different from what was shared in the past?" and spend a moment talking about what it's like to communicate.

Examples: Using "I" statements such as, "Am I correct in hearing you say..." or "I understand that you feel ____ when she/he ____" or "I understand how it may seem or feel that way to you..." or "I can see that you are angry right now..."

8. Detoxifying Information to Digest New or Discomforting Information Examples:

Aggression or violence expressed in a relationship causes 'confusion' or 'fear' and that becomes the problem as opposed to identifying the perpetrator of such behavior because one party generally instigates and the other acts out which means that both parties are 'guilty.'

Making overt the covert: Underscoring each party's contribution or negligence in any relationship versus Angel/Devil Characterizations

Affairs - Symptom of growing apart

Finances - Two households cost more to run than one.

Focusing on Parenting Plans that work for children and are developmentally sound, rather than parenting plans that work for parents.

When someone is expecting to be attacked: "We're in this together....This may be tough for you. What can we do about this?...

9. Normalizing Affect

Even positive change can be stressful

Reminding parties that statistically the first 18 months after physical separation is the 'crazy making time' in any divorce

It is statistically normal to experience the roller coaster of emotions up to 3 years post-separation

Using empathy "I know it's hard" to normalize situation

Examples: "I can appreciate why you feel that way, but..." or "You are not alone in feeling that way..." or "I appreciate your willingness to have these awkward discussions..." or "This is difficult but necessary territory to cover..."or "Your face changes when you talk about your kids..."

10. Introduce the idea of taking action consistent with one's Enlightened Self-Interest

Referring to a term coined by political economist Adam Smith in discussing the 'invisible hand' of efficiency

With divorcing couples how developing the benefit of doubt benefits oneself.

Helping the other party to help him/herself, i.e., if one party in a divorce is more content with an outcome that this benefit will flow back in a positive way to the first party, underscoring the two-way nature of conflict.

Examples: "What would help the other party to put this issue to rest, even if you don't think he/she deserves it?"...or..."What can you do to put the other party's mind at ease? How can I get on the other party's side to get him or her on my side?

11. In terms of the financial issues, how the discovery process is pre-emptive

The more forthcoming and co-operative the parties are, the more trustworthy one becomes and besides discovery is required anyway.

Discovery as an educational tool leading to increased trust and furthering agreements.

Using voluntary Discovery as another "enlightened self-interest" technique.

Example: "Is there an area of the family's finances that you took care of and did not explain fully to the other party?"...or..."Were there 'white lies' that worked in the marriage that need to be discussed now, like hidden expenses that enhance the quality of life but were never discussed?"...or..."What more can you tell me about your finances that is not on the disclosures?"...or...."How do you think the other party will view your disclosures?"

12. How to handle 'bad news' or sensitive topics

Reproach that is honest (not brutal) and delivered in a way that maintains the relationship, particularly if the parties value personal dignity and/or a coparenting relationship.

How to handle the facts that some parties will call 'none of your business'

Examples: Preparatory statements delivered with some humor- "We're going to be going into some very sensitive material now. Are you ready? If it gets to be too much, give the time-out sign and we'll take a break, knowing that we will come back to the discussion. Hold on to your hats. This is an E-ticket ride, for those of us who haven't been to Disneyland in awhile"...or..."This is the irony of divorce, it's these difficult discussions/boundaries that were and are still necessary to have/hold while you were married that were ignored/violated and that contributed to the demise of your relationship that brought you to the divorce today."

13. How to work with empathy and compassion to get co-operation.

Understanding another's perspective without the appearance of alignment-of particular concern to the individual lawyers who may be expected by the client to align with and empathize with their client only.

Differentiating between listening versus obeying.

Examples: "That's interesting. Can you tell me more?" or You may expect to be judged...I want to understand what it's like to be in your shoes."

"When did this happen and what else of significance was going on at the time?" though the conventional wisdom among therapists is that often taking history is a way of backing off the emotions present in the room.

14. Conclusion

There is the conventional wisdom that it is easier to part on bad rather than good terms, though this may run counter-intuitive to a smart settlement and emotional closure.

The desire to collaborate may not easily translate into settlement opportunities.

Deep communication on important issues does not come naturally particularly to people who are no longer invested in pleasing each other on a spousal or intimate basis.

Ambivalence about the divorce is to be expected even by the party who seems to be driving the case.

PERCEPTION OF TIME & PRIORITIES: POLYCHRONIC VS. MONOCHRONIC

Monochromatic Individuals	Polychromatic Individuals
Do one thing at a time and typically in a very linear thought process	Do many things at once without having to be in a defined sequence
Concentrate and focus on the job they have been assigned	Are highly distractible and subject to interruptions
Take time commitments (deadlines, schedules) very seriously	Consider time commitments as an objective to be achieved, if possible
Are low-context and need information	Are high-context and already have information
Are committed to the job and tend to avoid interaction with their fellow workers	Are committed to people and human relationships sometimes more than the task they have been assigned
Adhere religiously to plans	Change plans often and easily
Are concerned about not disturbing other; follow rules of privacy and consideration	Are more concerned with those who are closely related (family, friends, close business associates) than with privacy
Show great respect for private property; seldom borrow or lend	Community oriented; borrow and lend things more often and easily
Emphasize promptness	Base promptness on the relationship
Are accustomed to short-term relationships	Have strong tendency to build lifetime relationships

PRACTICE HINTS: PARENTING RESPONSIBILITIES ISSUES

OVERVIEW

For many parties, parenting responsibility issues will be relatively easy and the mediator's role will be to merely organize the specific issues that need to be decided. A checklist of those issues are set out in the Parenting Plan section of the Agreement format. However, some parties may need to be encouraged to consider the value of a "fall back", "worst case scenario" specific plan to be put into effect should serious conflict arise in the future so that the children are not inadvertently caught in the middle of parents' difficulties.

For many parties, and especially those for whom parenting issues are an identified source of stress, it will be important to lay-in groundwork before the actual negotiation occurs to minimize unnecessary conflicts that arise out of misinformation or lack of information. Those include:

- An overview of the issues that need to be decided and organization of issues- distinguish time arrangements from decision-making issues (pre-emptive education).
- Check understandings of terms, especially legal concepts such as "custody" and "joint" or "sole" custody. Most parties (lawyers and judges included) either don't understand or have different interpretations of the terms (pre-emptive education).
- Identify what both parties agree the children require from both parties and encourage parties to visualize theirs and the other parent's future relationship with the children (ground softening exercises).
- Lay negotiation format into place-what do each of you want/offer to accept and agree with the other.

Remember, the more difficult the issue, the greater the importance of breaking it up into manageable parts and perhaps shortening the sessions. As well, try to structure the process so that there is sufficient time between sessions for the parties to think about and assimilate the information.

Remember, words create realities-avoid using terms such as "custody", "visitation", "primary parent" and talk instead of parenting responsibilities, time arrangements, and both parents. Explain why you prefer the use of that language to clients when either of them use those words. (This should be begun at the first contact with the parties in mediation and continued throughout the process, not just at the time the parenting plan is being discussed.)

SYSTEMS PERSPECTIVE

The graphic of the family (genogram), done in the consultation session, is often helpful here for the parties to visually see their family as a system.

In difficult cases, the family hierarchy breaks down and the parents will often triangulate or form alliances with the children. Parents often abdicate responsibility and give too much power to children-"They can decide who they want to live with." The legal system (judges and lawyers) often contributes to the breakdown of the family hierarchy by concentrating on the "right" of a child to decide instead of the needs of a child.

- Certain operating assumptions need to be examined and, if appropriate, raised with the parties:
- Children are almost always "caught in the middle"-unwittingly or intentionally.
- Children will often say what they sense a parent wants to hear.
- Divorce may be more difficult for older children (adolescents) than younger children; that is when children are trying to figure out their own sexual identity and relationships. Adult children are also strongly affected by parental divorce.
- Parents tend to functionally neglect children in divorce.
- CHILDREN SHOULD NOT BE REFERRED TO AS "VICTIMS"-THAT SETS UP A "BLAME" SITUATION. IF THE CHILDREN ARE VICTIMS OF DIVORCE, THEN THE PERSON WHO WANTS THE DIVORCE IS TO BLAME.
- CHILDREN ARE FUNCTIONAL CONTRIBUTORS (OR MANIPULATORS?) OF THE CONFLICT-THEY ARE NOT INNOCENT OR GUILTY. (See Saposnek, D., Mediating Child Custody Disputes).
- How parents parent is often more a reflection of spousal relationship than a response to childrens' needs, e.g., if one parent is strict, other is likely to overcompensate by being permissive.
- Overgeneralization-men will control with money; women with children.

Co-parenting Food for Thought [14]

- What is your co-parenting style now?
- Where would you like to be six months from now?

Perfect Pals

- Co-parents who are friendly, cordial and civil.
- Co-parents who respect each other as people and parents.

[14] Adapted from Constance Ahrons, Ph.D., The Good Divorce, 1994

- Co-parents who are full partners in parenting and rely on each other for support and back-up for problem solving.
- Co-parents who collaborate on planning events and celebrations.

Co-operative Colleagues

- Co-parents who do not feel they have to like or accept each other.
- Co-parents who put their differences aside to compromise and work together for the sake of the children.
- Co-parents whose commitment to the children outweighs their negative feelings toward each other.
- Co-parents for whom the desire to minimize trauma to their children is foremost.
- Co-parents who respect each other's rights as parents.
- Co-parents who divide the time spent parenting.
- Co-parents who share in their children's activities and life events.
- Co-parents who reasonably negotiate disputes, but it always takes an effort.

Angry Associates

- Co-parents who allow bitter, resentful and/or antagonistic feelings to enter into all of their interactions.
- Co-parents who barely accept each other's rights to parent.
- Co-parents whose children are often caught in the middle as the parents compete for their loyalty.
- Co-parents whose life after separation is filled with predictably unpredictable blowups with the other parent.
- Co-parents who have not forgiven each other or healed emotionally.
- Co-parents whose children suffer from stress-related disorders.

Fiery Foes

- Co-parents who live in a war zone.
- Co-parents who focus on the wrongs and are hard-pressed to find good in the other parent or to recall good times as a family.
- Co-parents who view their former parent as the enemy and/or insane.
- Co-parents whose fights and legal battles become a chronic condition.
- Co-parents who show little or no respect for the other's right to parent.
- Co-parents whose battles are taken up by family members and friends.

- Co-parents for whom this battle is central in their lives even after the divorce.
- Co-parents whose children are caught in this struggle are often forced to choose sides and may end up losing a parent.

PRIMARY PHYSICAL CUSTODY

"Standard" Visitation - Examples

Week #	Monday	Tuesday	Wednesday	Thursday	Friday	Saturday	Sunday
1	Mom	Mom	Dad	Mom	Dad	Dad	Dad
2	Mom	Mom	Dad	Mom	Mom	Mom	Mom
3	Mom	Mom	Dad	Mom	Dad	Dad	Dad
4	Mom	Mom	Dad	Mom	Mom	Mom	Mom

Pros

- For children over age 7, who understand the concept of a week, this is a predictable schedule.
- Allows for flexibility with either Sunday evening or Monday morning return to school and
- mid-week time to the other parent for either overnights or evenings only.

Cons

- The non-custodial parent goes 6 days every other week w/out seeing the children.
- For children under 7, who don't yet understand the concept of a week, this may be too much time away from the non-custodial parent unless other means are used to stay in contact or times are made available either during the school day, during daycare hours or by way of involvement extra-curricular activities.

Standard Visitation with additional weekday time to the other parent after the custodial parent's weekend.

Week #	Monday	Tuesday	Wednesday	Thursday	Friday	Saturday	Sunday
1	Dad	Dad	Mom	Mom	Dad	Dad	Dad
2	Mom	Dad	Mom	Mom	Mom	Mom	Mom
3	Dad	Dad	Mom	Mom	Dad	Dad	Dad
4	Mom	Dad	Mom	Mom	Mom	Mom	Mom

Pros

- The non-custodial parent has continuous weekday time to be involved in the children's homework routines without substantially increasing the number of transitions between the parents' households.
- For children between ages 5 and 7, who understand the concept of 'the day after tomorrow,' they are not separated from the custodial parent for more time than they can conceptualize.

Cons

- Twice a month a child aged 5-7 is separated from the non-custodial parent one or two days more than they can conceptualize. In such cases, you may want to consider adding dinner on Thursday prior to mother's weekend as well as other times suggested above.

JOINT PHYSICAL CUSTODY

Split Week Plan for parents sharing children on weekdays and weekends

Week #	Monday	Tuesday	Wednesday	Thursday	Friday	Saturday	Sunday
1	Dad	Dad	Mom	Mom	Dad	Dad	Dad
2	Dad	Dad	Mom	Mom	Mom	Mom	Mom
3	Dad	Dad	Mom	Mom	Dad	Dad	Dad
4	Dad	Dad	Mom	Mom	Mom	Mom	Mom

Pros

- Works for children under age 5 who have equally good attachment to both parents.
- Works for temperamentally even-keeled children between ages of 5 to 12.
- This is a regularly recurring and consistent plan.

Cons

- Particularly for children under age 5, this plan may require the child to be away from the more involved parent for excessive periods of time.
- Conflict saturated transitions between parents' households are stressful particularly for immature and learning and/or emotional disabled children.

Alternating Week Plan for parents who want uninterrupted time with their children.

Week #	Monday	Tuesday	Wednesday	Thursday	Friday	Saturday	Sunday
1	Mom	Mom	Mom	Mom	Mom	Mom	Mom
2	Dad	Dad	Dad	Dad	Dad	Dad	Dad
3	Mom	Mom	Mom	Mom	Mom	Mom	Mom
4	Dad	Dad	Dad	Dad	Dad	Dad	Dad

Pros

- Works for children over age 7, who understand the concept of a "week" and "month."
- This plan may be preferred by teens and pre-teens who require fewer transitions.

Cons

- The child may express or experience the need to have mid-week contact with the other parent.
- Though this may be viewed as an interruption, it is highly recommended particularly for children under age 7, to have at least one face-to-face contact with the non-custodial parent, preferably at school if possible.

TOOLS FOR CREATING PARENTING SCHEDULE

HOLIDAY	TIME	DAD	MOM
Passover			
Easter			
Mother's Day			
Memorial Day			
Father's Day			
July 4th			
Labor Day			
Rosh Hashanah			
Yom Kippur			
Halloween			
Thanksgiving			
Hanukkah			
Christmas Eve/Day			
New Years Eve/Day			
Child's Birthday			
Child's Birthday			
Child's Birthday Party			
Parent Birthday			
Parent Birthday			
Grandparent Birthday			
Special Family Events			

Some Suggestions for Developing Your Holiday Parenting Schedule:

Holidays with Multiple Celebration Days: some holidays, like Christmas, Easter and Passover have 2 celebration days. For example, "Christmas" can be divided up with Christmas Eve and Christmas Day, "Easter" may be divided with Good Friday and Easter Sunday, and Passover may be divided with first night Seder and second night Seder. Other holidays, like Halloween, are also celebrated during the season with parties and events in addition to the actual date. While one day might be more widely celebrated, the second day also gives the other parent an opportunity to be involved in the holiday each year, even if he or she doesn't have the "primary" day in that particular year.

Federal Holidays: In the case of Federal holidays, which are generally celebrated on a Monday, many parents elect to extend the previous weekend by 24 hours. Also, if only one parent has off from work on the Federal holiday(s), it may also make for a natural extension of time.

Children's Birthdays: Children's birthdays may or may not supercede the regular parenting plan. Some parents prefer to give each parent the opportunity to see the child on his or her birthday, even if it's just for a short period of time. Other parents split the birthday with the actual day to one parent, and the following Saturday or Sunday to the other parent for the birthday party, alternating each year. Talking in advance about whether you'll invite each other, both extended families, and/or new partners to the child's party, and how you'll handle the stress surrounding this mix of relatives and friends, can make the event go more smoothly.

Alternating Holidays Each Year: Many parents alternate holidays, with one parent having a holiday in even-numbered years, and the other having the children in odd-numbered years. Or, if one family has a special event held each year (e.g., Uncle Fred's 4th of July Picnic), one parent may have the children on that holiday each year and the other parent has the children on another holiday each year. This allows you to create family traditions that are repeated each year.

Parent Birthdays: May parents elect to use the following language: At the birthday parent's option: children are with the birthday parent or with the other parent with 48 hours' notice to the other parent.

ONLINE PARENTING CALENDARS

By Keisha Chandler Director of Operations Peace Talks® Mediation Services, Inc. Copyright 2007

Juggling soccer practice, violin lessons, tutors, and everything else in between can be extremely difficult to manage for any family, but for divorcing parents it's all the more challenging.

Using programs like these will help give your children a sense of predictability. You can even enlist the help of your children to set up the initial information on the website. It is an opportunity for them to see how you manage time and schedules which is an excellent skill for a child of any age to participate in and observe. Take a look at all of the options and decide which features you will use given your family's needs.

Several websites offer online parenting calendars with various features and functions to make life easier. Each paid site offers a schedule, database for doctor and medical contact information, keeping track of expenses, school and homework info, and uploading photos to share. Subscription sites tend to be more complete, but the free calendars have benefits as well:

Sharekids.com

This program costs $200 per year for a joint account and $100 per year for an individual account. They also offer a lifetime fee structure which is $1000 for a joint account and $500 for an individual account. If you have young children, you may want to consider this option if you find this program works for you and your family. As an added bonus, they offer a 30 day free trial with absolutely no obligation to you.

Sharekids.com provides different options and permissions for every member of your family. For example, if your children have grandparents that play an active role in your children's lives, you can create an additional profile for them and give them access to only the sections you choose, like the children's sports schedules. Since grandparents don't need access to the accounting portion of the website or your own personal day to day schedule, you can limit their access to just the sections in which they're interested. This feature is especially useful for stepparents and blended families, nannies, personal assistants, or any other interested adults.

One of the most helpful sections Sharekids.com offers is a House Rules section. You can post house rules about computer use, TV, video game time, sleepovers, and bedtimes on the website. Just don't expect Grandma and Grandpa to follow them! ?

Best features: multiple users with different access, nice navigational menu

www.sharekids.com Our Family Wizard.com

This program costs $99.00 per year or about $8.65 per month. No free trial period.

This is the most comprehensive and organized program. It is also the most sophisticated of the products I reviewed. It allows you to input the basic schedule for up to three years in advance. The program has a basic calendar for scheduling events, but also has a great feature to facilitate pick up and drop off time for each parent using color coding.

The most helpful and advanced feature of this program is the management of scheduling conflicts and trading days between parents. When either situation presents itself, the program automatically posts this information to the Message Board which can be very helpful in avoiding miscommunications about events and appointments.

Best features: 3 year schedule, manages scheduling conflicts

www.ourfamilywizard.com

Custody Planner.com

This is a nice, clean, simple and easy to use site. Best of all, it's free. I particularly love the rules and exceptions section, and the ability to outline joint household rules. I could also see kids getting involved—they can read for themselves that both parents agree that there are no "R" rated movies in either household.

Lacking: No database section of contact info for children's doctors, dentists, other healthcare providers, teachers, school, even friends and names of friends' parents.

Best features: Free, rules and exceptions section

www.custodyplanner.com

Free Online Calendars (www.yahoo.com, www.aol.com, www.airset.com, www.hotmail.com)

These free calendars are simply calendars that you can share with other users. You can see days of the week, but you cannot input any set schedule for years or months in advance.

Since they're just calendars, these programs also do not allow you to keep track of expenses or keep information in one central place. There are other limitations, too. Neither Yahoo! nor Hotmail have the ability to create calendars in one central location with one user profile.

The best of the free general calendars is probably Airset. The Airset calendar allows you to have multiple calendars under one username. The interface allows you keep up to 1 GB of information. In that case, you can keep Word documents online with all the information pertaining to the kids on the Airset website. The Airset interface also offers a message board, a lists section, and a contacts section with permissions for other users similar to Sharekids.com. www.airset.com

There are a few other websites that I wasn't able to see a demonstration or free trial but are mentioned here for the sake of being complete:

- www.kidmate.com
- www.parentingtimecalendar.com

No matter which program you choose, each will be helpful in organizing your family's life post divorce, from schedule to doctors to uploading photos to share. Check out each to determine which features best suit your situation and price point.

Parenting Plan Model Language

A. _____________ shall share joint legal custody of the minor children _______________, born ____________, who shall have regular and ongoing contact with both parents in accordance with the parenting plan set forth below:

1. Both parents shall share the right and responsibility to make decisions relating to the health, education and welfare of the minor child(ren).

2. In exercising joint legal custody, it is explicitly required that the parents are in agreement in making decisions on the following matters for each minor child:

a. Enrollment or termination of attendance in school or university, marriage before the age of 18 years, and/or joining a branch of the military service;

b. Beginning or ending the regular practice of a religion. Both parents agree that the child(ren) will be raised in the _______ faith.

c. Commencing psychiatric, psychological, or other such mental health counseling or therapy including but not limited to educational testing;

d. Authorizing the issuance of the minor child's driver's license, and providing an automobile for the child to drive;

e. A passport application or issuance of a passport. Original documents for passport, birth certificate, Social Security card and immunization records shall be held by mother/father and copies shall be provided to the other parent;

f. Enrollment and participation in regularly occurring extracurricular activities;

g. Permission for tattoos, piercings, and any and all other permanent alterations of the child's body; and

h. Non-emergency medical, dental, or other elective care treatment, as well as routine checkups. Each party shall notify the other of the name and address of any health practitioner who examines or treats the minor child within one week of the commencement of the first such examination or treatment.

i. Employment prior to the age of 16 years, including but not limited to acting and modeling.

3. In emergency situations, each party is authorized to take any and all actions necessary to protect the health and welfare of the minor child including, but not limited to, consenting to emergency medical, dental and surgical procedures or treatment. Each party shall attempt to notify the other party within one hour of any such emergency situation and of all medical, dental or surgical procedure and treatment administered to the minor child. In the event of an emergency in which one party cannot reasonably be contacted, either party acting alone may continue to give his or her consent to any medically necessary emergency medical or dental care, test, treatment, service or procedure until the other party can be notified. The party consenting to treatment shall forthwith thereinafter have the other party's consent to treatment as stated above and if the other party can not be in contact with medical personnel, the party with the child shall

inform the other party about any care, test, treatment, service or procedure administered to the minor child.

4. Except upon prior agreement, each party shall avoid scheduling activities for the minor child that conflict with the other party's physical custody. Both parents are encouraged to attend their child's activities. Parents are responsible for keeping themselves advised and for advising each other of all school, athletic and social events in which the child participates.

5. Both parents shall have access to the minor child's medical, dental and school records, as more fully set forth in California Family Code Section 3025. The names of both parents shall be listed on class rosters, school records and extracurricular cards to be contacted in case of emergency. Each parent is expected to keep himself or herself informed of the school schedule and class activities via the school's web site and teacher e-mail. If either parent does not have internet access then that parent may request that the child's schools duplicate all materials and send them to both parents. The requesting parent shall provide self-addressed, stamped envelopes to the school in order to assist the school in carrying out this request.

6. The parents are ordered to confer in advance and in good faith on matters having to do with the health, education and welfare of the minor child including, without limitation, all matters listed in Paragraph IV A. above. If they do not agree, they shall consult with a mediator or appropriate professional first in an attempt to resolve the issue(s) prior to seeking the assistance of the Court, as more fully set forth below.

B. Physical Custody - The parents will share parenting time as follows:

1. The day-to-day schedule shall be as follows:

a. Weekends -

b. Weekdays -

c. Both parents agree to make-up or reschedule mother/father's time if the child is ill or otherwise unable to spend time with a parent during his or her regular custodial time, of if one or both parent's travel schedules require that the child misses his or her time with the mother/father.

2. Holidays - The holiday schedule shall supercede the regular schedule and the vacation schedule as follows:

3. Vacations: shall supersede the regular schedule but not the holiday schedule.

a. Each parent shall have the opportunity to exercise up to ____________ weeks of uninterrupted time with the child(ren) to go on vacation per calendar year commencing in _______ and every year thereafter until further agreement between the parents.

b. Winter Vacation shall be shared as follows: First half/second half to include or not include Christmas and/or New Year's holiday.

c. Spring Vacation shall be shared as follows: Share the week or alternate the year.

d. Summer Vacation shall be shared as follows:

e. Vacation times shall not interfere with school unless mutually agreed by both parents. Vacation time not taken by either or both parents in any given calendar year shall not accrue to the next year.

HOLIDAY	TIME	DAD	MOM
Passover			
Good Friday			
Easter Sunday			
Mother's Day		Xxx	With mother each year
Memorial Day/Weekend			
Father's Day		With father each year	X
July 4th			
Labor Day/Weekend			
Rosh Hashanah			
Yom Kippur			
Halloween			
Thanksgiving Day/Weekend			
Chanukah			
Christmas Eve			
Christmas Eve Overnight to Christmas Morning			
Christmas Day			
New Years Eve Overnight			
New Years Dday			
MLK Day/Weekend			
Child Birthday			
Child Birthday Party			
Parent Birthday	With the birthday parent or the other parent, at the birthday parent's option, with 48 hours notice to the other parent		
Special Family Events			
Other Three Day Weekends			

f. Each parent shall give as much notice as possible as to his or her intended vacation dates, and at least 30 days' notice of his or her intention to take vacation time with the child(ren). In the event of a disagreement as to vacation times, the mother will have first choice of dates in even-numbered years and the father shall have first choice of dates in odd numbered years.

g. The parent traveling shall give the other parent the itinerary, contact information, and telephone numbers so that both parents can be in contact with [child's name] and in case of emergency.

h. Both parents agree not to vacation in a location which the United States State Department has issued a travel hazard warning against during the 90 days prior to commencement of travel (http://travel.state.gov/travel/warnings.html). Foreign entry requirements are posted at www.travel.state.gov/visa/americans1html. Both parents are aware that for international travel, written, notarized permission must be given by both parents in order for children to travel with only one parent. Most airlines also recommend taking a copy of your parenting plan with you when you travel with your children.

i. When arriving at the intended vacation destination, the traveling parent shall insure that [child's name] makes telephone contact with the other parent either by direct telephone contact and/or telephone message.

C. Other Issues

1. Travel Schedules and Work Emergencies: Both parents will be flexible about each other's schedules, and will give the other parent as much notice as possible when he or she needs to be out of town or when he or she has an emergency which prevents the custodial parent from being with [child's name] during their time with the child. Both parents will exchange their emergency situation and travel schedules as soon as they are aware of them.

2. Childcare: For the present, will stay in the current placement or school, ____________________, which both parents agree is good and that [child's name] enjoys. Both parents shall have access to the childcare provider's name, address, and telephone number.

3. Right of First Option of Child Care: In the event that either parent will require child care during his or her custodial time for more than ____ hours or ____overnight(s), the other parent must be given the first opportunity, with as much notice as possible, to care for the children before other arrangements are made. The other parent is under no obligation to care for the children under these circumstances, and if the other parent is unwilling or unable to care for the children, then it is the parent seeking childcare during his or her custodial time that is responsible for finding suitable childcare. Unless specifically agreed or ordered by the court, this order does not include regular child care needed while a parent is working.

If the child(ren) is spending the night other than with the parent who has the child during that scheduled time, the custodial parent shall notify the other parent of the child's sleepover and the contact information where the child will be staying.

4. Transportation: The parents shall share transportation of the child approximately equally. Unless otherwise agreed, the parent commencing his or her custodial time shall pick the child up to begin the parenting time. When possible, the parents shall exchange the children at the children's school or activity whenever possible, so as to provide for a "blind transition" and minimize any stress the children might feel at the transfer. When a blind transition is not possible, then the parents will exchange the children at a neutral public place, such as the children's book department at Barnes & Noble or at Starbucks. If the pick up or drop off needs to be at either party's residence, the traveling parent will stop at the curb and the at-home parent will wait for the children at the door. The children will travel between the car and the house without the parents having direct contact.

5. Exposing [child's name] to Adult Disputes: Both parents shall minimize the child's exposure to their disputes with each other as well as new partners or other family members or friends. While it is inevitable that the parents may disagree with one another from time to time, such disagreements are to be expressed in a courteous and dignified fashion, and outside of the children's presence and hearing. Each parent is ordered to use his or her best efforts to keep all communication between them gracious, respectful and productive.

Neither party shall speak in a negative, disrespectful or derogatory manner to or about the other parent, especially in the minor child's presence or within hearing distance of the child. Both parents are ordered to use their best efforts to ensure that other family members and friends also comply with this order.

6. No Use of Children as Messengers: The parents shall develop a method of communicating with each other concerning the children, whether it is by in-person

meeting, telephone, fax, e-mail or other methods, and both parents agree that the children shall not be used as messengers between the parents.

7. Toys, Cell Phones, Lap Tops, IPods (other devices add or subtract) and Clothing: The parents are to cooperate to permit toys and clothing to move freely between households, whenever it is reasonable to do so. Toys and clothing are to be treated as the property of the children, not the parent who purchased them. Each parent is ordered to use his or her best efforts to ensure that items are available for each child's use where they will be needed or wanted. As each child gets older, [child's name] can be reasonably expected to remember to bring particular items that [child's name] may want. If one of the adults has a special request regarding return or use of a particular item, that request shall be made directly to the other parent, outside of the children's presence. The goal is to make sure that these items are fairly distributed and available for the children's use in a relaxed and natural way, so that the children do not become hyper-conscious of this issue and so that it does not become a cause of

tension between households.

8. Teenage Sexuality, Curfews and Substance Use: Unlike other household rules which each parent has greater latitude in setting in their respective households, parents agree to maintain a mutually consistent set of expectations and rules regarding teenage sexuality and substance use that they will both communicate to the child(ren) and apply in both houses. Once this set of expectations and rules has been established, it will be enforced the same way in both households.

With regards to teenage sexuality, such rules may include but not be limited to an 'open door policy' while entertaining child(ren)'s friends and partners in each home, restrictions surrounding sleepovers and protocols involving communication with the parents of child(ren)'s partners and friends, especially when the situation includes another minor child.

With regards to teenage substance use, such rules may include agreements with pre-planned consequences over curfews, agreements about using a parental residence for a party and parental party supervision, and what degree of tolerance over tobacco and substance use, if any, that each parent is comfortable with full knowledge and discussion with the teenager of what the law provides.

9. Telephone Contact : Each of the parents shall be entitled to reasonable, unlimited, unmonitored telephone access with the minor child during all periods when the child is with the other parent. Telephone contact is intended for parents to stay in touch with the child(ren) and not necessarily with each other.

10. New Partner Etiquette and other Protocols: Neither parent shall introduce [child's name] to new partners and/or their respective children without prior notice to the other parent. Both parents agree that they shall have a multi-step plan in place that may include, but not be limited to, the adults involved meeting prior to introducing [child's name] to the new partners and/or their respective children, having [child's name] meet the new partner and/or their respective children at neutral locations outside the children's home and school, and overnights occurring with the new partner and/or their respective children and [child's name] only after an initial time period has passed.

Discipline, both verbal and physical, shall only be administered by the parents, not by stepparents or new partners.

11. Parenting Log Book: The parents will maintain a "log book" and make sure that the book is sent with the child(ren) between their two homes to create a record of medication schedules, reactions to medications or missed doses, as well as any agreed upon behavioral consequences to be followed through with in both parent's homes. Using businesslike notes (no personal comments), parents will record information related to the health, education, and welfare issues for the children that arise during the time that the children have been with that parent. Once child(ren) are old enough they may be encouraged to participate in the note writing. The log book will also include the names,

addresses and telephone numbers of all of the children's doctors, dentists, healthcare providers, school, emergency contacts, and all of the parents' contact information. The log book will not be sued for requested changes to the parenting schedule.

12. House Rules: Both parents will/will not necessarily have the same house rules in each home concerning: computer access and internet supervision, supervision Re: television and video game time, content of movies and TV shows, chores, and how and when to leave children home alone, use of childcare providers, and time with grandparents.

13. Revisiting the Parenting Plan: Both parents agree to revisit the parenting plan contained herein on an as-needed basis/ at least every 12 months / not later than _____________________. In the event that controversy arises prior to a scheduled parenting plan review regarding major decisions, both parents shall first consult together in an attempt to resolve the dispute and if they are unable to reach a resolution on their own, they will meet and confer with an expert in the field related to the dispute, e.g., the child's doctor, teacher, counselor, etc. If the consultation does not resolve the dispute, the parents shall return together to mediation in an attempt to reach an agreement. Finally, if the dispute continues, it shall be submitted to the court for a decision. Until such time as this agreement is changed in writing by the parents, or these orders are modified by the Court, the existing order shall remain in effect.

14. Relocation:

a. Local Relocation: If either parent intends to move less than ____ miles from his or her current residence/ move far enough away that the parenting plan would need to be adjusted (how to quantify?) / move such that the children's school would be changed, he or she shall give the other parent at least ____ days advance written notice. Both parents shall work together in good faith to adjust the parenting plan to accommodate the move, and if they are unable to modify the parenting plan on their own, they agree to return to Peace Talks® Mediation Services or another mutually agreed-upon mediator to seek assistance in establishing a new parenting plan, and both parents agree to use Court action as a last resort, as more fully set forth in Paragraph XXIII below. Each parent is to provide the other with the address and telephone number where the minor child resides and is to notify the other in writing within 2 days prior to any change of address and/or telephone number.

b. Non-Local Relocation: If either parent intends to move more than ____ miles from his or her current residence / change the country, state or county of residence of the minor child(ren) he or she shall first obtain the written consent of the other parent or an order of the court permitting the move prior to moving. No move of this type shall be undertaken without written consent of the other parent, or further order of the court. Should either parent intend to move from his or her current residence, the other parent shall be given not less than 90 days written advance notice. The notification must state, to the extent known, the planned address of the child(ren) at the new residence. In the event that the parents are unable to work out a new parenting arrangement, they agree to contact Peace Talks® Mediation Services or another mutually agreed-upon mediator to seek assistance in establishing a new parenting plan, and both parents agree to use Court action as a last resort, as more fully set forth in Paragraph XXIII below. Each parent is to provide the other with the address and telephone number where the minor child resides and is to notify the other in writing within 2 days prior to any change of address and/or telephone number.

For purposes of a non-local "move away", both parents agree that they shall ask the court to use a "best interests" standard to evaluate the move, and not a "substantial change in circumstances" standard or decision based solely on time sharing in the parenting plan, irrespective of the current status of move-away law in California.

15. Final Custody Determination: The Court finds that this agreement concerning legal and physical custody is in the best interests of the child(ren) involved and is a final custody determination per Montenegro vs. Diaz and Marriage of Rose and Richardson (2002) 102 Cal. App. 4th 941. For purposes of any modification to this custody stipulation, both parents agree that they shall ask the court to use a "best interests" standard to evaluate the requested change(es), and not a "substantial change in circumstances" standard or decision based solely on time sharing in the parenting plan, irrespective of the current status modification law in California and despite the holdings in Montenegro and Rose and Richardson.

16. Jurisdiction and Findings:

a. Pursuant to California Family Code Section 3048, the court finds that the Superior Court of the State of California, County of Los Angeles, has jurisdiction over the parties and minor child(ren) under the Uniform Child Custody Jurisdiction and Enforcement Act, California Family Code Section 3400, et seq., as both parties and the minor child(ren) reside on the County of Los Angeles and within the State of California. Both parties and the minor child(ren) have lived in

the County of Los Angeles and within the State of California for at least the past 6 months. If parties have lived elsewhere during the last 6 months, state where they have lived. Venue shall stay with the Superior Court of the State of California, County of Los Angeles, Central Civil Courthouse, unless both parents no longer reside in said district or the Court declines jurisdiction under the UCCJEA.

b. The court finds that the manner in which notice and opportunity to be heard was according to the laws of the State of California. Service of the Summons (Family Law) and Petition was by Notice and Acknowledgement of Receipt, and both parties had the opportunity to secure counsel and to be heard on this matter prior to reaching this agreement.

c. A clear description of the custody and parenting rights of each party is set forth above in this Stipulated Judgment.

d. Each party is hereby advised and notified: VIOLATION OF THIS JUDGMENT MAY SUBJECT THE PARTY IN VIOLATION TO CIVIL AND/OR CRIMINAL PENALTIES.

The court finds that the "home state" of the minor child(ren) under the California Family Code Section 3402(g) is the State of California and that the country of "habitual residence" for the purposes of the Hague Convention for international law is the United States of America.

The approximate time share for parenting time with the child(ren) is ________ % with the father and ___________ % with the mother.

CHILD SUPPORT CHECKLIST*

1. Monetary payments for child support
   a. From whom to whom
   b. Amounts and how often
   c. Direct or through the court, court fees
   d. If direct, any coverage of legal costs for enforcement
   e. Any reduction of child support when children with other parent
   f. Child care expenses
   g. Other child-related expenses (clothing, activities, camp, etc.)
2. Medical insurance coverage for children
   a. Carried by whom
   b. Payments made by whom
   c. Change if parent carrying insurance not covered through employment
3. Medical costs not covered by insurance
   a. Paid for by whom
   b. What will be paid for - hospital, medical, optical, dental, orthodontic, counseling, psychological, psychiatric
4. Life insurance to cover obligations to children in case of death of parent
   a. How much to go for this obligation
   b. For how long
   c. Who will be the beneficiary
   d. Should there be a life insurance trust
5. Income tax exemptions for children and signing of waiver
6. Post-high school education of children
   a. Any minimum guarantees to children
   b. Any agreement on contributions by parents

CALIFORNIA CHILD SUPPORT GUIDELINES (ABRIDGED)

Cal Fam Code § 4055 (2004) **At Peace Talks®, we have a computer program that will do these calculations for you**

§ 4055. Formula for statewide uniform guideline for determining child support

The statewide uniform guideline for determining child support orders is as follows: CS = K [HN - (H%) (TN)].

(1) The components of the formula are as follows:

CS = child support amount.

K = amount of both parents' income to be allocated for child support as set forth in paragraph (3).

HN = high earner's net monthly disposable income.

H% = approximate percentage of time that the high earner has or will have primary physical responsibility for the children compared to the other parent. In cases in which parents have different time-sharing arrangements for different children, H% equals the average of the approximate percentages of time the high earner parent spends with each child.

TN = total net monthly disposable income of both parties.

(2) To compute net disposable income, see Section 4059.

(3) K (amount of both parents' income allocated for child support) equals one plus H% (if H% is less than or equal to 50 percent) or two minus H% (if H% is greater than 50 percent) times the following fraction:

Total Net Disposable Income Per Month	K
$ 0-800	0.20 + TN/16,000
$ 801-6,666	0.25
$ 6,667-10,000	0.10 + 1,000/TN
Over $ 10,000	0.12 + 800/TN

For example, if H 7.986117e-222quals 20 percent and the total monthly net disposable income of the parents is $ 1,000, K = (1 + 0.20) x 0.25, or 0.30. If H% equals 80 percent and the total monthly net disposable income of the parents is $ 1,000, K = (2 - 0.80) x 0.25, or 0.30.

(4) For more than one child, multiply CS by:

# of Children	Multiplier	# of Children	Multiplier
2	1.6	**7**	2.75
3	2	**8**	2.813
4	2.3	**9**	2.844
5	2.5	**10**	2.86
6	2.625		

(5) If the amount calculated under the formula results in a positive number, the higher earner shall pay that amount to the lower earner. If the amount calculated under the formula results in a negative number, the lower earner shall pay the absolute value of that amount to the higher earner. ******

(c) If a court uses a computer to calculate the child support order, the computer program shall not automatically default affirmatively or negatively on whether a low-income adjustment is to be applied. If the low-income adjustment is applied, the computer program shall not provide the amount of the low-income adjustment. Instead, the computer program shall ask the user whether or not to apply the low-income adjustment, and if answered affirmatively, the computer program shall provide the range of the adjustment permitted by paragraph (7) of subdivision (b).

SUMMARY LETTERS AS MEDIATION TOOLS

We insist on doing summary letters after all of our mediation sessions. The letter sets forth the agenda, the tentative agreements, and the issues and things to think about before the next mediation session as well as a detailed to-do list. The letters are long and time-consuming to draft, despite some model language we use about often-cited topics, but we think it's a valuable part of the mediation process.

Since the summary letter isn't legally binding, and it's simply a record of the session, we tell clients:

> These tentative agreements and offers are exactly that-tentative. Nothing is final until it's signed by both of you and submitted to the court. Please think of this letter as a starting place, or a set of building blocks, building toward your ultimate agreement. You may change your mind about some of the agreements or discussions-that's okay. Our only request is that if you do change your mind, please have some alternatives in mind that will work for you when you come to the next session. This letter is provided as a basis for further discussions, and we hope that it will help you to measure the considerable progress you made in the first session.

Because mediation is confidential, we also are clear about how we hope clients will use the letters: Although these summary letters are confidential and not admissible in court, we fully expect that you will share them with your lawyer, accountant, therapist or other advisors.

In our practice, it used to be optional, but in the name of saving a few dollars too many clients went without the summary letter and too many mediations fell apart between sessions because neither client had an accurate record of what went on during the session. Our case management compromise (so far) is that we bill for about an hour for the summary letter, even though in reality it takes us 2-3 hours to write. It's worth it to us not to have the mediations fall apart, and the clients see it as a manageable expense. We also don't give them the option of refusing a summary letter-it's just too valuable a tool both for the clients and the mediators.

What the mediation summary letter does: The summary letter accomplishes multiple goals: giving clients an opportunity to think about agreements before they become binding, providing an institutional memory of the session, fleshing out discussions that were not finished, encouraging clients to think of creative solutions between sessions and underscoring progress made during the sessions.

To avoid pressuring people to make a decision about an important issue on the day of the mediation, we often leave the agreement about the issue as simply that they will investigate their options. The summary letter will outline the discussion, delineate questions to ask their advisors, and set forth a to-do list so that the clients don't have to take copious notes during the session. For clients interested in saving money and doing as much as possible outside of the session, the to-do list can give them some guidance.

Another advantage of the summary letter is that it gives both the clients and the mediator an "institutional memory" of what went on at the session. A good, detailed summary letter can eliminate much of the he said/she said. Even if the mediator makes a mistake in the summary, at least everyone is starting from the same place.

The summary letter can also flesh out discussions that didn't quite get finished, or which might be too technical to be of use during the session. A good example of this is the explanation of how Qualified Domestic Relations Orders work. "There's a special court order you can use to divide up a pension, so don't worry about how that will happen," might suffice for the mediation session itself, but ultimately the client will need more detail than that. The summary letter is a good place to make sure the clients get the information they need to make a good decision.

We also use the summary letters to ask the clients to expand their range of options between sessions. We'll ask them to think of different ways to resolve things, or whether they would consider a particular solution, even on a temporary basis. The summary letter is also an opportunity to acknowledge high points in the mediation, point out progress made, and gently encourage clients to keep thinking about certain issues.

Sometimes it's hard to convey the benefits of the summary letters to clients before they've actually seen one, but most are grateful that you've insisted once they see the finished product. It makes case management and mediation session planning easier because you have a great summary of the last meeting, and it helps clients stay organized, too.

EVALUATION OF MEDIATION SESSION

Purpose: The purpose behind doing mediator evaluations of each mediation session is to:

- Encourage self-reflection on the mediation sessions
- Create a learning tool for the mediators involved
- Helping Peace Talks® to plan mediator trainings
- Encourage mindfulness in the mediation room

Evaluations are due within 48 hours of the end of the session.

Mediation Session Evaluation:

- My name:
- Clients' Name(s):
- Session Date:

Please answer with a short sentence or two:

- What I liked best about this session....
- About the session in general
- About what my co-mediator did
- About what I did

What I'd like to see next time.......

- About the session in general
- About what my co-mediator did
- About what I did

Mediation Scorecard: Rate 1-5, with 5 being "strongly agree" and 1 being "strongly disagree"

Example

I evaluate this mediation session as follows:

Clients made an appropriate amount of progress given who they are and where they are in the process Co-mediators worked together effectively I felt supported by my co-mediator Co-mediation team prepared effectively for session Co-mediation team de-briefed effectively after session We used mediation techniques and session structure to clients' benefit We provided clear directions to the parties re: the mediation process and session structure

I think that clients would evaluate this mediation session as follows:

We made an appropriate amount of progress given who we are and where we are in the process

Co-mediators worked together effectively I understood what the session structure would be We stayed on our agenda or made a specific choice to deviate from our agenda

I evaluate my co-mediator:

- Displayed empathy and developed trust
- Demonstrated neutrality and even-handedness
- Elicited important information
- Refined Questioning and Listening Skills-Professional Reframing
- Assisted in identifying issues, interests, and options, and in reaching agreements
- Effective session pacing
- Managed client interactions, including "dirty tricks" and emotional outbursts:
- Communicated & kept confidentiality boundaries
- Encouraged Collaboration

I'd like to see my co-mediator improve skills in ___________.

I evaluate myself:

- I took appropriate notes
- Displayed empathy and developed trust
- Demonstrated neutrality and even-handedness
- Elicited important information
- Refined Questioning and Listening Skills-Professional Reframing
- Assisted in identifying issues, interests, and options, and in reaching agreements
- Effective session pacing
- Managed client interactions, including "dirty tricks" and emotional outbursts:
- Communicated & kept confidentiality boundaries
- Encouraged Collaboration
- My Interaction with Co-Mediator

I'd like to improve my skills in __________ .

Answer if applicable:

- My co-mediator collaborated with and managed the parties' attorneys effectively

- I collaborated with and managed the parties' attorneys effectively
- We used caucuses effectively

Session Information, please respond Yes or No:

- Clients came in for separate sessions
- Clients spent time in caucus
- Single mediator rate applied for some of the mediation time (other than summary letter)
- Is there anything else you'd like to share about this session, yourself or your comediator, this case, Peace Talks® Mediation procedures, or anything else?

PRACTICE HINTS: PREPARING AN EFFECTIVE WRITTEN MEMORANDUM

A written memorandum is the tangible product of the mediation process, and therefore, a critical task for the mediator. How thorough and specific the agreement will often mean the difference between whether or not the mediated agreement holds, especially in the face of attorney review. The agreement format is used throughout the mediation process by the mediator as a detailed checklist of the issues to be addressed. It is designed to minimize the need for mediator note-taking in session and the amount of effort necessary to prepare a memorandum of understanding out of session. NOTE the following suggestions:

1. THE MEMORANDUM IS NEVER SIGNED BY THE PARTIES IN THE COURSE OF MEDIATION. The mediator is not preparing a legal document for signature; this should blunt most criticisms of the unauthorized practice of law.

NOTES FOR MEDIATORS WHO ARE NOT ATTORNEYS:

The point in the mediation process where those who are not attorneys are most vulnerable to the charge of "unauthorized practice of law" is in the preparation of memoranda of understanding. In addition to not allowing clients to sign the memorandum, thereby treating it as a legal agreement per se, the mediator may want to consider doing the following:

a. Leave off the style of the case (p. 1, top) that makes the document look like a formal legal document.
b. Leave out the signature spaces (p. 34) to avoid any confusion in that the draft of the agreement is intended for signature in mediation.
c. Call the document a memorandum of understanding not an agreement; the terms are effectively the same, although agreement has more of a formal tinge of legal meaning. In the final document, after attorney review, the term "agreement" can be subtitled back for "memorandum."

2. The mediator can maintain a draft of the memorandum on his or her office word processor and bring into the mediation process any issues lawyers may raise over wording.

This also offers a "selling point" for mediation in that the lawyers will not need to duplicate any work done in mediation.

3. THE MEMORANDUM FORMAT IS NEVER GIVEN TO THE PARTIES. There is a risk they will turn mediation into a "fill-in the blanks" exercise. However, if particular issues have been difficult, (eg. parenting responsibility) a rough draft of the particular section recording their tentative understandings of that issue may be prepared.

4. AN AGREEMENT IS ONLY AS GOOD OR AS EFFECTIVE AS THE PROCESS USED TO DEVELOP THE AGREEMENT. There is a "Zen" of agreements: The more you need a written agreement to define and insure rights, the less protection there will be. There is an inverse correlation between length and detail of an agreement and its effective enforceability and value as a working document. A written agreement has a "working life" of approximately 35 years. The parties must be disabused of the belief that this agreement is forever (Myth of Finality); that there will never be any need for modification and that every future circumstance can be provided for and that if the agreement is written exactly there will be no further conflict or dispute. The agreement should address major "what ifs..." likely to occur in the future, not every "what if..." Finally, do not try to spell out future details, rather focus on general principles and process. For example, the section or college expenses provides a process for planning for and allocating financial responsibilities, not an exact formula.

THE CASE FOR BRIEF CONFIDENTIAL EVALUATIONS IN CHILD CUSTODY DISPUTES

by Tara Fass, LMFT, Richard Gilbert, Ph.D.,and Diana Mercer, J.D., copyright 2005

Court mandated child custody evaluations (CCEs), Civil Code 730, are well-intended investigative instruments designed to aid bench officers in resolving custody issues. They have numerous shortcomings, however. By way of background, in the past, a CCE would start within a few weeks of the original order and take approximately 6-8 weeks to conduct publicly through Family Court Services or through private practitioners, and settle either in or out of court. In Los Angeles, the current wait time varies, but is never less than two, and can be up to, four or more months to commence. Civil Code 1257.3 was adopted in 1999, ushering in the present era of court ordered partial evaluations, which are known in the field by several different names. The court's version is the Fast-Track Evaluation which routinely includes oral testimony, but not a written report, by the evaluator. This quickly replaced the term Mini-Evaluations because the nomenclature was roundly viewed by everyone as having the connotation of inferiority. Allen Gottfried and Kay Bathurst developed the methodology and coined the term for Focused Issue Evaluations, which generally includes only a written report, while Rapid Response and Limited Scope Evaluations are yet other terms in use.

The idea behinds partial evaluations came into being as a practical and clinical solution to the problem of the overwhelming case load leading to delays in decision making as well as the fact that some CCE's involved non-clinical parents and specific, time-sensitive issues such as whether or not overnights should be granted to the non-custodial parent of an infant, where a child would go to school or would a child be allowed to move-away from the legal jurisdiction. The goal was for these shorter evaluations to be completed and heard within one or two weeks of the initial court order requesting it. Ironically, these instruments are also in such high demand that the waiting time in court to start the fast-track evaluations is as long, or longer, than what used to be the optimal timeframe for conducting the full CCE. Paradoxically, approximately a quarter of all court generated fast-track evaluations recommend full evaluations as part of the evaluator's testimony and recommendation.

Additionally, for some time now it has been recognized that all too often, an unintended consequence of the full and partial CCEs has been that the evaluative process, in itself, not only prolongs the time and money spent in court, but also adds to the despair and dysfunction families experience as they struggle to heal and regain stability post-separation. The conventional wisdom increasingly is that court-ordered processes have become iatragenic to divided families, meaning that the 'cure' worsens the 'condition.' A by-product, or dual purpose, of the partial CCE's was the hope it would address the harsh reality that the family court system needed to find ways to speed up its work because it could not increase its capacity fast enough to keep up with the burgeoning case load and that many cases bound for a CCE were not clinical type cases. The increasing awareness is that while these newer instruments are clinically and legally interesting in terms of approaching divided family issues, the problem remains that it takes place within the system that appears to be not only iatragenic, but collapsing under its own weight, particularly in light of today's looming budget deficits.

This is why the promise and purpose of mediation, which is to resolve disputes by means other than litigation, has been the best idea in family law for the last twenty years. It is true though that at times, couples involved in mediation find themselves deadlocked regarding important issues of custody and/or visitation. In response, one or both parties may wonder what the disposition of these issues might be if they were litigated rather than resolved through mediation. Forrest Mosten in his textbook, The Complete Guide to Mediation (1997), proposes the use of a hybrid mini-evaluation, called the Confidential Mini Evaluation. We propose calling this new and promising tool in the field of mediation a Brief Confidential Evaluation (BCE) because it highlights the brevity and confidentiality of this instrument. From an attorney's and a client's perspective a BCE has a number of significant advantages over court-ordered custody evaluations.

First there is the issue of confidentiality: BCEs are private and discreet, whereas, in contrast, court-ordered custody evaluations are conducted in a public forum. Privacy is particularly important if your client has a high-profile or engages in an eccentric or questionable lifestyle. No portion of the BCE would be admissible as evidence in court and the evaluator could never be called as an expert witness in the case. The BCE could be seen as an excellent discovery technique and could reduce the risk of miscalculating your client's ability to "win."

Second, you and your client define the parameters, the timing, whether or not there is a written report and if collaterals or the children are interviewed. Unless there is a compelling need that is endorsed by both parties, the child or children who are the subject of the dispute are not included in the BCE. While information obtained from the child or children is always included in a court-ordered evaluation, and can be helpful and important, BCEs make every effort to shield the child or children in question from the stress and loyalty issues often generated by a formal custody evaluation.

By having a BCE, conducted by an evaluator with experience in court-ordered evaluations, the parties can learn the process, and likely outcome, of a litigated approach to the contested custody issues without having to go to court or leave the mediation process behind. In many cases, the knowledge derived from the BCE can help break the existing impasse and increase the likelihood of finding a mediated solution to the relevant issues. In this way, the parties can avoid the considerable time commitment, cost, stress and exposure involved in pursuing a court action. If nothing else, perhaps the parties can gain a perspective on their situation that had not previously occurred to them.

Even if the mediator has a sense what the root causes of contested issues might be, in order not to develop and dual relationship and to maintain neutrality, the mediator can not deliver such insights or information. Besides, most mediators in family law are not child development specialists informed of the current research in child development and divorce-related issues. In choosing an evaluator, the parties must be confident that great value is placed on conducting evaluations which are fair and impartial toward each party, respect the value of both parent-child relationships, and maintain a consistent focus on the best interests of the child or children that are the subject of the evaluation.

Added value to the BCE, and congruent with one of the fundamental values of mediation, is that to the extent possible, the parties should be self-determining. For instance, if one of the recommendations is for one or both parents to have therapy or parenting classes, if the parties can grasp the wisdom of those recommendations they can maintain face and pride by voluntarily entering into treatment, without having to be ordered, and not risking tainting the treatment or the mediation. The attorney has strengthened the case by having more manageable as well as more presentable clients. If the case were to litigate, the evaluative process would have to start over, though there could be an opportunity to mediate after the BCE and before court.

Thirdly, BCEs offer rapid results at a lower cost than a full CCE. The entire BCE, from the initial interviews with each party to the communication of findings and recommendations, can be completed in one to two weeks, based upon the availability of the parties. This is in contrast to court-ordered custody evaluations which often take six months or more from the time the evaluation is ordered to the submission of findings and can be extremely expensive, often costing seven or eight thousand dollars or more, without any guarantee of the final expense. Because it is customary to bill full evaluation services on an hourly basis, the parties are unaware at the outset what the eventual cost will be.

In contrast to the BCE, there is a fixed cost for 10 hours of service, generally in the ballpark of $2750. This cost covers all interviews with the parties and collateral contacts, administrative expenses incurred by the evaluator, time spent reviewing the parties' questionnaires and any written materials, as well as a feedback session to go over the findings and recommendations with their mediation team. Thus, BCEs avoid having the parties go through a protracted period of stress and contention while having the child or children remain in a custody and/or visitation arrangement for an extended time that may not be in their best interests.

The steps leading to a BCE are simple and straightforward. After a divorcing couple decides to initiate a BCE, each party is sent a questionnaire to fill out. The questionnaire asks them to provide information regarding their personal, family, and marital history, their perceptions of the child or children's developmental needs, and their views regarding the most desirable custody or visitation arrangements. In addition, parents are asked to provide contact information for important collateral relationships in the child or children's lives (e.g., a nanny or other important, substitute-care provider; a pediatrician; a teacher; a therapist, etc.) and release granting approval for the evaluator to speak with these individuals.

After completing the questionnaire and collateral contact information, the parties forward their written materials to the evaluator along with full payment for the evaluation. The evaluator will then contact each party and arrange initial, individual meetings. The purpose of the initial interviews is to review, clarify, and expand upon the information provided in the written materials. The initial interviews generally take about 1.5 to 2 hours each. After the initial interviews, the evaluator will conduct telephone interviews with relevant collateral contacts and then arrange an hour-long follow-up interview with each party, including the children, if the parents agree that is necessary. Finally, the evaluator will organize the findings and recommendations of the evaluation and arrange a conjoint meeting with the parties and the mediation team to orally communicate the results.

Time Estimates for Steps in a CME

TASK	TIME ESTIMATE
Review Questionnaire/Written Materials	1 hour
Initial Interviews with each party	4 hours
Telephone Interviews with Collateral Contacts	1.5 hours
Telephone Follow-up Interviews with each party	1.5 hours
Organization of Findings/Preparation for Feedback Session	1 hour
Feedback Session with the Mediation Team	1 hour
Total	10 hours

CALIFORNIA FAMILY CODE: SPOUSAL SUPPORT LAW § 4320.

Circumstances to be considered in ordering spousal support

In ordering spousal support under this part, the court shall consider all of the following circumstances:

(a) The extent to which the earning capacity of each party is sufficient to maintain the standard of living established during the marriage, taking into account all of the following:

(1) The marketable skills of the supported party; the job market for those skills; the time and expenses required for the supported party to acquire the appropriate education or training to develop those skills; and the possible need for retraining or education to acquire other, more marketable skills or employment.

(2) The extent to which the supported party's present or future earning capacity is impaired by periods of unemployment that were incurred during the marriage to permit the supported party to devote time to domestic duties.

(b) The extent to which the supported party contributed to the attainment of an education, training, a career position, or a license by the supporting party.

(c) The ability to pay of the supporting party, taking into account the supporting party's earning capacity, earned and unearned income, assets, and standard of living.

(d) The needs of each party based on the standard of living established during the marriage.

(e) The obligations and assets, including the separate property, of each party.

(f) The duration of the marriage.

(g) The ability of the supported party to engage in gainful employment without unduly interfering with the interests of dependent children in the custody of the party.

(h) The age and health of the parties, including, but not limited to, consideration of emotional distress resulting from domestic violence perpetrated against the supported party by the supporting party where the court finds documented evidence of a history of domestic violence, as defined in Section 6211, against the supported party by the supporting party.

(i) The immediate and specific tax consequences to each party.

(j) The balance of the hardships to each party.

(k) The goal that the supported party shall be self-supporting within a reasonable period of time. Except in the case of a marriage of long duration as described in Section 4336, a "reasonable period of time" for purposes of this section generally shall be one-half the length of the marriage. However, nothing in this section is intended to limit the court's discretion to order support for a greater or lesser length of time, based on any of the other factors listed in this section, Section 4336, and the circumstances of the parties.

(l) Any other factors the court determines are just and equitable.

ISSUES IN DETERMINING A LUMP SUM SPOUSAL SUPPORT BUY-OUT

Determining an exact figure for a fair spousal support buy-out number is difficult because there are so many factors. To give you an idea of what needs to be considered, here is a list of some of the variables that go into a buy-out calculation:

- Amount of spousal support which would be paid is not absolutely clear unless there's already a court order;
- Chances that spousal support would be modified in the future:
    - Increase;
    - Decrease;
    - Anticipated retirement.
- Length of time spousal support would be paid;
- Early termination: death of either party, remarriage of recipient;
- Risk that spousal support is not paid:
    - Disability or decrease in income for person paying support;
    - Person paying support fails to pay or disappears.
- Earning capacity;
- Duty to be self-supporting;
- Tax ramifications: ordinarily spousal support is tax deductible by the person paying and included in the income of the recipient, but lump sums are not taxed;
- Time value of money:
    - Advantage to having the money in one lump sum;
    - Anticipated rate of return if lump sum was invested.

Non-Monetary Factors:

- Peace of mind and closure;
- No need to modify spousal support later;
- Privacy with regard to your financial situation in the future;
- Each party has incentive to prosper financially without penalty;
- Easier to co-parent when you're not worried about each other's earning capacity;
- Decreased anxiety associated with ongoing litigation.

Don't forget to add: the cost of litigation in order to find out what the spousal support order will be if you cannot settle on the terms.

CLOSING

As the negotiations progress, the mediator summarizes areas of agreement to motivate the parties toward a final settlement. If the parties move to common positions on all or certain portions of the issues and are ready to execute a written document, the mediator will typically assist in the crafting of the draft/final agreement by monitoring it for common pitfalls of poorly written settlement agreements.

The mediated agreement may be executed on the spot or held pending review by counsel. It may be a private agreement or incorporated into a consent judgment in pending litigation. There may be an enforcement clause that provides for monitoring by the mediator or another party and specifies what the parties will do if they believe the agreement has been violated. Contract disputes are perhaps best concluded with an agreement that is based on money, product, or other tangible asset, not based on further relationships between the parties unless relationship interests were a primary goal of the mediation. Complete releases from one party to the other on any future claim may be more important to the parties than the actual dollar or asset settlement.

If the parties fail to agree on all issues, the mediator may try to salvage the positive result of the mediation. The parties may be able to stipulate certain facts, cooperate in discovery, or agree to another way to resolve the dispute. They may have learned to negotiate better and may, in fact, settle unresolved issues themselves later.

Whatever the agreement stipulates, it is only a good agreement if it endures. For an agreement to be durable, it should be satisfying to both parties, procedurally, substantially, and psychologically. This can be accomplished when the parties make an informed decision visa vie a well organized and orchestrated mediation.

CLOSING TASK

- To bring closure - Get it over with .
- Create value on the issues that have been resolved .
- Create value on the issues not resolved by emphasizing the conflict can be over .
- Do the parties understand their agreement to settle? .
- Reminding the parties of problems if they don't settle
- Summarize the positives
- Command progress if necessary
- Evaluation by the mediator if necessary
- Entice closure . Focus on the 'Deal'
- Concentrate on providing fair and controlled closure

- Develop a resolution scenario which will be durable
- Monitor satisfaction of the parties
- Remind parties and their advocates of their commitment to confidentiality……
………………
- … (FOR FUTURE IDEAS)

CLOSING ACTION

- Offer opinions about the options of resolution
- Perform reality check
- Remind the parties of the positives
- Remind the parties of how good it will feel when its over
- If the final negotiations become heated and seemingly at impasse try:
    - Moving locations
    - Taking recesses
    - Threaten to quit
    - Encourage splitting the difference
    - Bribe the parties
    - Change the currency
    - Barter
    - Ask, "Do you want resolution, or do you want conflict?"
    - Create urgency
    - Change styles
    - Revisit worst case scenarios
    - Play Russian roulette
    - Flip a coin
- Set agreement in writing
- … (FOR FUTURE IDEAS)

CLOSING RESULT

- An informed decision leads to a durable conclusion
- The disputants were treated fair
- The disputants were treated well
- The disputants were treated with respect
- The disputants were treated with empathy
- The disputants were satisfied with the process

- They have a written agreement
- A confidential, private settlement
- . . . (FOR FUTURE IDEAS)

SUGGESTIONS FOR MEDIATED WRITTEN AGREEMENTS

1. The mediator is to avoid being the author of the settlement agreement but should monitor the crafting of such an agreement to assist the parties in a document which has the basic requirements of an contract/agreement and will be final and durable.
2. Encourage them to write in a language and sentence structure the parties can easily read and understand. Be sensitive to the needs of parties who don't read very well or don't have a good command of English.
3. Avoid references to the parties as "complainant/plaintiff" or "respondent/defendant" in the agreement. Use the names they have used throughout the mediation session. If the agreement is going to be forwarded to a referring court you may want them to use full legal names throughout.
4. Make sure there is only one agreement item in each numbered statement, and assist them in avoiding an agreement conditional on an act of the other party.
5. Have each party to the dispute agree to each individual clause. Encourage them to avoid writing "we agree to," but rather "John agrees to.....," and in a separate item, "Mary agrees to....."
6. If payments are a part of the agreement, make sure the scribe includes specifics about where and how they are to be made. In general it is not a good idea to have payment made by personal check. Ask the parties to use certified checks, money orders, or cash with appropriate receipts whenever possible.
7. Help them be specific as possible in wording agreements about future behaviors. Avoid phrases such as "will not harass" since they may be understood differently by each party and lead to further disagreement.
8. Attempt to have them balance the agreement as much as possible. If the situation is one-sided, you can help them balance clauses by asking one party to agree to accept what the other is agreeing to do. (e.g. "Jones agrees to accept this method of payment.")
9. Remember that the agreement belongs to the parties. Encourage the use of their word choice when it is clear and mutually understood. Check the wording of each item with each of the parties to make sure they are writing what they agree to.
10. Consider what the impact of the wording of the agreement will be if the parties read it a month after the mediation session. Have they written a clause that implies guilt or blame? Will all the clauses be clear to the parties and to anyone else to whom the agreement is shown?

11. Help them to avoid admission of guilt or blame and/or a party to giving up his/her right to legal advice. Discourage agreements which consent to withdrawal of a criminal complaint, unless the court has specifically empowered them or the scribe to do this.
12. Be sure the agreement reflects the same issues in original dispute that were submitted, or change the submitted form.

SETTLEMENT AGREEMENT

____________________________ and ____________________________ met with ________________________, mediator, to resolve their dispute. The parties have agreed to the following.

The parties acknowledge that the terms stated above accurately reflect their statement agreement. The parties further agree to abide by the finding, terms, and conditions set forth above.

The parties (do ___) (do not ___) choose to make this agreement admissible and enforceable in a court of law.

Date signed: ______________________, 20___.

____

____

Mediator

MEDIATOR ETHICS: ROLES AND FUNCTIONS

By Diana Mercer and Tara Fass, copyright 2005 Peace Talks® Mediation Services 8055 W. Manchester Ave., Suite 201 Playa del Rey CA 90293

In any given case, a professional has one role but may have multiple functions. Many mediation professionals offer multiple services in keeping with their non-mediation education and training: arbitration, litigation, expert opinions, custody evaluations and therapy to name a few. Keeping your services within the role for which you've been hired in any particular case is key to staying out of ethical trouble.

The first step is to define the difference between your Role and your Function.

Role: The professional's role is the position for which he or she has been hired. Some examples: a professional might be a mediator, therapist for adult or child, therapist-coach, collaborative law therapist-coach, evaluator, collateral contact therapist in an evaluation, litigation attorney, mediation support attorney, collaborative attorney, business valuation expert.

Trouble starts when roles begin to blur within a single case. A therapist-mediator cannot also be a treating therapist for one of the parties or the couple. A lawyer-mediator cannot also be one party's individual attorney. A business valuation expert cannot also give tax strategies and advice. Although some mediators practice an evaluative style, they cannot act as arbitrators or ultimate decision-makers. Although many of us are hired for different roles in different cases, each of us has only one role for each case.

Function: Although the professional has been hired for a discrete role: his or her position or task in a case (therapist-mediator, litigation attorney), he or she may also be able to use different skills from his or her professional background and have different functions, which are necessary or helpful to the client(s) within that one case, consistent with his or her role in that case.

What functions you will be comfortable providing within any given role are discretionary within the ethical boundaries of your underlying profession. The examples we've provided below are guidelines only, and are not necessarily where you'd set your individual boundaries with respect to functions you'd fulfill within any given role.

Attorney-mediator: Role is mediator

Appropriate functions for attorney-mediator	Inappropriate functions
Providing both clients with copies of statutes	Giving legal advice on a given issue to one party
making settlement suggestions	insisting on a settlement option
pointing out where differences of opinion might exist	endorsing one option without acknowledgment others exist
referring both parties to several attorneys	if mediation breaks down, and stepping down from case representing one party if mediation breaks down

Permissible functions are completely dependent on the role for which the professional was hired. You'll note that the "inappropriate functions" in this example are inappropriate for an attorney-mediator, but that many of them would be appropriate if the attorney was hired as a litigation attorney or advocate. Likewise, the "inappropriate functions" for the therapist-mediator would be appropriate for an individual's, couple's and/or child's therapist, depending on how the parties originally contracted for treatment with that therapist.

When you're hired for a case, be sure and define your individual role in that case, and base your functions on those which are appropriate for your role. For client requests that fall outside of your role, be prepared with solid referrals to appropriate professionals so that your role is never blurred. You'll preserve the nature of the professionalism of your role, you'll stay out of ethical trouble and you'll also provide better service for your client.

PRACTICE ETHICS FOR MEDIATORS

ETHIC 1	Competency **The mediator shall maintain professional competency in mediation skills and, where s/he lacks the skills necessary for a particular case, shall decline to serve or withdraw from serving as Mediator.**
ETHIC 2	Impartiality A Mediator shall, in word and action, maintain impartiality toward the parties and on the issues in dispute, and where his/her impartiality is in question, shall decline to serve or withdraw from serving as Mediator.
ETHIC 3	Confidentiality A Mediator shall, unless statutorily obligated to the contrary, maintain the confidentiality of all communications made to him/her by the parties within the mediation process.
ETHIC 4	Consent A Mediator shall make reasonable efforts to ensure that each party understands the operation of the mediation process and the options available to them and that each party is free and able to make whatever choices s/he desires regarding participation in mediation generally and regarding specific ssettlement options.
ETHIC 5	Self-Determination A Mediator shall respect and encourage self-determination by the parties in their decision whether, and on what terms, to resolve their dispute, and shall refrain from being directive and judgmental regarding the issues ub dispute and options for settlement.
ETHIC 6	Separation Of Mediation From Counseling And Legal Advice A Mediator shall limit him/herself solely to the role of Mediator, and shall refrain from giving legal advice or other advice and otherwise engaging in counseling or advocacy during mediation.
ETHIC 7	Promotion Of Respect And Control Of Abuse A Mediator shall encourage mutual respect between the parties, and shall take reasonable steps, subject to the principle of self-determination, to limit abuses of the mediation process.
ETHIC 8	Conflicts Of Interest A Mediator shall, as far as possible, avoid conflicts of interest, and shall in any event resolve all such conflicts in favor of his/her primary obligation to impartially serve the parties to the dispute.

MEDIATION PRACTICE STANDARDS

Here are the generally accepted Standards of Mediation Practice of the American Bar Association, American Arbitration Association and Association for Conflict Resolution. You should also identify relevant state standards of practice.

These are the standards of mediation practice jointly defined by the American Bar Association (ABA), Association for Conflict Resolution (ACR) and the American Arbitration Association (AAA) and are generally applicable to the mediation of legal disputes.

The purpose of this initiative was to develop a set of standards to serve as a general framework for the practice of mediation. The effort is a step in the development of the field and a tool to assist practitioners in it--a beginning, not an end. The model standards are intended to apply to all types of mediation. It is recognized, however, that in some cases laws or contractual agreements may affect the application of these standards.

Preface

The model standards of conduct for mediators are intended to perform three major functions: to serve as a guide for the conduct of mediators; to inform the mediating parties; and to promote public confidence in mediation as a process for resolving disputes. The standards draw on existing codes of conduct for mediators and take into account issues and problems that have surfaced in mediation practice. They are offered in the hope that they will serve an educational function and provide assistance to individuals, organizations, and institutions involved in mediation.

I. Self-Determination: A Mediator Shall Recognize that Mediation is Based on the Principle of Self-Determination by the Parties.

Self-determination is the fundamental principle of mediation. It requires that the mediation process rely upon the ability of the parties to reach a voluntary, uncoerced agreement. Any party may withdraw from mediation at any time.

COMMENTS:

The mediator may provide information about the process, raise issues, and help parties explore options. The primary role of the mediator is to facilitate a voluntary resolution of a dispute. Parties shall be given the opportunity to consider all proposed options.

A mediator cannot personally ensure that each party has made a fully informed choice to reach a particular agreement, but is a good practice for the mediator to make the parties aware of the importance of consulting other professionals, where appropriate, to help them make informed decisions.

II. Impartiality: A Mediator Shall Conduct the Mediation in an Impartial Manner.

The concept of mediator impartiality is central to the mediation process. A mediator shall mediate only those matters in which she or he can remain impartial and evenhanded. If at any time the mediator is unable to conduct the process in an impartial manner, the mediator is obligated to withdraw.

COMMENTS:

A mediator shall avoid conduct that gives the appearance of partiality toward one of the parties. The quality of the mediation process is enhanced when the parties have confidence in the impartiality of the mediator.

When mediators are appointed by a court or institution, the appointing agency shall make reasonable efforts to ensure that mediators serve impartially.

A mediator should guard against partiality or prejudice based on the parties' personal characteristics, background or performance at the mediation.

III. Conflicts of Interest: A Mediator Shall Disclose all Actual and Potential Conflicts of Interest Reasonably Known to the Mediator. After Disclosure, the Mediator shall Decline to Mediate unless all Parties Choose to Retain the Mediator. The Need to Protect Against Conflicts of Interest also Governs Conduct that Occurs During and After the Mediation.

A conflict of interest is a dealing or relationship that might create an impression of possible bias. The basic approach to questions of conflict of interest is consistent with the concept of self-determination. The mediator has a responsibility to disclose all actual and potential conflicts that are reasonably known to the mediator and could reasonably be seen as raising a question about impartiality. If all parties agree to mediate after being informed of conflicts, the mediator may proceed with the mediation. If, however, the conflict of interest casts serious doubt on the integrity of the process, the mediator shall decline to proceed.

A mediator must avoid the appearance of conflict of interest both during and after the mediation. Without the consent of all parties, a mediator shall not subsequently establish a professional relationship with one of the parties in a related matter, or in an unrelated matter under circumstances which would raise legitimate questions about the integrity of the mediation process.

COMMENTS:

A mediator shall avoid conflicts of interest in recommending the services of other professionals. A mediator may make reference to professional referral services or associations which maintain rosters of qualified professionals.

Potential conflicts of interest may arise between administrators of mediation programs and mediators and there may be strong pressures on the mediator to settle a particular case or cases. The mediator's commitment must be to the parties and the process. Pressure from outside of the mediation process should never influence the mediator to coerce parties to settle.

IV. Competence: A Mediator Shall Mediate Only When the Mediator has the Necessary Qualifications to Satisfy the Reasonable Expectations of the Parties.

Any person may be selected as a mediator, provided that the parties are satisfied with the mediator's qualifications. Training and experience in mediation, however, are often necessary for effective mediation. A person who offers herself or himself as available to serve as a mediator gives parties and the public the expectation that she or he has the competency to mediate effectively. In court-connected or other forms of mandated mediation, it is essential that mediators assigned to the parties have the requisite training and experience.

COMMENTS:

Mediators should have information available for the parties regarding their relevant training, education and experience.

The requirements for appearing on the list of mediators must be made public and available to interested persons.

When mediators are appointed by a court or institution, the appointing agency shall make reasonable efforts to ensure that each mediator is qualified for the particular mediation.

V. Confidentiality: A Mediator Shall Maintain the Reasonable Expectations of the Parties with Regard to Confidentiality.

The reasonable expectations of the parties with regard to confidentiality shall be met by the mediator. The parties' expectations of confidentiality depend on the circumstances of the mediation and any agreements they may make. The mediator shall not disclose any matter that a party expects to be confidential unless given permission by all parties or unless required by law or other public policy.

COMMENTS:

The parties may make their own rules with respect to confidentiality, or other accepted practice of an individual mediator or institution may dictate a particular set of expectations. Since the parties' expectations regarding confidentiality are important, the mediator should discuss these expectations with the parties.

If the mediator holds private sessions with a party, the nature of these sessions with regard to confidentiality should be discussed prior to undertaking such sessions.

In order to protect the integrity of the mediation, a mediator should avoid communicating information about how the parties acted in the mediation process, the merits of the case, or settlement offers. The mediator may report, if required, whether parties appeared at a scheduled mediation.

Where the parties have agreed that all or a portion of the information disclosed during a mediation is confidential, the parties' agreement should be respected by the mediator. Confidentiality should not be construed to limit or prohibit the effective monitoring, research, or evaluation of mediation programs by responsible persons. Under appropriate circumstances, researchers may be permitted to obtain access to the statistical data and, with the permission of the parties, to individual case files, observations of live mediations, and interviews with participants.

VI. Quality of the Process: A Mediator Shall Conduct the Mediation Fairly, Diligently, and in a Manner Consistent with the Principle of Self-Determination by the Parties.

A mediator shall work to ensure a quality process and to encourage mutual respect among the parties. A quality process requires a commitment by the mediator to diligence and procedural fairness. There should be adequate opportunity for each party in the mediation to participate in the discussions. The parties decide when and under what conditions they will reach an agreement or terminate a mediation.

COMMENTS:

A mediator may agree to mediate only when he or she is prepared to commit the attention essential to an effective mediation.

Mediators should only accept cases when they can satisfy the reasonable expectations of the parties concerning the timing of the process. A mediator should not allow a mediation to be unduly delayed by the parties or their representatives.

The presence or absence of persons at a mediation depends on the agreement of the parties and the mediator. The parties and mediator may agree that others may be excluded from particular sessions or from the entire mediation process.

The primary purpose of a mediator is to facilitate the parties' voluntary agreement. This role differs substantially from other professional-client relationships. Mixing the role of a mediator and the role of a professional advising a client is problematic, and mediators must strive to distinguish between the roles. A mediator should, therefore, refrain from providing professional advice. Where appropriate, a mediator should recommend that parties seek outside professional advice, or consider resolving their dispute through arbitration, counseling, neutral evaluation, or other processes. A mediator who undertakes, at the request of the parties, an additional dispute resolution role in the same matter assumes increased responsibilities and obligations that may be governed by the standards of other processes.

A mediator shall withdraw from a mediation when incapable of serving or when unable to remain impartial.

A mediator shall withdraw from a mediation or postpone a session if the mediation is being used to further illegal conduct, or if a party is unable to participate due to drug, alcohol, or other physical or mental incapacity.

Mediators should not permit their behavior in the mediation process to be guided by a desire for a high settlement rate.

VII. Advertising and Solicitation: A Mediator Shall be Truthful in Advertising and Solicitation for Mediation

Advertising or any other communication with the public concerning services offered or regarding the education, training, and expertise of the mediator shall be truthful. Mediators shall refrain from promises and guarantees of results.

COMMENTS:

It is imperative that communication with the public educates and instills confidence in the process. In an advertisement or other communication to the public, a mediator may make reference to meeting state, national, or private organization qualifications only if the entity referred to has a procedure for qualifying mediators and the mediator has been duly granted the requisite status.

VIII. Fees: A Mediator Shall Fully Disclose and Explain the Basis of Compensation, Fees, and Charges to the Parties.

The parties should be provided sufficient information about fees at the outset of a mediation to determine if they wish to retain the services of a mediator. If a mediator charges fees, the fees shall be reasonable, considering among other things, the mediation service, the type and complexity of the matter, the expertise of the mediator, the time required, and the rates customary in the community. The better practice in reaching an understanding about fees is to set down the arrangements in a written agreement.

COMMENTS: A mediator who withdraws from a mediation should return any unearned fee to the parties. A mediator should not enter into a fee agreement that is contingent upon the result of the mediation or amount of the settlement.

Co-mediators who share a fee should hold to standards of reasonableness in determining the allocation of fees.

A mediator should not accept a fee for referral of a matter to another mediator or to any other person.

IX. Obligations to the Mediation Process: Mediators have a Duty to Improve the Practice of Mediation.

COMMENT:

Mediators are regarded as knowledgeable in the process of mediation. They have an obligation to use their knowledge to help educate the public about mediation; to make mediation accessible to those who would like to use it; to correct abuses; and to improve their professional skills and abilities.

PRACTICE HINTS: THE ECONOMICS OF PRACTICE AND THE MARKETING OF MEDIATION

ECONOMICS OF PRACTICE: ISSUES TO CONSIDER:

1. OFFICE: Placement and style of office. Generally, do not need separate office for mediation. Style and arrangement is personal choice.
2. BILLING: How much; hourly or session rate; payment per meeting or monthly; retainer requested.
3. STATIONERY: Separate stationery for mediation practice is advisable to avoid confusion.
4. FORMS: (See this book.)
5. ADVERTISING BUDGET: (See below.)
6. MALPRACTICE INSURANCE: (See Ethics, 14.12)

MARKETING MEDIATION AND PUBLIC EDUCATION

The key to the development of mediation as a viable option will be marketing and public education. The single biggest obstacle to the spread of mediation is that too few people know of it as an available option. Mediators cannot wait for parties to come to them as they might do as lawyers and therapists. Generally, referrals will not come easily from other professionals; both lawyers and counselors view mediation as threatening to their livelihood.

Three points to keep in mind:

- Develop a marketing strategy that reaches the general public; don't ignore professionals and professional groups, but don't rely on them either.
- Remember, as you must in the mediation process itself, that often parties are afraid to take responsibility for their own lives. Your marketing strategy must present mediation as a competent, protected process where parties cannot get hurt legally or personally.
- Sell mediation as a businesslike, sensible and thoughtful way to settle disputes, not as the humanistic "right thing to do."

Other considerations in marketing:

1. Distinguishing public relations and education from advertising, the use of media and public relations experts.
2. The demographics of divorce and marketing strategies

3. Setting goals and objectives: target referral groups
4. Using and managing the media: creating press events; press releases and press packages
5. Advertising: radio, TV, Newspapers, other periodicals
6. Speaking engagements: How to prepare and what to present
7. Publications: brochures, graphics, logos
8. The cost of public relations ad advertisings: How to take advantage of free advertisement

SELECTED BIBLIOGRAPHY:

Big Ideas for Small Businesses: How to Successfully Advertise, Publicize & Maximize Your Business of Professional Practice. Marilyn and Tom Ross. Communication Creativity, 1994.

Marketing Strategies for Small Businesses. Richard F. Gerson, PhD, U.S. Chamber of Commerce, Small Business Institute, Crisp Publications, 1994.

Guerilla Marketing: Secrets for Making Big Profits from Your Small Business. Jay Conrad Levinson. Houghton Mifflin Co., 3rd Rev & Ex edition (October 1998).

Guerrilla Marketing With Technology: Unleashing the Full Potential of Your Small Business. Jay Conrad Levinson. Perseus Press, 1997.

WEBLIOGRAPHY - All sites are preceded by http://

- www.profitzone.com
- www.artofselfpromotion.com
- www.albertabusiness.com/books/marketing/Default.htm
- www.ama.org
- www.americanexpress.com/smallbusiness/
- www.vbizine.com/news.htm
- www.canadaone.com
- www.capstonecomm.com
- www.delphi.com/babco
- www.gmarketing.com
- www.deasiteforbusinessplan/
- www.inc.com/idx/idx t Vc.html
- www.jenntech.com/businessplan/
- www.liraz.com
- www.marketingtips.com
- www.morebusiness.com/running your business/marketing

- www.pertinent.com
- www.quicken.com/small business/marketing/
- www.smallbizhelpt.net/marketing.htm
- www.smalltownmarketing.com
- www.smartbiz.com/sbs/cats/mktggen.htm
- www.web9000.com/bus/resource/
- www.yudkin.com/marketing.htm

SETTING UP A MEDIATION-FRIENDLY OFFICE[15]

1. Be vigilant about how offices are arranged: are client needs and comfort take into consideration?
2. Plan out where settlement discussions are to be conducted within the office
3. Have all the necessary settlement propos on hand: white board, flip charts, round tables
4. Use flip charts to preserve writing-they can be posted around the room to reinforce progress achieved and kept for later sessions
5. Windows can be used as substitutes for white boards
6. Survey your office to set up space for breakout or caucus rooms
7. If you're using a professional designer, don't limit your choice to only those with law office or therapy office experience
8. Consider establishing a client library in your office. If you do not have a full room to devote to a library, think about putting client-friendly space with books and a VCR with headphones in a corner of your waiting room.
9. Develop materials with sufficient copies on hand to send to clients. Arrange materials into client packages that can both educate and sell clients on the mediation process.
10. Maintain packets from several mediators to send to future clients as the needs arise.
11. Train staff to ask whether the other spouse has requested mediation information before sending it. Also ask whether lawyers are involved and if they also should receive copies of materials.
12. Articulate that client service is the top priority of your firm and reward employees for actions that reinforce client service.

[15] Adapted from and used by permission: The Complete Guide to Mediation by Forrest S. Mosten, ABA Publications, copyright 1997.

HOW DO I BECOME A MEDIATOR?

People from a wide variety of backgrounds can make good mediators. Presently, California has no mediator licensing requirements, which makes the answer to the question "How do I become a mediator?" as individual as the mediators themselves.

Before embarking on the journey to become a mediator, there are some questions you may wish to ask yourself in order to have a realistic approach in developing a career in mediation. Going from mediation training to a full-time mediation practice is difficult road, like building any quality business. Before you get started, ask yourself:

- Why do I want to become a mediator?
- What do I hope to accomplish?
- What will I use my mediation skills to do?
- How will my background contribute to my future practice in mediation?
- Do I need a steady paycheck, or do I prefer to be self-employed?
- Do I want to mediate full-time, part-time, or as an adjunct service to my existing career or practice?
- Do I want to be paid for my services, or do I prefer to mediate as a volunteer?

Once you've answered these questions for yourself, you're going to need some training. Most people start out with a 40-hour basic mediation class, but before investing your time and money in a class, you may wish to read The Mediation Process, by Christopher Moore (2nd Edition, Wiley/Jossey-Bass 2002). This book is a classic in the mediation field, and describes the process from beginning to end. While there are many great mediation titles available, no other book takes the process from start to finish like

The Mediation Process.

From there, you may wish to sign up for a 40-hour course. Most mediation panels, both volunteer and paid, require at least that much training in order to join. A 40 hour course is a great place to start to acquire, develop and hone your mediation skills. How much or how little training you wish to receive is up to you, but you'll want to start out with programs certified by the Association for Conflict Resolution (ACR), as well as your local mediator organization, like the Southern California Mediation Association (SCMA). Even though there's no formal certification process for mediators in California, solid training is essential.

Many mediators train and re-train throughout their lifetimes, enjoying the new perspective that each conference or training course gives. There are many quality courses offered in California, some privately and some through government agencies. The Association for Conflict Resolution lists certified training courses on its web site, http://www.acrnet.org. Training classes are also listed on Mediate.com and the Southern California Mediation

Association's web site, http://www.scmediation.org. ACR holds an annual conference, as does the SCMA. Although the ACR conference is a national conference, held in different states each year, you can find more local conferences like the California Bar Association's ADR South Committee's one-day conference, held each year at Pepperdine University in Malibu. These are just a few of the places you might look for a taste of what a career in mediation might look like.

You'll also want to join professional organizations, like the Dispute Resolution Section of the American Bar Association, the ADR Section of the California Bar Association, and your local bar associations as well as ACR and the California Dispute Resolution Council, to keep abreast of developments in the field as well as to network and form study groups. Join a few professional organizations, and volunteer on the committees. You'll get the opportunity to propose legislation that affects the mediation field, you'll help the group offer training in mediation or specialized skill areas that affect mediation, and you'll increase your profile in the field. Even if you're new to mediation, you have skills which you can offer to these professional organizations which will help you advance your mediation skills while helping the organization itself. For example, as a new member of SCMA, I volunteered to co-chair the Los Angeles Roundtable. As I helped to organize each meeting, I met the area's top mediators and had an intimate opportunity to hear them speak. I didn't know much about mediation when I started, but by the end of the year I'd learned the best tips from the top practitioners in Los Angeles.

You may find that the professional organization for your underlying field also has a mediation committee, such as the Alternative Dispute Resolution Committee for the local Bar Association, Therapists' Association, or Construction Contractors' Association. And, if your underlying field does not have an ADR Committee, here's your change to get one started!

Once you've got your training, the next question most people ask is "how do I get started in mediating actual conflicts?" There are as many ways to get started mediating as there are paths to the profession itself. Many people choose to join volunteer panels and community mediation programs. Some examples of these are the programs offered by the Equal Employment Opportunity Commission, the Centinela Valley Juvenile Diversion Program, the United States Postal Service, and the Superior Court. There are also several local for-profit panels of mediators, as well as nationally known panels like JAMS and the American Arbitration Association. Most beginning mediators start out on a smaller local panel or volunteer panel, however. Many of these programs offer mentoring programs, or you can sign up for a mentor through your local bar association or mediator association.

Except for the large panels and in-house corporate or government positions, mediation practices are, by and large, boutique firms or solo practices. The opportunities for being employed by one of these firms are few and far between, but there are nevertheless opportunities. The SCMA web site has a listing of job offers, but networking through professional organizations is a great way to hear about these [often unadvertised] jobs. Starting and building your own practice is also a choice many mediators ultimately make. Adding mediation to your existing career is where many mediators start their transition into a mediation career.

Once you've been to a mediation training, you can start to implement your mediation skills on a daily basis in your current work situation, form helping manage employee conflicts, or offering mediation as one of your services to existing clients. You may wish to take a mediation marketing course, such as the courses offered by Golden Media, Mosten Mediation Training, or the Straus Institute of Dispute Resolution at Pepperdine. There are also several books on the subject, such as *Mediation Career Guide* (Wiley/Jossey Bass 2002) by Forrest S. Mosten and *Becoming a Mediator: Your Guide to Career Opportunities* (Nolo Press 2004) by Peter Lovenheim.

There are also opportunities to work in mediation with a paycheck in private industry or government service, such as:

- Ombudsperson for a corporation;
- Teaching and training;
- Teaching and training in schools and peer mediation programs;
- Human resources departments;
- Conciliation Court (Family Court Services, Superior Court);
- Non-profit organizations and community mediation programs administration;
- As a volunteer, e.g., Centinela Valley Juvenile Diversion Program, US Postal Service;
- Government agencies like the EEOC;
- Mediation coach or consultant.

While it would be impossible to explore every avenue available toward becoming a mediator in this short article, but it provides some food for thought as to how you might approach becoming a mediator.

Opportunities in Mediation

Can Mediation be my Day Job?

Web Sites With Job Opportunities

- Southern California Mediation Association (http://www.scmediation.org)
- Golden Media (www.marketingmediation.com)
- Peace Talks® Mediation Services, Inc. (www.Peace-Talks.com)

- Mediate.com (www.mediate.com)
- Association for Conflict Resolution (www.acresolution.org)
- Los Angeles Superior Court (http://www.lasuperiorcourt.org/HR/)

Volunteer Opportunities in Mediation

- Centinela Valley Juvenile Diversion Program
- Families Able to Resolve Situations (FARS-parents & teenagers)
- Victim-Offender Mediation (VORS) 11633 Hawthorne Blvd., Suite 501 Hawthorne, CA 9025, (310) 675-8700 (They provide a very nice training program if you volunteer ($50 is cost))
- Los Angeles Superior Court (http://www.lasuperiorcourt.org/adr/) 111 N. Hill Street Los Angeles, CA 90012, (213) 974-5425 (has panels for family and civil mediations. Also has internship program.)

Training

- Institute for Conflict Management, LLC (www.icmadr.com)
- Conferences and Training, Association for Conflict Resolution (http://www.acresolution.org/research.nsf/key/conferences) ADR degrees & certificate programs, SCMA (http://www.scmediation.org/adr_cert_program.html)
- List of accredited training programs (http://www.mediate.com/training/)

Opportunities in Mediation

Question # 1: Do I need a steady paycheck, or do I prefer to be self-employed?

Question # 2: Do I want to mediate full time, part time, as part of my practice, or as a volunteer?

Question # 3: How will I get training to be a mediator?

Some ideas.....

Conflict Resolution Careers With or Without a Paycheck

- Ombudsperson
- Teaching & Training
- Teaching & Training in schools-peer mediation programs
- Private Practice
- Human Resources

- Conciliation Court (Superior Court)
- Non-Profit Organizations and Community Mediation Programs
- As a volunteer, e.g., FARS & VORS, US Postal Service
- Mediation panels like Mosten Mediation Center and Mediator Network
- Jayne Major's new program (Breakthrough Parenting)
- Government and EEOC, DFEH
- Mediation coach or consultant

Mediation Training Options

- 40 hour courses: Mosten Mediation Training, Ken Cloke
- Certificate programs like at Pepperdine
- Conferences - ACR in San Diego in August, SCMA in Malibu November
- Volunteer programs like FARS, VORS and the post office
- Mentoring
- SCMA Roundtable
- Self-study-Christopher Moore's *The Mediation Process* (Jossey-Bass)

APPENDIX 1: ROLE PLAYS

40 Hour Role Play

Husband: John Freeman, age 55

Business manager, entertainment attorney

Wife: Sharon Coochi, age 38

Stay at home mother, former hotel sales and marketing executive

Children: Son, Tyler, age 8, 2nd grade

Twin Daughters, Jody and Jill, age 5, Kindergarten

Date of Marriage: June 15, 1999

Date of Separation: June 1, 2008

Date of Meeting #1: April 15, 2008

John Freeman, age 51, and Sharon, age 39, have decided to divorce after a year of therapy and 9 years of marriage. John is a licensed attorney and business manager with an impressive roster of clients. When they met 15 years ago in Las Vegas, John who was based in Los Angeles and Toronto, had an international reputation as a 'man about town.' Sharon had just moved to Las Vegas for a job promotion from San Francisco where she had been a mid-level public relations and sales manager for an internationally known security services firm. When they met, Sharon was on the fast track to upper management just having launched a very successful marketing campaign for the global hotel chain where John booked so much business he attained the level of a corporate guest.

They kept separate residences and had a very satisfying long distance open relationship for the first two years. For the next two years they lived together in a committed but part-time relationship in a home they bought together in Las Vegas. They sold that house and bought a new house in Los Angeles that they moved into after they got married when Sharon was 5 months pregnant with Tyler who wasn't planned. Sharon went back to work in the hotel management business 6 weeks after giving birth to Tyler. Three years later they went through in-vitro fertilization (IVF) after one year of trying to get pregnant without luck and were blessed with two healthy twins. Sharon is now a stay at home mom. They have 3 children, Tyler age 8 and twin daughters, Jody and Jill, age 5, who will be starting kindergarten in the fall. Paul earns $375,000 a year with a rather generous business personal expense account.

In 2006, John invested $400,000 of community savings to purchase raw land half way between Los Angeles and Orange County to develop 200 single family dwellings in a planned housing development with the agreement that John would receive 5% net profit from every unit sold. In 2007, John also invested $250,000 of community savings with the goal of developing an urban mixed-use work/live/shop real estate venture including condominiums for sale and commercial office and retail space for lease. For every lease signed John would receive 1% of the net profit on rents collected and 1% for the first time each condo unit sold for as long as the initial $250,000 investment was tied up in the business. Both of these projects have been undertaken with a consortium of other partners, each of whom has their own separate deals. The man who brought all the partners together is a real estate developer, and John's good friend from Toronto who is the husband of one of his biggest clients also a native of Toronto.

The bank that financed both of the projects has now tightened up its lending practices. As a result, the former project is at a complete stand still. John's contract doesn't give him the ability to force the sale of the land or to back out the money for 10 years with 0% interest which will be in 2016. And though there is steady interest in the urban mixed use projects, breaking ground on construction has been delayed because of a fall out with a neighborhood association who found violations of traffic abatement standards. That deal also expires in 10 years (2017) when John can pull out their money under the same conditions.

John and Sharon started marriage counseling approximately once a month starting in June of 2006 that ended in March 2007. Sharon had found out in May that John had been spending money on and off on another woman since 2005. John admits he was only half-heartedly courting this other woman. It was more that she was in dire financial straits and it felt good to be so appreciated for helping her but that she refused to be intimate with him because he was a married man and father. John is adamant that he stopped giving the other woman money or gifts early in 2006. He also denies, as Sharon charges, that John was unfaithful during her pregnancy with the twins. John admits that until the twins started walking and talking their life together had been 'perfect.' Though they had household help, the feeling of personal responsibility and level of mental and physical energy output required of John exceeded his limits. While they were in marital counseling they maintained separate bedrooms in the same house but admitted to being intimate. John was travelling quite a bit during this time as well. Sharon refused to continue counseling after their last session in March 2008 when John was asked by the therapist if he loved Sharon and it took him too long -she thought - to answer.

Sharon admits to having spent freely since they've been married without complaint from John and particularly in the last few years as a way to cope with her marital grief and to help her when John was out of town travelling first class. John defends his business entertainment expenses as normal, regular, customary and reimbursed by clients. The jointly owned home was refinanced into an interest only loan to pay off the equity line of credit and high interest credit cards against Sharon's wishes and they have been making minimum payments on the house for the last 18 months. Now they agree it is time to sell the house that has depreciated about 20% in one year and is now worth about $2 million which leaves them with about $300,000 net profit.

Sharon has taken a joint bank account with $60,000 in it and has deposited $20,000 in each of the children's accounts that they both have access to. Paul will leave it this way and additionally will give Sharon 80% of the proceeds of the sale of their house in lieu of Sharon backing off her request for a summary of John's personal business expenses.

They agree of a move out date of May 1st and have agreed to a tentative step up parenting plan so that the twins can get used to seeing John without mom 2-3 times per week and sleeping over John's house at least once a week, once they start school in the Fall. John will take all the children for 5 days on an extended family vacation in Canada where there will be a high adult to child ratio. The parents agree that Tyler might be able to have extra overnights with John starting in the summer of 2008. John stresses that though he'd like a regular schedule for caring for the children that he needs flexibility. Settling on a mutual definition of flexibility is a bone of contention.

Sharon has a 401(k) valued at $150,000 and is invested in safe index funds. Paul has a SEP IRA valued at $200,000 and is invested in highly speculative mutual funds.

Child and spousal support will start once the house is sold. Until then John will continue to pay Sharon's bills.

Date of Meeting #2: July 15, 2008

The deal on the table to sell the house has fallen through.

John's move out of the family residence occurred one month later than expected on June 1, 2008. John's sister Sue is paying his apartment rent and he is looking for an investment property for Sue to buy that he will be able to live in. Sharon wonders why Sue doesn't buy a place for her and the children to live in so that the children don't have to change their school district as the public schools where they are just fine. In a lower rent neighborhood, there may then be the issue of private school.

Sharon states that without John's disclosure of his summary of accounting she will not be able to continue the healing process in the divorce. Besides, if there was tax fraud she wants to know since she signed off on the tax returns too. Sharon also wonders if John's secretary is totally honest because in the past she has found some purchases at a local supplies store unusually high. John states that if he must produce the records that Sharon says are readily available this will only serve to hurt Sharon's feelings and not reveal any new information. Sharon isn't so sure. She thinks John is paying for the Mercedes lease of a new girlfriend. If Sharon persists in her requests, John's offer over the kids' accounts and the home equity split is off the table.

The family dog, Rex, is old and has been diagnosed gall stones which if removed will cost $1800. If not removed, Rex may not survive another episode in which he must pass them naturally.

Sharon and John agree to split the proceeds of the real estate investment deals should they come through.

Date of Meeting #3: September 15, 2008

Support Summary

Calculated on October 09, 2008 with the CalSupport™ program, version 2008-1.3, dated January 21, 2008, using tax year 2007.Tax tables and support laws are subject to change so if this report is old please contact your service provider to inquire whether it is still accurate. CalSupport has been certified accurate by the California Judicial Council and by law its results must be accepted in all California courts.

Figures in the report are Monthly

CALCULATED RESULTS:	Guideline	Family Support
Monthly support payment from Doug to Liz	1,344	1,710
Spouse (deductible) support <Santa Clara>	328	1,304
Child (non-deductible) support (CA Guideline)	1,016	406
CS add-ons shared <50/50>	0	0
Net disposable income - Liz	6,116	6,121
Net disposable income - Doug	5,603	5,610

Net disposable income = income after taxes, support and authorized deductions. See Net Income Report for detailed analysis. Family Support figure assumes Doug releases 0 exemptions to Liz

Support is based on figures and options supplied by both parties
as summarized below. Accuracy of result depends on accuracy of information entered. Check carefully. Each party is entitled by law to examine current tax returns, wage stubs, and financial documents of the other party to verify figures. Best if each party uses a copy of this program to examine entries and calculations; otherwise, use with printout of glossary. Numbers in headings below correspond to screens in the program.

	Doug	Liz
Screen 1-Family Information		
Number of children (of this relationship) living primarily with	0	1
Percent of time other parent has primary care of children	20.0%	0.0%
Which party will be the Petitioner	Respondent	Petitioner
Screen 2-Gross Income Information		
Earned income: wages, salary, bonus, commissions	10,833	0
Self-employment income after appropriate business expenses	0	6,250
Income from rents and royalties after appropriate business expenses	0	0
Tax free income due to depreciation and other business expenses	0	0
Unearned income (interest, dividends, pension, etc)	0	0
Social Security retirement income	0	0
Tax-free income (government bonds, military pension, etc)	0	0
Spousal support actually being received from other parties	0	0
Capital gains, short-term	0	0
Capital gains, long-term	0	0
Screen 3-Authorized Deductions from Income		
Health insurance for self and children	200	0
Mandatory deductions from pay checks:		
Union dues paid as a condition of employment	0	0
Retirement paid as a condition of employment	0	0
Support actually being paid to other relationships:		
Child support for children of other relationships	0	0
Spouse support per court order to spouse of other marriage	0	0

Prepared with the assistance of Peace Talks Mediation Services, Phone: (310) 301-2100
CalSupport's tax computations have been certified by Michael S. Thompson, CPA, San Jose.
CalSupport™ Professional Version 2008-1.3

Screen 4-Discretionary Deductions from Income	**Doug**	**Liz**
These items can be deducted from income only if agreed by parties or ordered by Judge after evidence presented in court:		
Necessary job-related expenses	0	0
Extraordinary health expenses	0	0
Uninsured catastrophic losses: amount to help recover	0	0
Deduction for live-in children of other relationships	0	0
Screen 5-Add-On Costs Shared by Parents		
If these expenses are actually being paid, they will be shared 50/50 unless parties agree (or Judge decides) to share in proportion to net incomes.		
Child care expense to allow parents to work, seek work, or for education or training leading to employment	0	0
Uninsured health care expenses for children, actually being paid	0	0
Expenses below, if agreed by parties or ordered by Judge, to be shared 50/50 unless parties agree (or Judge decides) to share in proportion to net incomes:		
Educational or other special needs of children	0	0
Travel exp. for child or parent required for visitation	0	0
Screen 6-Tax Information		
Tax filing status (assume not married to this party)	Single	Head of House
Total number of exemptions that will be claimed	1	2
Exempt from deductions (for certain public employees)	Not Exempt	Not Exempt
State of residence for taxes	California	California
State income taxes	Calculated	Calculated
Amount used to secure retirement or disability in lieu of FICA	0	0
Screen 7-Tax Deductions		
Tax deduction method.	Standard	Itemized
Voluntary contrib to retirement (IRA, Keogh, 401k)	0	0
User-Entered itemized expenses:		
a. Deductible medical, dental, drug expenses	0	0
b. Taxes: Real and personal property	0	157
c. Interest (paid on mortgages, other recurring loans)	0	1,400
d. Charitable contributions	0	0
e. Job related expenses	0	0
f. Misc. deductions	0	0
Federal Tax Credits applied to both parties are:		
Child & Dependent Care, Child Tax Credit, Additional Child Tax Credit, Earned Income Credit		
Number of qualifying persons for the Child and Dependent Care Credit	0	1
Additional Child and Dependent Care Expenses	0	0
Number of qualifying children for the Child Tax Credit	0	1
Number of qualifying children for the Earned Income Credit	0	1
Non-taxable earned income other than voluntary retirement	0	0
Additional tax credits	0	0
State tax credits applied	JCHH	JCHH
California Child & Dependent Care Credit applied to both parties		
Other State tax credits	0	0

Prepared with the assistance of Peace Talks Mediation Services, Phone: (310) 301-2100
CalSupport's tax computations have been certified by Michael S. Thompson, CPA, San Jose.
CalSupport™ Professional Version 2008-1.3

Support Summary

Calculated on October 09, 2008 with the CalSupport™ program, version 2008-1.3, dated January 21, 2008, using tax year 2007. Tax tables and support laws are subject to change so if this report is old please contact your service provider to inquire whether it is still accurate. CalSupport has been certified accurate by the California Judicial Council and by law its results must be accepted in all California courts.

Figures in the report are Monthly

CALCULATED RESULTS:	Guideline	Family Support
Monthly support payment from Doug to Liz	2,886	3,695
Spouse (deductible) support <Santa Clara>	1,513	3,678
Child (non-deductible) support (CA Guideline)	1,373	17
CS add-ons shared <50/50>	0	0
Net disposable income - Liz	7,263	7,310
Net disposable income - Doug	7,015	7,062

Net disposable income = income after taxes, support and authorized deductions. See Net Income Report for detailed analysis. Family Support figure assumes Doug releases 0 exemptions to Liz

Support is based on figures and options supplied by both parties
as summarized below. Accuracy of result depends on accuracy of information entered. Check carefully. Each party is entitled by law to examine current tax returns, wage stubs, and financial documents of the other party to verify figures. Best if each party uses a copy of this program to examine entries and calculations; otherwise, use with printout of glossary. Numbers in headings below correspond to screens in the program.

Screen 1-Family Information	**Doug**	**Liz**
Number of children (of this relationship) living primarily with	0	1
Percent of time other parent has primary care of children	20.0%	0.0%
Which party will be the Petitioner	Respondent	Petitioner
Screen 2-Gross Income Information		
Earned income: wages, salary, bonus, commissions	15,000	0
Self-employment income after appropriate business expenses	0	6,250
Income from rents and royalties after appropriate business expenses	0	0
Tax free income due to depreciation and other business expenses	0	0
Unearned income (interest, dividends, pension, etc)	0	0
Social Security retirement income	0	0
Tax-free income (government bonds, military pension, etc)	0	0
Spousal support actually being received from other parties	0	0
Capital gains, short-term	0	0
Capital gains, long-term	0	0
Screen 3-Authorized Deductions from Income		
Health insurance for self and children	200	0
Mandatory deductions from pay checks:		
Union dues paid as a condition of employment	0	0
Retirement paid as a condition of employment	0	0
Support actually being paid to other relationships:		
Child support for children of other relationships	0	0
Spouse support per court order to spouse of other marriage	0	0

Prepared with the assistance of Peace Talks Mediation Services, Phone: (310) 301-2100
CalSupport's tax computations have been certified by Michael S. Thompson, CPA, San Jose.
CalSupport™ Professional Version 2008-1.3

Support Summary

Calculated on October 09, 2008 with the CalSupport™ program, version 2008-1.3, dated January 21, 2008, using tax year 2007 Tax tables and support laws are subject to change so if this report is old please contact your service provider to inquire whether it is still accurate. CalSupport has been certified accurate by the California Judicial Council and by law its results must be accepted in all California courts.

Figures in the report are Monthly

CALCULATED RESULTS:	Guideline	Family Support
Monthly support payment from Doug to Liz	612	698
Spouse (deductible) support <Santa Clara>	303	524
Child (non-deductible) support (CA Guideline)	309	175
CS add-ons shared <50/50>	0	0
Net disposable income - Liz	5,392	5,397
Net disposable income - Doug	6,324	6,330

Net disposable income = income after taxes, support and authorized deductions. See Net Income Report for detailed analysis. Family Support figure assumes Doug releases 0 exemptions to Liz

Support is based on figures and options supplied by both parties
as summarized below. Accuracy of result depends on accuracy of information entered. Check carefully. Each party is entitled by law to examine current tax returns, wage stubs, and financial documents of the other party to verify figures. Best if each party uses a copy of this program to examine entries and calculations; otherwise, use with printout of glossary. Numbers in headings below correspond to screens in the program.

Screen 1-Family Information	**Doug**	**Liz**
Number of children (of this relationship) living primarily with	0	1
Percent of time other parent has primary care of children	49.0%	0.0%
Which party will be the Petitioner	Respondent	Petitioner
Screen 2-Gross Income Information		
Earned income: wages, salary, bonus, commissions	10,833	0
Self-employment income after appropriate business expenses	0	6,250
Income from rents and royalties after appropriate business expenses	0	0
Tax free income due to depreciation and other business expenses	0	0
Unearned income (interest, dividends, pension, etc)	0	0
Social Security retirement income	0	0
Tax-free income (government bonds, military pension, etc)	0	0
Spousal support actually being received from other parties	0	0
Capital gains, short-term	0	0
Capital gains, long-term	0	0
Screen 3-Authorized Deductions from Income		
Health insurance for self and children	200	0
Mandatory deductions from pay checks:		
Union dues paid as a condition of employment	0	0
Retirement paid as a condition of employment	0	0
Support actually being paid to other relationships:		
Child support for children of other relationships	0	0
Spouse support per court order to spouse of other marriage	0	0

Prepared with the assistance of Peace Talks Mediation Services, Phone: (310) 301-2100
CalSupport's tax computations have been certified by Michael S. Thompson, CPA, San Jose.
CalSupport™ Professional Version 2008-1.3

Page 1 of 4

Support Summary

Calculated on October 09, 2008 with the CalSupport™ program, version 2008-1.3, dated January 21, 2008, using tax year 2007. Tax tables and support laws are subject to change so if this report is old please contact your service provider to inquire whether it is still accurate. CalSupport has been certified accurate by the California Judicial Council and by law its results must be accepted in all California courts.

Figures in the report are Monthly

CALCULATED RESULTS:	**Guideline**	**Family Support**
Monthly support payment from Doug to Liz	2,029	2,450
Spouse (deductible) support <Santa Clara>	1,406	2,434
Child (non-deductible) support (CA Guideline)	623	16
CS add-ons shared <50/50>	0	0
Net disposable income - Liz	6,448	6,463
Net disposable income - Doug	7,827	7,842

Net disposable income = income after taxes, support and authorized deductions. See Net Income Report for detailed analysis. Family Support figure assumes Doug releases 0 exemptions to Liz

Support is based on figures and options supplied by both parties
as summarized below. Accuracy of result depends on accuracy of information entered. Check carefully. Each party is entitled by law to examine current tax returns, wage stubs, and financial documents of the other party to verify figures. Best if each party uses a copy of this program to examine entries and calculations; otherwise, use with printout of glossary. Numbers in headings below correspond to screens in the program.

Screen 1-Family Information	**Doug**	**Liz**
Number of children (of this relationship) living primarily with	0	1
Percent of time other parent has primary care of children	49.0%	0.0%
Which party will be the Petitioner	Respondent	Petitioner
Screen 2-Gross Income Information		
Earned income: wages, salary, bonus, commissions	15,000	0
Self-employment income after appropriate business expenses	0	6,250
Income from rents and royalties after appropriate business expenses	0	0
Tax free income due to depreciation and other business expenses	0	0
Unearned income (interest, dividends, pension, etc)	0	0
Social Security retirement income	0	0
Tax-free income (government bonds, military pension, etc)	0	0
Spousal support actually being received from other parties	0	0
Capital gains, short-term	0	0
Capital gains, long-term	0	0
Screen 3-Authorized Deductions from Income		
Health insurance for self and children	200	0
Mandatory deductions from pay checks:		
Union dues paid as a condition of employment	0	0
Retirement paid as a condition of employment	0	0
Support actually being paid to other relationships:		
Child support for children of other relationships	0	0
Spouse support per court order to spouse of other marriage	0	0

Prepared with the assistance of Peace Talks Mediation Services, Phone: (310) 301-2100
CalSupport's tax computations have been certified by Michael S. Thompson, CPA, San Jose.
CalSupport™ Professional Version 2008-1.3

Division of Marital Property

Property division report for Doug Sample and Liz Sample.

		Doug Amount	Pct	Liz Amount	Pct	Total Amount
Real Estate Equity						
Condo		$0		$112,000		$112,000
Total Value	$350,000					
1st Mortgage	$175,000					
2nd Mortgage	$63,000					
Equity	$112,000					
Total Real Estate Equity		$0	0%	$112,000	100%	$112,000
Businesses						
Graphic Arts		$0		$0		$0
Total Businesses		$0	0%	$0	0%	$0
Subtotal Non-Retirement		**$0**	**0%**	**$112,000**	**100%**	**$112,000**
IRAs and 401(k)s						
Liz's SEP IRA		$0		$5,000		$5,000
Liz's 401k		$0		$20,000		$20,000
Doug's 401k		$40,000		$0		$40,000
Total IRAs and 401(k)s		$40,000	62%	$25,000	38%	$65,000
Defined Benefit Pensions						
Doug's Pension		$0		$0		$0
Total Pensions		$0	0%	$0	0%	$0
Subtotal Retirement		**$40,000**	**62%**	**$25,000**	**38%**	**$65,000**
Total Assets		**$40,000**	**23%**	**$137,000**	**77%**	**$177,000**
Debts						
Joint CC		($15,000)		$0		($15,000)
Liz's CC		$0		($40,000)		($40,000)
Doug's		($8,500)		$0		($8,500)
Total Debt		($23,500)	37%	($40,000)	63%	($63,500)
Total Debts		**($23,500)**	**37%**	**($40,000)**	**63%**	**($63,500)**
Total Assets		**$40,000**	**23%**	**$137,000**	**77%**	**$177,000**
Total Debts		**($23,500)**	**37%**	**($40,000)**	**63%**	**($63,500)**
Total Property		**$16,500**	**15%**	**$97,000**	**85%**	**$113,500**
Equalization Payment		$40,250		($40,250)		
Total Marital After Payment		**$56,750**	**50%**	**$56,750**	**50%**	

Note: "Total Amount" column may not add due to rounding.

Budget Report for 2008

Budget Report for Doug Sample and Liz Sample for 2008

This report shows Doug's and Liz's income, taxes, expenses, excluding spousal support and child support.

	Doug Monthly	Liz Monthly
Income		
Insurance Agency	$7,500	$0
Liz's Employer #1	0	0
Bonuses	5,000	0
Total Wage and Non-Wage Income	$12,500	$0
Business Income		
Graphic Arts	$0	$6,250
Total Business Income	$0	$6,250
TOTAL INCOME	**$12,500**	**$6,250**

	Doug Monthly	Liz Monthly
Mortgage Payments		
Condo	$0	$2,000
Total Mortgage Payments	$0	$2,000
Household		
Maid / cleaning service	$0	$400
Rent	1,300	0
Tax - Property Tax	0	156
Utilities - Other	500	0
Other Household	0	1,344
Living Expenses - Household	$1,800	$1,900
Transportation		
Car Payments	$0	$325
Car Other	0	975
Living Expenses - Transportation	$0	$1,300
Child		
Child Care - Day Care	$0	$400
Child Care - Sitters	100	0
Child Medical Medication	200	0
Living Expenses - Child	$300	$400
Personal		
Clothes	$100	$500
Education for Party	0	200
Food / Groceries	100	600
Restaurants	1,800	0
Therapist / counselor	1,000	0
Vacations	200	600
Living Expenses - Personal	$3,200	$1,900

Budget Report (cont.)

	Doug Monthly	Liz Monthly
Health and Medical		
Medical/Doctor Exp	$0	$200
Living Expenses - Health and Medical	$0	$200
Total Living Expenses	$5,300	$5,700
Major Expenses		
Preschool	$600	$600
Total Major Expenses	$600	$600
Payments on Debt		
Joint CC	$200	$0
Liz's CC	0	500
Doug's	300	0
Total Payments on Debt	$500	$500
TOTAL EXPENSES	**$6,400**	**$8,800**
Taxes		
Federal Taxes	$2,588	$1,390
FICA & Medicare	$708	$0
State Taxes	$843	$169
TOTAL TAXES	**$4,140**	**$1,559**
Total Income	**$12,500**	**$6,250**
Minus Total Expenses	**(6,400)**	**(8,800)**
Minus Total Taxes	**(4,140)**	**(1,559)**
FINAL BUDGET	**$1,960**	**$(4,110)**

APPENDIX 2: COURSE POWERPOINT PRESENTATION

Family Law Mediation

From Intake to Agreement:
40 Hours to Mediation Mastery

The Institute for Conflict Management
and
Peace Talks Mediation Services, Inc.

Introductions Exercise

2 minutes: introduce yourself to your partner

2 minutes: your partner introduces himself or herself to you

1 minute each: you introduce your partner to the class in 60 seconds or less

Ask: did I get it right?

Who Are We?

- Your name, and what you like to be called
- Your best personal attribute
- Your core life value
- How your core life value determines one aspect of your mediation signature style
- What you'd like to learn from this class
- Each person will then have 60 seconds to introduce his or her partner to the group

Why Are We Here?

- What are you here to learn?
- How will you use it later?

Our First Mediation

How would you like to handle our ground rules?

- o Cell phones
- o Text messaging
- o Laptops
- o Room temperature
- o Health issues

Break:
See you at 10:45am!

Why Mediation?

- What we'll do in this training
- Value, benefits and results of mediation
- Uses for mediation skills
- Who is a mediator?
- Mediation styles and signatures
- Other types of ADR

What We'll Do in this Training

- Start to finish mediation of a family law case
- Practical orientation
- Emphasis on applications
- Overview of conflict resolution theory

GOAL: You will be able to mediate a case when you get back to your office

Mediation Cost Savings

Mediation Benefits

PROS AND CONS OF DIVORCE COURT vs. MEDIATION

Divorce Courts	Divorce Mediation or Custody Mediation

Mediation vs. Court

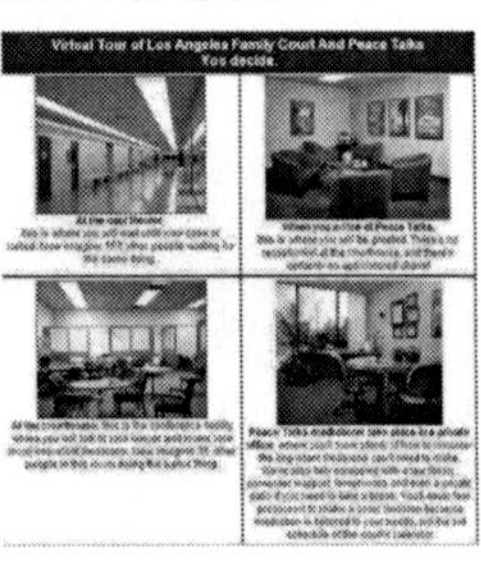

Family Health
Divergence During Divorce
Wendy Hutchins Cook, Ph.D.

Family Health Baseline Criteria

Goal of Mediation

Satisfaction of parties that they have a:

- Chance to make an informed decision
- Settlement that is durable
- Future without conflict
- Conflict prevention tools

Using Your Mediation Skills

- As part of your practice
- At home
- On the job
- HR
- Ombudsperson
- Camel Story
- Orange Story

Camel Story

Dad's estate plan: divide my camels between my 3 sons:

1/2 to the eldest

1/3 to the middle son

1/9 to the youngest son

17 camels. How to solve?

Anthropologist William Ury's story….

Dividing the Orange

2 kids, one orange. Each wants the orange.

Mom comes home and slices orange in half & gives half to each kid.

Both kids unhappy.

Why?

Reinventing Neutrality

- All mediators talk about being *neutral*
- No parties want their mediator to be neutral
- Neutrality in mediation = *invested but not aligned*

Mediators are *empathic guides*

Mediation Styles and Signatures

- Evaluative
- Facilitative
- Transformative
- Settlement conferences
- A mix of styles
- Your signature style

Other Types of ADR

- Arbitration
- Mediation/Arbitration
- Collaborative Divorce

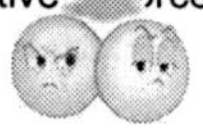

5 Steps in Mediation

- **Convene:** Get the parties to the table
- **Open:** Parties feel secure that it's safe
- **Communicate:** Get their stories
- **Negotiate:** encourage flexibility and innovation
- **Close:** Agreements and informed decisions

Benjamin's 5 Key Steps to Success

- Gain commitment to the process
- Facts and the story (managing the dialogue)
- Clarify the issues
- Negotiation and options
- Confirm understanding of the agreement

Robert Benjamin, Indiana Association of Mediators, September 26, 2008

Moore's 12 Stages of Mediation

1. Establish a relationship w/parties
2. Select a strategy
3. Collect/analyze background info
4. Design a plan for mediation
5. Build trust & cooperation
6. Begin the session

The Mediation Process, by Christopher Moore, Jossey Bass 2003, 3rd edition

Moore's 12 Stages (cont.)

7. Define issues and set agenda
8. Uncover hidden interests
9. Generate options for settlement
10. Assess options for settlement
11. Final bargaining
12. Formal settlement

The Mediation Process, by Christopher Moore, Jossey Bass 2003, 3rd edition

Mediation Becomes Mainstream

- ADR programs at court
- FARS and VORS
- Community programs
- Divorce, prenups
- Disputes with few law-based solutions
  - Unmarried couples
  - Child custody
- Harassment & discrimination claims
- Fostering ongoing relationships

Why?

- Distrust of lawyers
- More self-determination
- Cost control
- Damage control
- Confidential
- Publicity

A Mediator's Roles

- Convener
- Reality tester
- Alternative generator
- Gainer of closure
- Educator
- Communication Facilitator
- Creator of Options
- Process provider
- Referee
- Trust builder

Lunch:
See you at 1:30 pm!

First Steps in Mediation

- Convening
- Orientations
- Session structure
- When clients arrive
- Ground rules and Agreement to Mediate
- Therapeutic intake
- Setting the Agenda

Convening Mediations

Getting parties to the table

Convening Mediations

- Handling initial contact
- Approaching the reluctant spouse
- Information packets

How to Convene Cases

- Know how you are "selling" mediation
  - Be clear what your firm does & does not do
    - *e.g.*, Do you prepare and file legal paperwork?
- Mission statement of the firm
- Be clear that the professionals represent the mediation process, not the individuals involved

Convening Cases (continued)

- In convening, convey the idea of a client-centered mediation firm
- Float the idea of the mediation orientation to end the endless questions
  - Be ready for information to mail if reluctant to come in, *e.g.*, mediation profile, resume, brochure

Terminology is Important

- How would you feel as the guest of honor in a "malpractice mediation"?
- Would it feel better if it was a mediation about "appropriate treatment disputes"?

Be aware of the words you use. What do they set up in people's minds?

Mediation Orientation Sessions

Conspiracy Theorists

- No mediator contact before both parties have arrived
- Leave the room if one participant leaves unless you have specific permission to stay

Mediation Orientations

- Let's start with your questions
- Why mediation works
- Mediation format and structure
- Timing and cost
- Mediator styles
- Information vs. advice
- Product vs. Process
- FAQ

Discussion of Settlement Range

Worst Case | Mythical 50/50 "fair" resolution | Best case

Discussion of Settlement Range

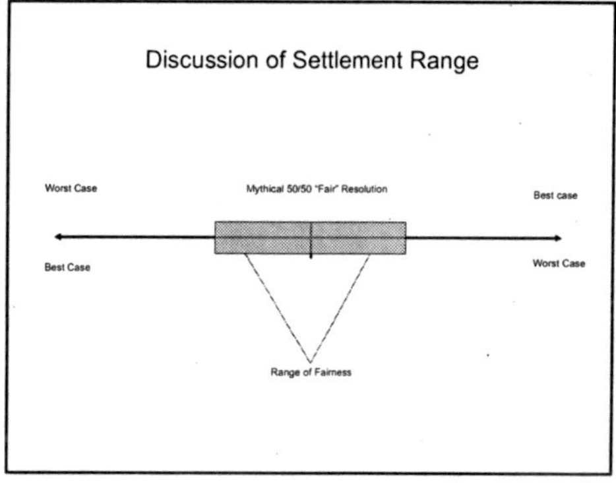

Continuum of Mediator Styles

Facilitative | Evaluative

Range of Mediator Styles

- Mediator arranges a neutral venue
- Mediator in the room but silent
- Mediator listens and summarizes
- Mediator interprets, comments
- Mediator facilitates discussion
- Mediator tests parties' positions
- Mediator helps generate options

Complete Guide to Mediation, by Forrest S. Mosten (1997 ABA)

Range of Styles (cont).

- Mediator works to expand range of options
- Mediator offers own ideas and proposals
- Mediator gives opinion as to MLATNA
- Mediator tells parties correct legal position and predicts outcome
- Mediation suggests position or action
- Mediator instructs parties to agree to same

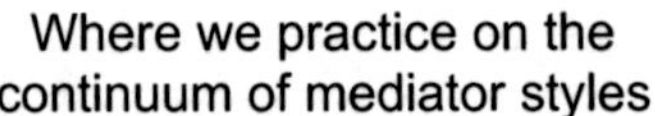

Where we practice on the continuum of mediator styles

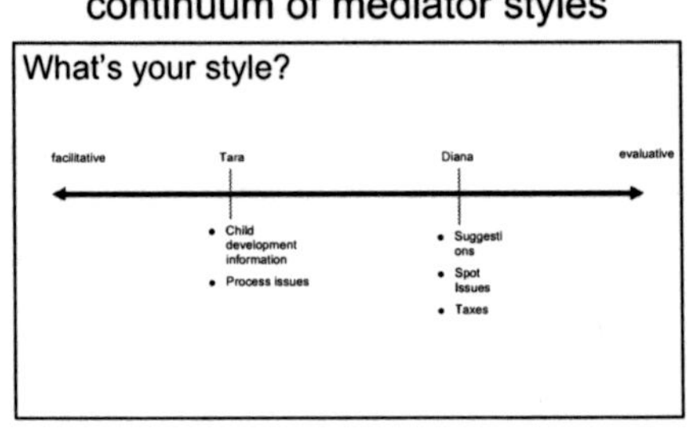

" You can make an unconventional decision in mediation, but in our office you won't make an uninformed decision."

Where does legal information cross the line into legal advice?

The Psycho-Legal Approach to Mediation

Where Product and Process Meet

Where do Product and Process Meet?

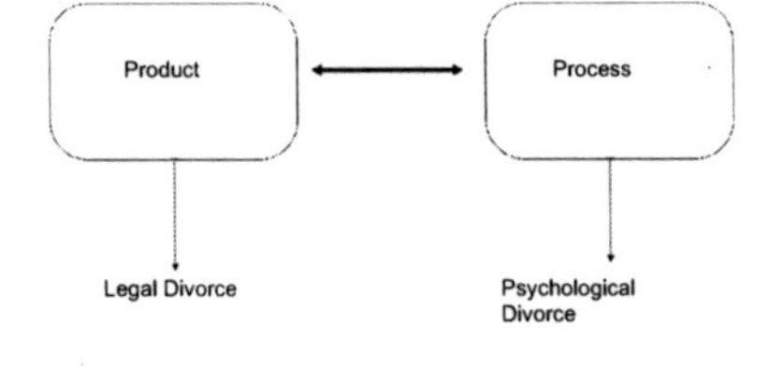

Session Structure

How will you set up your sessions for success?

- One mediator or more? Background?
- Initial individual sessions?
- Joint or individual sessions during the mediation?
- Who to include?
- If attorneys, what role do they play?

Mediation Planning

Preparing for a Mediation Session

- Debriefing by convener
- Set the physical environment for calm and peace
- When clients arrive, do your best to make them feel at home
- Hypothesis and agenda: Strategic Mediation

Peace Talks Mediation Services

Peace Talks Mediation Services

Mediator Process of Building and Testing a Hypothesis

1. Collect data about dispute through observation, secondary sources, or interviews with parties
2. Develop hypothesis about critical situations faced by parties and causes of conflict
3. Search for theories that explain conflict and that suggest interventions
4. Select theory and implied intervention; develop hypothesis about what intervention should accomplish
5. Make intervention (test hypothesis)
6. Verify or nullify hypothesis

The Role of Diversity in Mediation Planning

Diversity is more that just gender, race, and/or socio-economic issues

The Role of Diversity in Mediation Planning

Consider the following:

- Cultures torn by war
- Traumatized cultures
- Geographic differences (*e.g.* Farmer vs. Urbanite)
- Religious differences
- Sexual orientation differences

The Role of Diversity in Mediation Planning

Other nuances exist which are influenced by these issues:

- Mores about openness to helping professions
- Trust in government
- Acceptable gender roles
- Tolerance for conflict

The First Mediation Session

Intake

- How to do an effective intake
- What you are looking for
- How to use that information during a mediation session

Intake vs. Venting

You'll hear a lot of about venting and opening statements in mediation trainings.

We think that the psycho-legal intake accomplishes the goals of venting without disregulating the parties and gives mediators useful information.

Intake vs. Opening Statements

Opening Statements:

- Nobody's listening to the other side
- If they are, they're just getting more angry and entrenched
- Opening statements make things worse
- Don't tell anyone we said this

Robert Benjamin, Indiana Association of Mediators Conference, September 26, 2008

A Note about Ground Rules...

Most mediation trainings teach about ground rules: no interrupting, no swearing....etc.

Ground rules are BS. Don't tell anyone we told you that. This is our little secret.

Unintended consequence: you may suppress what they really want or need to say.

Why Shouting is Good

Flare ups tell you where the pressure points are and where it hurts.

By giving rules mediators are trying to make themselves feel better but it suckers you into being a 5th grade teacher.

The Psycho-Legal Intake

- Ask the clients' ages. Ask nicely.
- Ask them how they met. Get as much detail as possible:
  - When they met
  - The speed of the relationship
  - Details of engagement
  - Family support
- The demise of the relationship
  - What was done about it

The Psycho-Legal Intake (continued)

- Children and Parenting
  - Decision to have children
    - Planned or unplanned
  - The course of the pregnancy
  - Child rearing
    - Division of labor
  - Ask about the children
  - Blended family
  - Medications for children
    - Chronic conditions
    - Therapy

The Psycho-Legal Intake (continued)

- Post Separation
  - Parenting schedule
- The role of anniversaries
  - Construct timeline including various milestones and ruptures in the lives of the parties, children, and family
  - What are you looking for?
    - Traumas of all kinds
    - Dates in the history of their relationship
    - Wedding anniversaries
    - Children's birthdays
    - Anniversary of the death of a parent

When you're asking seemingly innocuous questions, here's what you are looking for:

- See if the words match the body language; if not, sensitively talk about it
- Avoidant attached people will gloss over subject material
- Anxious/preoccupied will **catastrophize**
- Clients may find subject matter taboo. It's you job to address it

Managed Dialogue

Another way to handle the intake:

- I'd like to hear from both of you what you understand the facts to be
- Start with a few questions and make sure each party adds to the answers
- Use a flip chart to keep track of what they agree upon and where the issues are
- Manage the dialogue

Robert Benjamin, Indiana Association of Mediators Conference, September 26, 2008

Psychological Threads in the Breakdown of a Marriage

6 Common Trauma Points

- Unplanned Pregnancy
- Affairs
- Unilateral Decision to Divorce
- Birth of the First Child
- Launching of the Last Child
- Other Life Altering Events

Agendas

Agendas are brainstorming exercises

- Easy and hard issues
- Small and big issues

All belong on one mutual agenda

All are framed in neutral language

Getting the Agenda Started

- Ask clients first but be prepared to get the discussion going
- Stay on task. No discussions yet.
- If you can't resolve these simple process issues, you won't be able to resolve the actual issues

Keys to Success

- Baby steps
- No rushing
- Hold boundaries

Break: See you at 3:45pm

Let's meet our family!

Role Play Intake to Agenda

- Break up into groups of four (co-mediators) or three (one mediator, two parties);
- Decide for the first round who is each party, *e.g.*, who is the wife, who is the husband, who is the mediator;
- Take each role for 10 minutes at a time;
- When you switch roles, pick up where the last person left off;
- Make up facts if you don't know or remember them;
- We will let you know when it is time to switch roles.

Role Play De-Briefing

- What I liked best was....
- What I'll do differently next time
- I have questions about....

Feedback from the *clients*

- How did it feel to be a participant?
- What was particularly effective or helpful?

See you Tomorrow!

Summary of Day One

Overnight thoughts and questions

Recap and Summary

- What is one thing you learned yesterday that you will put into practice?
- Did yesterday's discussion raise in questions for you?

What is Conflict?

- Our values surrounding conflict
- Moore's 5 sources of conflict
- The nature of family conflict
- Conflict resolution strategies

Group Discussion

What are our values surrounding conflict?

Resistance to Negotiation and Mediation

- Cultural resistance
- Moral resistance
- Psychological resistance

If mediation is so great, why aren't people lining up to mediate?

Negotiating Values

- Negotiation seen as weakness. No dominant power starts with "let's negotiate"
- Negotiation is impolite in some cultures
- Negotiation as morality issue or moral hierarchy (*e.g.*, children are most important)
- Negotiation assumed in some cultures
- Everyone has a negotiating ritual based on gender, culture, all kinds of things

Assess *Your* Values Surrounding Conflict

- How do I feel about conflict?
- Am I structuring the mediation sessions to address my needs or the parties'?
- Mediation based on what you're comfortable with (*e.g.,* a legalistic approach) may or may not be the best approach in any given case
- Your concept of rationality, bias, fear of conflict, your feelings about negotiation…

If You're Going to Help….

You need to know:

- How you feel about conflict
- Your own biases in negotiating
- That what the conflict is about is not necessarily the articulated issues

Moore's 5 Sources of Conflict

- Data conflicts
- Relationship conflicts
- Structural conflicts
- Interest conflicts
- Value conflicts

Data Conflicts

Data Conflicts are caused by:

Lack of information
Misinformation
Different views on what's relevant
Different interpretations of data
Different assessment procedures

Data Conflict Interventions

- Decide what data are important
- Agree on process to collect data
- Develop criteria to assess data
- Use 3rd party experts for neutral opinions or to break deadlocks

Relationship Conflicts

Relationship conflicts are caused by:
Strong emotions
Misperceptions & stereotypes
Poor communication & miscommunication
Repetitive negative behavior

Relationship Conflict Interventions

- Improve quality & quantity of communication
- Encourage problem-solving attitudes
- Control expression of emotions with procedures, ground rules, caucuses, etc.
- Promote expression of emotions through process and validating feelings
- Block negative repetitive behavior by changing structure

Structural Conflicts

Structural conflicts are caused by:

Destructive patterns of behavior/interaction

Unequal control, ownership or distribution of resources

Unequal power and authority

Geographical, physical, or environmental factors that hinder cooperation

Time constraints

Structural Conflict Interventions

- Clearly define and change roles
- Replace destructive behavior patterns
- Reallocate ownership or control of resources
- Establish mutually acceptable decision-making process
- Focus on interest-based bargaining
- Change physical/environmental relationship of parties

Interest Conflicts

Interest conflicts are caused by:

Perceived or actual competition over substantive (content) interests

Procedural interests

Psychological interests

Interest Conflict Interventions

- Focus on interests, not positions
- Look for ways to expand options and resources
- Develop tradeoffs to satisfy interests
- Look of objective standards to guide solution development

Value Conflicts

Value conflicts are caused by:

Different criteria for evaluating ideas or behavior

Exclusive intrinsically valuable goals

Different ways of life, ideology or religion

Value Conflict Interventions

- All parties to agree to disagree
- Create spheres of influence in which each dominates (exclusively)
- Search for larger goal all parties share
- Avoid defining problem in terms of value
- You'll never get people to change their values

Strategic Mediation

What's the next step or action to create baby steps of progress?

Create awareness

Motivate discussion

Guide, don't direct

Give them the best opportunity to agree

Commonality

Strive to find commonality. Examples:

- They both care about the children
- It works for both of them if unemployed spouse goes back to work or finishes degree

Resolving Conflict

- The truth is irrelevant. How each person views the facts is more important than the facts themselves.
- Readiness for Resolution: People must believe settling is better than not settling.
- Focus on strategy, not results.
- Find each person's incentive to move on.
- Search for common ground.

Basic Tools

- Ask an outcome question: "How would you like for this to work out?"
- Where do you want to be a year from now?
- How do you think we can get you there?
- What are some of the agreements we'll need to make?

Positions vs. Labels

Get away from labels by asking **why** they want what they've requested, **what** that will accomplish for them and what need it will meet.

Start a conversation.

Empathic Identification

Let them know that you understand their struggle.

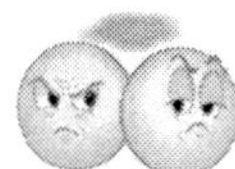

Normalization

Let them know that lots of people struggle with these issues and that it will get better.

Solvability: "You can do this" encourages them to keep going. Your confidence in them is important.

Break:
See you at 10:45am!

Peace Talks Mediation Services

Logic is Ineffective

Logic is the least effective way of convincing anyone of anything.

Mediators play into it, though, assuming people make decisions rationally.

All of our neuroscience proves that people's decisions are always attached to emotion.

Most decisions are predictably irrational.

Robert Benjamin, Indiana Association of Mediators, September 26, 2008

Negotiation Techniques

- Interest based negotiations
- BATNA and WATNA
- Reality testing
- Doubt and dissonance
- Psycho-legal approach
- Bias and impartiality
- Neutrality redefined, invested not aligned
- Pacing and transitions

Interest Based Negotiations

Get away from the stated position and get to what the underlying goal is. Then establish commonality from that goal.

Interest Based Negotiations

- Labels vs. Goals
- Expanding the options
- Prioritize
- Win/Lose outcomes
- Impasse outcomes
- Compromise outcomes
- Win/Win outcomes

Mediator Intervention: De-Positioning

- Accurately restating position
- Ask, "Imagine if a judge were to accept your position: How would that benefit you?"
  - Squeeze those benefits dry
- Restate and summarize all of the benefits
  - Ask, "If a settlement encompassed all of these concerns, would you consider settling?"

Parties must feel heard before their position can be changed.

The Keys to Success of This Intervention are:

- Be accurate
- Bend over backwards to accept the party' s stated goals, even if you don't agree
- Seize the baby step toward agreement
- Don't rush to the agreement
- Create a readiness to come to agreement

De-Positioning

- Get party to realize that to achieve settlement, it must be an agreement that the other party will sign
  - Create an openness to the other's needs
  - Low cost and little time to explore the other party's needs
  - Listening is not obeying

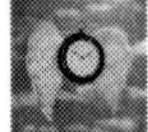

BATNA

- BATNA: Best alternative to a negotiated agreement
- WATNA: Worst alternative to a negotiated agreement
- MLATNA: Most likely alternative to a negotiated agreement

Reality Testing

- "Have you thought/talked about how that might work?"
- Break down to the details
- Talk about ranges
- Meet clients where they are. No rushing

Plan A Includes Plan B

What if things don't turn out the way you think they will?

How will it work if Plan A doesn't happen?

Consider adding Plan C, too. Anticipate all realistic fall back positions.

When Plan C is too Much....

Some clients will want to talk endlessly about all possibilities in order to avoid letting go of the relationship and the finality the agreement represents.

Like everything else, it's a balancing act for the mediators.

Doubt and Dissonance

- The client is sure about his or her position and unwilling to consider alternatives
- Discussion of ranges of outcome
- Acknowledgment that there may be more than one solution or outcome
- Enlist help of others for backup opinions
- Written guarantees for "my lawyer said" promises

Psycho Legal Approach

No 2 people come to the decision to divorce on the same emotional timeline

Often expressed using terms like *flexibility* vs. *structure* re: children

Emotional pain in exchange for financial generosity

Listen to the unmet needs between their words

Psycho Legal Approach

Listen for ambivalence

We're coming in on the middle of an old, unproductive conversation

Make peace with your own discomfort around fighting couples

How many sparks are too many and when is it not enough?

Bias and Impartiality

Clients want to feel connected, heard and held but not exclusively

Mediators are invested but not aligned

Keep the process balanced:

- Check in with each
- No one-sided conversations
- Ask them to let you know if it feels unbalanced

Bias and Impartiality

Don't lose your sense of humor

Lightness without diminishing their pain

Acknowledge when you're asking them to stretch out of their comfort zone

When you're leading them to the obvious, let *them* say it, not you

Bias and Impartiality

If you find yourself biased toward one party:

- What are they stirring up in you?
- For that party to succeed the agreement must be fair enough for the other to sign

Good Phrases for Bad News

- With all due respect.....
- I'd be doing you a disservice if I didn't....
- I know it's hard for you to think about it from the other's point of view, but.....
- If only we could turn back the hands of time......
- We don't get here alone....
- Where does that leave you?

Lunch:
See you at 1:30 pm!

Mediation Planning

- Setting up for success
- Setting the intention
- Client-centered approach
- Case conferencing
- Evaluation and feedback

Setting the Intention

- Room and office set up
- Staff trained to anticipate issues and answer questions
- Mediators prepared for session
- Tone of generosity, calm and compassion
- No unilateral contact with mediators
- Neutral but not aloof
- Clients know they are important

Case Conferencing

Study group of colleagues to talk over challenges and interventions

Commitment to lifelong learning and continuous improvement

Learning to give and take constructive criticism

Evaluation of Sessions

- What I liked best was...
- What I'd do differently next time....

Working Through the Agenda

Order of Agenda

- Tackle the easiest issues first
- Work up to the more difficult issues
- Momentum is important
- Familiarize clients with the mediation process
- Settle into the rhythm of the process
- Let them see they are making progress

Working up to the more difficult issues allows you to accumulate all of the facts, predict where the difficult issues are and identify the potential for impasse.

Resistance to Agenda Order

- Starting with the most contentious issue can lead to clients "taking the low road".
- We don't know enough about the clients to help them manage their behavior or overcome impasse.
- The clients don't trust us enough yet to believe our impartiality and that we have their best interests in mind.

The Value of Smaller Issues

Smaller issues like personal property can be a good opportunity to teach the parties how to negotiate and communicate.

Mediators' impatience with smaller issues misses an important opportunity.

Break: See you at 3:45pm!

Peace Talks Mediation Services

First Agenda Items Role Play

- Break up into groups of four (co-mediators) or three (one mediator, two parties);
- Decide for the first round who is each party, *e. g.*, who is the wife, who is the husband, who is the mediator;
- Take each role for 10 minutes at a time;
- When you switch roles, pick up where the last person left off;
- Make up facts if you don't know or remember them;
- We will let you know when it is time to switch roles.

Role Play De-Briefing

- What I liked best was….
- What I'll do differently next time
- I have questions about….

Feedback from the *clients*

- How did it feel to be a participant?
- What was particularly effective or helpful?

Summary of Day Two

Overnight thoughts and questions

Recap and Summary

- What is one thing you learned yesterday that you will put into practice?
- Did yesterday's discussion raise in questions for you?

Peace Talks Mediation Services

Communication in Mediation

- Mediator goals when listening
- Mediator goals when speaking
- Communication techniques
  - Active listening
  - Summarizing—reframing, rephrasing
  - Empathy
  - Naming & making the hidden transparent
  - Neutral Language

Goals when Listening

- Ambivalence
- The mismatches
- The taboo subjects
- Do what you're hearing and what you're seeing match?

Goals when Speaking

- Balancing act—the art of keeping the dialogue balanced while moving toward compromise
- Using your words to neutralize and repair
- Letting them know you hear and understand
- Letting them know you're with them and they're not alone
- Letting them know they matter and impact you
- Everyone is pulling together for the solution

Putting Listening & Speaking Together

- Helping clients feel felt
- Making room for them in your mind
- Helping them articulate & make sense of the experience
- Empathic guide
- Expand the conversation so each can include the other

Communication Techniques

Active Listening

Encouraging: "Can you tell me more?"

Clarifying: "When did this happen?"

Summarizing: "Let me see if I understand what you just said…."

More Active Listening

Acknowledging: "I can see you are feeling pretty angry right now."

Open Questions: "Why? What would you like to see happen?"

Responding: "I see it this way….how do you see it?"

Active Listening

Soliciting: "I would like your advice about how we can resolve this."

Encouraging: "How would you feel it if were you?"

Normalizing: "Many people feel the way you do."

Active Listening

Empathizing: "I can appreciate why you feel that way."

Reframing: "I understand that you feel ___ when he/she ____."

Validating: "I appreciate your willingness to be here..."

Avoid.....

- Ordering
- Threatening
- Preaching
- Lecturing
- Giving answers
- Judging
- Prying
- Labeling
- Manipulating
- Diagnosing
- Excusing

More to Avoid....

And help the parties avoid....

- "You must" and "you should"
- "You always..."
- Pointing, finger wagging
- Aggressive body language

Reframing and Summarizing

It's very powerful to use the actual vocabulary they've used without parroting

It helps them to know that you have heard them and understood

Active Listening is Patronizing

Yes, we've just spent a long time talking about the importance of active listening.

And it's still important....but the advanced mediator uses it energetically as well as verbally.

Pacing with the client: matching their tone and intensity and then bringing it down to a conversational level.

Calm & Rational is a Trap

By trying to keep everything in a rational frame (ground rules, reflective listening, "let' s calm down here"...) you just inflame the irrational.

The more dispassionate the mediator is the more it ramps up the emotion.

Making the Hidden Transparent

Calling out behavior or talk which is counter-productive: the elephant in the room

"So what's really going on here?"

asked in a non-threatening way or in caucus

Neutral Language

Reframe agenda items, positions and interests as bi-lateral

"Liz's over-spending" becomes "credit card debt" on the agenda

"My child" becomes "our child"

Positive Language

- *Custody* implies someone's in jail. Parenting Plan names what it really is.
- *Visitation* implies someone's in the hospital. Parenting time or parenting responsibility names what it really is.

Questions

- *Why* questions entrench positions and create defensive answers.
- *How* and *what* questions create solutions

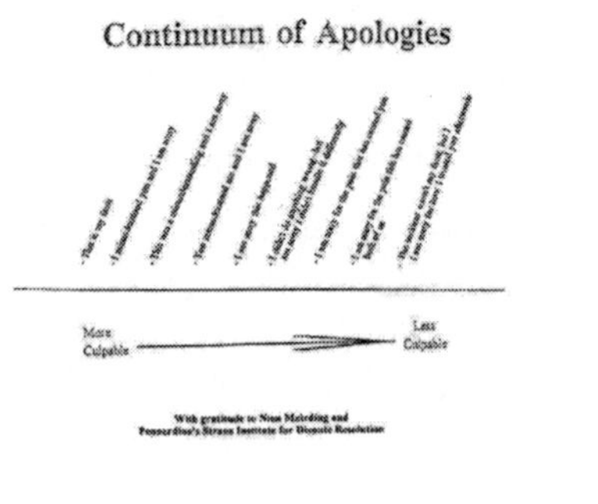

Break:
See you at 10:45am !

Peace Talks Mediation Services

Helping Clients Through the Process

- Mediation readiness
- Support systems
  - Forms, handouts, copies ready
  - Trained staff
  - Referral lists
- Setting the intention

Hypothesis Neutrality

When you have a hypothesis, ask "what are other plausible hypotheses?"

- Pull up your natural inclination and don't try to pretend
- Formulate alternative hypotheses
- Always operate on the most benign first & work your way up to less benign

Working Through the Agenda

- How to navigate the more difficult agenda items
- Impasse
- Caucuses
- The threatened walkout ☹
- Mediator techniques
- Counter-intuitive logic
- Mediation planning and de-briefing between sessions
- Case consultations and use of consultation groups

Navigating the Tough Stuff

- If clients become agitated, don't push them.
- **Never underestimate how the client's physiological reaction will impact his or her decision making capabilities.**

When the Going Gets Tough:

Mediator Strategies and Interventions

When the Going Gets Tough

- Impasse
- Threatened Walk Out ☹
- Caucuses

Top 10 Ways for Breaking an Impasse

- Examine the power structure
- Explore payoffs from being in conflict
- The Hot Seat
- Distinguish between stylistic, personality, and/or values differences
- Express needs in language that the other can hear
- Use irony to point out commonalities
- Address the emotional/physical toll of the conflict
- Listening vs. Obeying
- Perception vs. Reality
- Client's needs vs. Client's wants

Paradoxical Injunction

Giving clients permission to do what they say they want to do takes away their necessity to do it.

Manage the energy of the conflict.

Aikido in Mediation

Direction and channeling of force:

- Attack is how it starts
- Acknowledge and connect
- Come up alongside:
  - "Thank you for raising that"....
  - Follow through ("will that work for you")
- Take the energy in a different direction ("here is my concern for you…may I suggest for right now"…)

Robert Benjamin, Indiana Association of Mediators, September 26, 2008

Benjamin Tips

- Give people permission to do what they say they want to do. Your saying "no" only makes them fight you back.
- Logic can be your enemy. "Yes, but." People's inclination is to automatically disagree.
- Aggressive (non threatening) communication is communication. Clients are helping you. Being polite/ignoring doesn't help.

"I Understand" is Dismissive

"I understand" is a cut-off. You may be able to *appreciate* what they're going through but "I understand" is dismissive. Nobody feels understood when you say "I understand."

Clients need to feel that you appreciate their reality....you've got to grab the core before you can start to change their perspective.

Using Caucuses

- Caucuses can be helpful:
  - Self-soothing
  - Trust building with the mediator
  - Helping clients reality test
  - Helping clients prioritize their goals
  - Letting clients articulate their potentially unmanageable feelings

Why Are You Using a Caucus?

Examine why you want to use a caucus:

- Is it for your own comfort level?
- Is it for the attorneys involved?
- Is it in the client's best interests?

Before you jump to using a caucus, make sure you're doing it for the right reasons.

Drawbacks to Caucusing

- Increases cost
- May increase complexity
- Decreases opportunities for developing empathy
- Misses opportunity for clients to learn to communicate better
- Breeds conspiracy theories

The Biggest Drawback to Caucuses

- Rare is the client okay with sitting alone
  - "I'm fine sitting here by myself" is untrue.
- We split up the mediation team
  - No one sits alone in our office.

Working Through the Agenda (continued)

- Necessary awkward conversations
- Counter-intuitive logic
  - Speeding up by slowing down; caucuses, etc.
- Why the tough agenda items are tough
- Listening for echoes in your intake

Necessary Awkward Conversations

- Address taboo subject matter; note how clients (both mutually and individually) move away from subject
- Discuss the fundamentals of buyer's remorse
- Imbalance of power
- Legally controversial issues

Counter-Intuitive Logic

- Addressing ambivalence
- Courage to have necessary uncomfortable conversations
- Take a break when emotions run high
- Content to process shift
- Making the hidden transparent
- Warning people they are close to agreement
- Mediator's choice or stronger suggestions

Why is the tough stuff tough?

- Ambivalence
- Entrenched avoidance
- Anxiety and fear
- Value conflicts
- Structural conflicts

Listening for Echoes in Your Intake

- DABDA
- Trauma points
- Re-traumatization
- The importance of anniversaries
- Strategies to overcome impasse based on the client information

"What to do if….?"

Interventions for even the most experienced mediators

Parties Do Not See Progress: Therapist's Perspective

- Acknowledge frustration
- Articulate "lack of progress"
- Identify progress they see
- Explore the meaning
- What do they think is standing in the way
- What can be done to clear the path
- Explore what progress looks like
- Explore what progress feels like

Parties Do Not See Progress: Lawyer's Perspective

- Reiterate all they have accomplished
- Summary letter
- Be clear about lack of progress real time
- Suggest caucus to stop fighting
- Ask what do they hope to accomplish
- Alternative strategies: ask for help
- Reminder: litigation is slower

Clients want to stay in joint session, but you think is it counter-productive

- Talk about your own physical and emotional discomfort
- Ask each client if they are comfortable
- Make the hidden transparent
- If this doesn't work, insist on a caucus

Client Wants to Bamboozle the Other Party

- Full financial disclosure required by law
- Explain office policy about legal information
- Articulate your concerns in the summary letter
- Explore with each client what they think is going on
- Re-screen for domestic violence, controlling behavior and/or power imbalance
- Be prepared to let go of the case

How to Help Clients Harness Emotions

- Clients value the experience of being heard and understood more than being right or getting their way
- Reiterate that timing must be right for mediation
- Separate behavior from person

A Client is Out of Control

- Caucus or end session early
- Take a break
- Self-soothing technique
- Talk about your own discomfort
- Panic button!!!!!!

Attorney Wrangling

"The entire legal profession…has become so mesmerized with the stimulation of the courtroom contest that we forget that we should be healers of conflict. For many claims trial by adversarial contest will in time to the way of the ancient trial by battle and blood. Our system is too costly, too painful, too destructive for truly civilized people."

Former Chief Justice Warren Burger,
1984 State of Judiciary Address

Attorney Wrangling
Getting Attorneys to Buy Into the Process

- Excessive posturing
- Giving attorneys what they need from the process
- Gentle education about the process
- Authorizations to speak with attorneys
- Boundaries boundaries boundaries

Signs You Should Slow Down

- Ask, take the temperature
- One or both clients showing emotional distress
- One or both wearing their wedding bands
- Watch for detached facial expressions
  - right side of the face
- Acknowledge agitated behaviors
- Note the date of the intake and the date of appointment (*e.g.* anniversaries of death, birth or both)
- Client giving up too much, too often

Signs You Should Speed Up

- Never!
- Never work harder at reaching an agreement than the clients are working
- Tabling an issue
  - When you return, and still make no progress, make a suggestion or mediator's choice
- Ask why clients aren't speaking

Lunch: See you at 1:30 pm!

Emotional Divorce

- Ambivalence
- Grief
- Re-traumatization
- Recapitulation

Ambivalence

- Ambivalence
  - The simultaneous back and forth conflicted feelings that most divorcing clients seem to experience
- The underlying force of some the toughest cases
- What does ambivalence look like?

Making the Hidden Transparent

- Name the unspoken
- Acknowledge the taboo material
- Attend to body language

Mourning the Relationship

- When humans suffer grief and loss, current conventional wisdom is that they go through 5 basic stages of grief and loss
- Elizabeth Kubler-Ross defined these stages in her book, *On Death and Dying* originally published in 1969

DABDA: Stages of Grief

- **D**enial
  - This is not happening to me.
- **A**nger
  - How *dare* this happen to me!
- **B**argaining
  - How can I change what is happening to me?
- **D**epression
  - Why has this happened to me?
- **A**cceptance
  - I take responsibility for the role I play in what has happened to me.

" The fight, the unresolved conflict, is usually an unconscious attempt to hold on, like two fighters locked in a ring trying to stall the bell. Fighting is a form of forced intimacy, when one or both are stuck in the anger phase to delay the dreaded depression and feelings of loss associated with the end of a relationship. "

-Lisa LaCorte-Kring, LSCW

Product vs. Process:

Pacing a Case

Definition: Optimal Contingency

Giving clients what they ask for *and* what we know they need in a way they can hear it.

Range of Optimal Contingency

adapting Bebe and Lachmann's Model

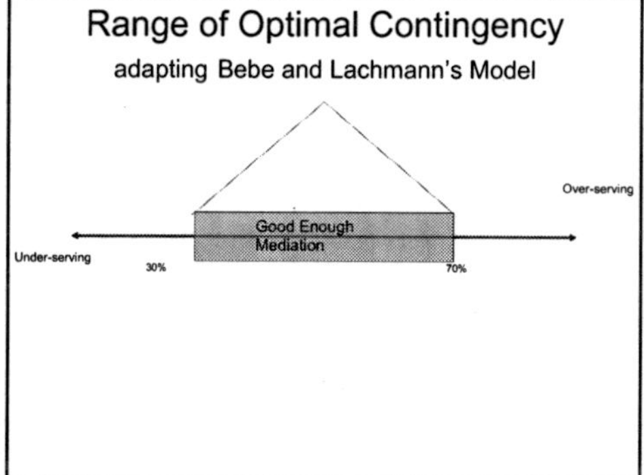

Good Enough Mediation

adapting D.W. Winnicott's model of Good Enough Parenting

What you need

What you want

Abuse — Neglect — Good Enough — Overindulgence

The Buy In

- Translate the experience
- Narrate the change
- Permission to proceed
- Build trust by moving from less to more difficult agenda items

Meta-Communication

Technique for Tuning Into the Right Brain

"All happy families resemble each other, each unhappy family is unhappy in its own way."

Leo Tolstoy, *Anna Karenina*

Conflict and the Human Brain:

An Introduction to Neuropsychobiology and Why It's Useful in the Context of Mediation

Being in conflict creates specific changes in the brain.

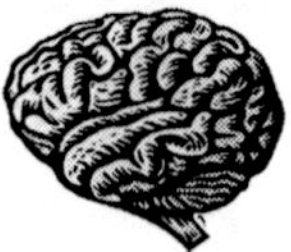

Neutrality:

Responding to clients in an empathetic yet unbiased way

The manner in which mediators encourage participants to express themselves can restore the parties' capacity for agreement.

Flipping One's Lid

The Low Road vs. The High Road

What happens in the brain when someone "flips their lid"?

- The Low Road:
  - Attuned communication decreases
  - Regulated emotions decrease
  - Response flexibility decreases
  - Empathy decreases
  - Self-awareness decreases
  - Extinction of fear decreases
- This behavior is rooted in the brain, and in this state people are less capable of moving from argument to dialogue.

Is All Hope Lost When Clients Take The Low Road? No!

- Intuition and gut feelings increase which can result in self-awareness
- By tuning into the right brain experience, we can help clients achieve clarity

Hand Model of the Brain

Parenting Plans

Be ready:

If too many of these pretty straightforward tasks become really difficult be ready to refer back to your therapeutic intake and what needs to be said but hasn't been said.

We'll get to that later....

Parenting Plans

Components:

- Decision making (legal custody)
- Day-to-day schedule (physical custody)
- Holidays and vacations
- Parenting protocols
- Move-aways

Legal Custody

- Education
- Healthcare
- Religion
- Decisions on how to raise a child

Day-to-Day Schedules

- Sample parenting plans
- Questions:
  - What are you doing now?
  - What's working and what isn't?
  - How is your child doing?
- As the mediator, what are the answers you are looking for which will guide the discussion?

Holidays and Vacations

- Pin down times, dates, travel, notice provisions
- Success or failure is in the details

If the clients' discussion is *only* about the details then know something else may be going on, *e.g.*, closure in the relationship.

Parenting Protocols

- Sharing the driving
- Toys & clothing
- New partners
- Household rules

Model Language: Agreement Innovations in Parenting Plans

- New Partner Protocols
- Step Up Plans
- Enforceable College Provisions
- Extensive Legal Custody and Other Issues Language
- Relocation Language

Move Aways

- How far is too far?
- How much notice is sufficient?
- What kind of schedule if move is imminent?
- ADR before court
- Brief confidential evaluations
- Case law changes with the tide

Break: See you at 3:45pm !

Peace Talks Mediation Services

Role Play of Parenting Plan

- Break up into groups of four (co-mediators) or three (one mediator, two parties);
- Decide for the first round who is each party, *e.g.* , who is the wife, who is the husband, who is the mediator;
- Take each role for 10 minutes at a time;
- When you switch roles, pick up where the last person left off;
- Make up facts if you don't know or remember them;
- We will let you know when it is time to switch roles.

Role Play De-Briefing

- What I liked best was….
- What I'll do differently next time
- I have questions about….

Feedback from the *clients*
- How did it feel to be a participant?
- What was particularly effective or helpful?

Summary of Day Three

Overnight thoughts and questions

Recap and Summary

- What is one thing you learned yesterday that you will put into practice?
- Did yesterday's discussion raise in questions for you?

Peace Talks Mediation Services

Legal Divorce

- Child support
- Spousal support (alimony)
- Property division
- Drafting agreements

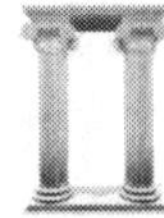

Child Support

- Set by statute
- Use software (Dissomaster ™)
- Based on a combination of net incomes and parenting time
- Also facilitate a needs-based discussion

Success in Negotiations

- Meet the parties where they are
- Run a variety of scenarios
- You're looking for a *range*
- Use each party's lowest and highest income
- Use lowest and highest parenting timeshare percentages

Spousal Support

- Every state has a statute
- Basic factors are age, health, education, ability to work, needs, etc.
- Negotiable
- Consider a lump sum buyout
- California *unofficially* uses software and some basic rules of thumb

Success in Negotiations

Look for tradeoffs:

- Assets (I'll waive spousal support if....)
- More $$ but shorter duration
- Buy out
- Tuition or startup time for a new job can be a win/win
- Floors, ceilings and ranges

Break:
See you at 10:45am !

Peace Talks Mediation Services

Property Division

- 50 states, 50 sets of rules
- Good news: not that different
- **Community property** means 50/50 for assets & debts accumulated during the marriage with lots of very rule-bound exceptions
- **Equitable division** means the judge decides what to divide but generally heavily based on $$$ during marriage

No Fault Divorce

California is *no fault*, meaning:

- Bad acts don't influence support or property division
- Fault not important in court
- Fault often VERY important to the parties, however.

When Fault Matters

- Some states permit judges to consider fault in property division and spousal support
- Generally doesn't weigh that heavily. Judges know marriages break down for a reason
- 10% swing either direction a typical max
- Fault always matters to the parties

Lunch:
See you at 1:30 pm!

Domestic Violence

Generally this is a screening issue.

Chronic domestic violence victims and perpetrators generally don't self-refer to mediation and when they do mediate, they often can't stay with the process.

Discussion

- **What is "domestic violence" and where will you draw the line?**
- **How will you know when you've got a domestic violence issue?**

DV Statistics

Type of Violence or Incident / Est. % of Total DV

- Ongoing/episodic male battering 10-18%
- Female initiated violence 13-15%
- Male-controlling interactive violence 20%
- Separation & post-divorce trauma 17-25%
- Psychotic and paranoid reactions 5%

Screening

Ways to ask about domestic abuse:

- Is there any reason why you & the other party should not sit down to try & work out [any issue]?
- Do you have concerns about sitting in the same room as the other party?
- Do you have concerns for your safety?
- Do you have any orders for protection in effect? Have you ever gotten an order of protection?
- Are you afraid of the other party?
- Has the other party ever threatened or hurt you?

Mediation Risks?

What are the risks in mediations where there has been domestic violence between the parties?

- For you
- For them
- For the process

Will You Mediate DV Cases?

- Pros and cons
- What's in between?
- No—never appropriate
- Yes—if the abused party is clear about wanting to mediate
- Yes—if screening and you feel the abuse wasn't that severe
- Yes—always, with safeguards

Is Court Really Better?

What does saying "no" to handling those kinds of mediations mean:

- For you and your practice
- For the participants

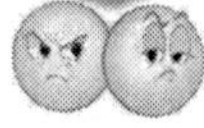

Before Mediating a DV Case

- Use screening techniques
- Be prepared to make referrals if mediation isn't appropriate
- Make sure mediation session won't violate TRO or Domestic Abuse orders---if the parties still wish to mediate, enter into written agreement & file with court that mediation will not violate "no contact" orders. This agreement protects both sides.

Drafting Agreements

Peace Talks Mediation Services

Language is Important

- Neutral and universal, not divisive
- Parenting plan, not custody
- Plain English, not legalese or jargon

What Kinds of Agreements Will You Draft?

- Summary letters
- Deal memos
- Letter Agreements
- Stipulations
- Stipulations to be signed only filed if necessary
- Court Judgments

Our Job as Mediators

Divorces have 100's of issues when you break it down to the most basic details.

Part of our job as mediators is to raise the issues the parties don't know about, and those issues which the court might gloss over.

Defining a divorce within the legal frame *only* is too narrow.

Agreement Drafting Tips

Write it down and pin it down:

- Amounts
- Deadlines
- Responsibilities
- Plan B
- ADR clause
- The court retains jurisdiction…..

Break: See you at 3:45pm !

Peace Talks Mediation Services

Financial Issues Role Play

- Break up into groups of four (co-mediators) or three (one mediator, two parties);
- Decide for the first round who is each party, *e. g.*, who is the wife, who is the husband, who is the mediator;
- Take each role for 10 minutes at a time;
- When you switch roles, pick up where the last person left off;
- Make up facts if you don't know or remember them;
- We will let you know when it is time to switch roles.

Role Play De-Briefing

- What I liked best was….
- What I'll do differently next time
- I have questions about….

Feedback from the *clients*

- How did it feel to be a participant?
- What was particularly effective or helpful?

Summary of Day Four

Overnight thoughts and questions

Recap and Summary

- What is one thing you learned yesterday that you will put into practice?
- Did yesterday's discussion raise in questions for you?
- ***Where do you want to go today?***

Peace Talks Mediation Services

Hot Topics in Mediation

- Ethics: Mediator Roles and Functions
- Reporting Requirements
- Mediation Confidentiality
- Professional Development
- Practice Development
- Future Trends
- Career Opportunities

Ethics

Roles and Functions

Role vs. Function

In any given case, a professional has one role, but may have multiple functions

The Professional's Role

- The position for which he or she has been hired
- Trouble starts when roles begin to blur within a single case
  - Although each of us may be hired for different roles in different cases, **each of us has only one role for each case**

The Professional's Function

- Although the professional has been hired for a discrete *role* , he or she may be able to use different skills from his or her professional background and have different *functions*
- Those functions must be consistent with his or her role in that case

Therapist-Mediator: Role is Mediator

- Appropriate functions for Therapist-Mediator
  - Taking a detailed family history for the purpose of understanding the circumstances of the children's lives
- Inappropriate functions
  - Treating the children

Attorney-Mediator Role is Mediator

- Appropriate functions
  - Pointing out where differences of opinion might exist
- Inappropriate functions
  - Endorsing one option without acknowledging others exist

The Ethics of Advanced Family Mediation

Is it Legal?

Will it stand up in court?

The Ethics of Agreement Innovations:

Answering the Hard Questions

Is it Conventional?

Is it Informed?

Summary Letters as Mediation Tools

- Used to be optional
- Mediations often fell apart between sessions
- Neither client had a record of the session

What the Summary Letter Does:

- Outlines the discussion
- Defines questions to ask their advisors
- Gives them a "to do list"
- Creates an "institutional memory" of session
- Fleshes out unfinished discussions
- Asks clients to explore options
- Points out progress, celebrates baby steps, encourages thinking further about the issues

Break: See you at 2:45pm !

Peace Talks Mediation Services

Role Play: Mediation to Agreement!

- Break up into groups of four (co-mediators) or three (one mediator, two parties);
- Decide for the first round who is each party, *e.g.* , who is the wife, who is the husband, who is the mediator;
- Take each role for 30 minutes at a time;
- When you switch roles, pick up where the last person left off;
- Make up facts if you don't know or remember them;
- We will let you know when it is time to switch roles.

Peace Talks Mediation Services

Role Play De-Briefing

- What I liked best was....
- What I'll do differently next time
- I have questions about....

Feedback from the *clients*

- How did it feel to be a participant?
- What was particularly effective or helpful?

Break:
See you at 3:45pm !

Peace Talks Mediation Services

Last Thoughts

.............and remaining questions

Peace Talks Mediation Services

Advanced Mediation Skills

Peace Talks Mediation Services

Advanced Mediation Skills

- Mediator's Choice
- Promoting self-soothing and self-regulation
- Caucuses
- Content-to-process shift
- De-positioning through self interest
- Turning business away
- Developing your signature style
- Party presentation of offers
- Changing the perception of the gap

Peace Talks Mediation Services

Mediator's Choice

- Mediator independently formulates proposal barely appealing to both sides: the last dollar each *might* accept or give
- Present proposal to each side in caucus
  - Don't reveal either side's answer unless *both* answer yes and there is an agreement
  - The stipulation is signed
  - No renegotiation of any terms

Peace Talks Mediation Services

Self-Soothing and Self-Confrontation

Peace Talks Mediation Services

Self-Soothing

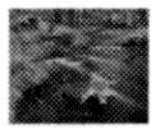

- "What can you do to make yourself feel better?"
- Acknowledge the pain and fear of the underlying conflict
- Get client to make commitment to get a grip
- Ask what has worked in the past
- Make sure client is out of ideas before you make a suggestion
- Suspend all negotiations until the party has calmed down
- Use focusing technique

Peace Talks Mediation Services

Self-Confrontation

In caucus, after self-soothing, ask, "What can you do to take responsibility for improving your (or your spouse's) willingness to negotiate?"

Peace Talks Mediation Services

Content to Process Shift

When the content is too controversial or is a" hot button" topic, think about what tools you could use to diffuse the tension.

Peace Talks Mediation Services

Party Presentation of Offers

- Mediator accompanies party to caucus room
- Once the offer is presented, there is no discussion except for clarification
- When the presenting party is done, he or she returns to their original caucus room
- Mediator stays with party receiving offer to discuss the pros and cons

Peace Talks Mediation Services

Why Does This Work?

- Facilitate discussion, but remove risk
- Limiting the reaction gives recipient a chance to think about the offer before making a knee jerk reaction
- Since you are in the room after the offer is made, you can help generate a thoughtful response

Peace Talks Mediation Services

Changing the Perception of the Gap

- Use the flip chart to:
  - o Delineate the gap
  - o Assess the probable outcome
  - o Assess the soft costs and emotional cost
  - o Examine the transaction costs of not settling
  - o Do the math to delineate the remaining gap
  - o Set strategies for closure
- Encourage them to *under* estimate (because they know the numbers are actually worse than what you're writing down)

Peace Talks Mediation Services

Changing the Perception of the Gap (continued)

- After you have done the steps above, ask the clients to :
  - o Assess the possibility of winning his or her position
  - o Define amount of money to make him or her feel better
  - o Calculate the cost of trial
  - o Assess financial benefit to keeping the relationship
  - o Agree estimate have been conservative

Peace Talks Mediation Services

Changing the Perception of the Gap (continued)

Remember you're taking baby steps:

- Be modest in your strategy goal
- Stop before pushing the client
- Do this exercise in the light most favorable to the client
- No hammering the client to accept **any** of this

Peace Talks Mediation Services

Throwing the Hail Mary Pass

- Collaborative Law or other ADR process
- Reality test what a Child Custody Evaluation or trial would be like
- Refer to other related professionals:
  - Accountant
  - Mediation friendly attorney
  - Another mediator
- Mediation door is always open
- Reassure client of their ability to resolve the situation independent of litigation, even if it doesn't include our office

Demonstration of Advanced Skills

 When to Let Clients Go 

- Suspects, not prospects
- Using mediation to avoid mediation
- Using mediation to circumvent legal realities

The Down and Dirty of Attachment Styles

Attachment Theory

- Describes and explains enduring patterns of relationships from birth to death
- Attachment styles describe ways of dealing with attachment, separation, and loss in close personal relationships
- Helps mediator predict response to conflict

Secure Attachment

- Find it easy to get close to others
- Comfortable depending on others and having others depend on them

Earned Secure

Coined by Daniel Siegel, M.D.

- After 5 years in a marriage with a securely attached person an insecurely attached person may achieve a state of secure attachment known as "earned secure"
- Other relationships and environments can also promote "earned secure" attachments

Preoccupied/Anxious

- Others are reluctant to get as close as they would like
- Worried that their partner doesn't really love them

Avoidant

- Somewhat uncomfortable being close to others
- Difficult to trust others
- Nervous when others get too close

Peace Talks Mediation Services

Disorganized Attachment

Framework in which to understand those who present a confusing pattern of relatedness

- The client may:
  - Alter responses
  - Show elements of preoccupation and anxiety
  - You may feel a sense of connectedness only to see a sudden retreat.
    - Expressed by silence, argumentativeness, or missed appointments

Peace Talks Mediation Services

Attachment Theory as a Predictor

- Avoidantly attached may dismiss and does not recognize emotional issues and dismiss the other person's concerns
- Labeling these types (silently and privately) can help the mediator anticipate the nature of the conflicts in the session

Peace Talks Mediation Services

Reading Between the Lines:

How attachment theory helps you listen more closely to what people are saying

Made in the USA